Herbert Stude
1966

Chicago, Ill.

THE STRUCTURE
OF NATIONS AND EMPIRES

The Structure
of
Nations and Empires

A STUDY OF THE RECURRING PATTERNS
AND PROBLEMS OF THE POLITICAL ORDER
IN RELATION TO THE UNIQUE PROBLEMS
OF THE NUCLEAR AGE

by

REINHOLD NIEBUHR

CHARLES SCRIBNER'S SONS

New York

TO

CHARLES C. BURLINGHAM,

counsellor of judges and statesmen,
civic reformer and pillar of his church,
who in the century of his life has shown us
how to combine realism with civic virtue and the sense
of justice.

Preface

THIS study of the perennial patterns, recurring problems and varied, but similar structures of the political order was undertaken with an eye on our present perplexities. It was prompted by the conviction that our generation, which faced the seemingly novel perplexities of the nuclear stalemate and of our encounter with the new secular religion of communism, might be tempted to forget the lessons which the past history of man offers every new generation. I thought the temptation to overestimate the novelty of the present situation was particularly great in a young nation, suddenly flung to a position of world responsibility by its great power. I am well aware that only an amateur would be sufficiently ignorant of the complexities of history and of the varied interpretations of historical events to have the temerity to undertake so ambitious a project. I therefore crave the indulgence of the specialists in the various fields of thought and of action, which I have traversed, if I have not done justice either to the obvious facts or to important differences in the interpretation of those facts in their several fields.

I would like to express my gratitude to the Rockefeller Foundation for the grant which made a leave for the study possible; and to the Institute for Advanced Study for the invitation to undertake it under its auspices and for furnishing every facility for scholarly pursuits, and particularly to Dr. Robert Oppenheimer for his interest in, and sympathetic understanding of, the purport of my study. I wish also to thank my colleagues on the Faculty of Union Theological Seminary, who granted me the leave, even though the time for it was only two years from my retirement.

I owe special thanks to my friends who read and criticized some or all of the chapters of the manuscript. Professor Arthur Schlesinger Jr., Professor Will Herberg, Professor Frederick Heymann, and Professor Daniel Williams read some of the chapters. Professor John Bennett, Dr. Kenneth Thompson, Professor Hans Morgenthau, Sir Llewellyn Woodward, and Professor George Kennan read the whole manuscript and not only made valuable criticisms and offered important corrections but gave interest and time for the discussion of the theme. I know that no one will hold them responsible for any remaining errors of facts or interpretation of the historical events.

I am grateful to the officials of the Firestone Library of Princeton University and of Speer Library of Princeton Theological Seminary who extended every helpful courtesy to myself and my wife. I owe my wife more gratitude than thankful husbands are wont to give helpful wives because she took a year's leave from her teaching post at Barnard College to help me in the preparation of this volume. She helped me in every stage of the work but her help was particularly valuable in the revision of the manuscript chapter by chapter. She challenged every long or involved sentence and every infelicity of style or obscurity of thought. If therefore this volume should be more lucid, as I hope it will be, than my previous books, the credit will belong to her. She could not, of course, change basic defects in my mode of thought.

I must also express my special gratitude for the staff of the Institute and particularly to the secretaries, Miss Dorothy Hessman and Miss Elizabeth Horton, who copied and recopied my manuscript with such accuracy and precision of detail that they earned both my admiration and lasting gratitude for their efficiency.

REINHOLD NIEBUHR

Table of Contents

CHAPTER I

Introduction

THE communities of mankind, like every human achievement and contrivance, are subject to endless variety and progression. The progression from the primitive community to city-state, empire, nation, and modern super-state is obvious. The variety of forms in which men have achieved integral, parochial communities and have enlarged the community to imperial dimensions is also clear. An analysis of this variety always presupposes, or ends in, the question: is there any consistency, any perennial pattern or permanent force in man's search for community? Is there a permanent pattern in the anatomy of community which may be discerned in such diverse communities as the tribe, the city-state, or the ancient or modern empire? Can one make any significant generalization about the attitudes and motives of action of communities which would be equally valid for autocracies and democracies; or were the philosophers of the eighteenth century right in assuming that the "selfishness" or the "aggressiveness" of nations and empires was due to the "rulers" and not to the people? Can one discern any consistency in the patterns by which the strong communities relate themselves to weak ones? Is imperialism merely the pattern of traditional power which expands by the force of military might or by some other instrument of superiority in organization or techniques until it *annuls* the sovereignty of weaker peoples? Is imperialism a pattern of the past, outmoded by the decline of absolute monarchy, as the liberal idealists of the eighteenth and nineteenth centuries believed; or was it annulled by the destruction of a "capitalistic" society, as the modern communists believe? If empire be a thing of the past, what significance can we assign to the curious fact in the history of community that the progress of community proceeded from city-states to the empires of ancient civilization; that empires of various types existed from the dawn of civilization to the beginning of the modern era; that the autonomous nation is a late arrival in history? Shall we assume, with Woodrow Wilson and the liberals of the nineteenth century, that modern history has room only for the integral community of the modern nation-state and for the universal community of mankind, expressing itself in the principle of "collective security" after having granted the parochial community all rights in the principle of "self-determination"?

If it should appear, upon analysis, that empire by military aggression has been outmoded by the pacific tendencies of commercial and industrial communities, and that "exploitation" has become less possible owing to the capacity for self-defense possessed by the subordinate communities, would any pattern of the stable relation of strength to weakness remain, though obvious "aggression" and "exploitation" were eliminated? Is there no place in the modern scheme of things for the responsible use of power? Are the principles both of liberal democracy and of Marxism, of the "equal sovereignty" of all nations embodied in the charter of the League of Nations and now repeated in every statement of Soviet policy, merely a fraud, or do they express valid principles of equal justice which the incidence of irrelevant coagulations of power is bound to contradict in both domestic and foreign policy?

If this contradiction be not due merely to the pretensions of the hegemonic nations or the "ruling" classes within the nations, may we discern a permanent moral embarrassment in men's search for —and achievement of—community on the level of both the integral parochial community (the nation) or the wider community (the empire)? Or shall we say for the latter the "super-nation," in order not to raise questions prematurely about the dubious connotations of the word "empire"? The word is dubious and embarrassing in the context of modern culture, whether liberal or Marxist, because it connotes a seemingly outmoded form of social organization or identifies the ventures of power and aggrandizement in which the European nations engaged, from the sixteenth to the nineteenth centuries, on the virgin soil of the Americas or upon the technically weak nations of Asia and Africa. But the question remains whether there is a recurring pattern of empire in history in the sense that strong nations exercise authority over weaker nations; and whether such authority is compounded inevitably in the present, as it has been in the past, of both force and prestige. Is the source of prestige always derived from the religious claim of the relation of the ruler's dominion or the nation's power to divine providence, or are there modern secular analogies for this source of prestige in traditional societies? If there are analogies, are there significant differences in the analogies of Marxist and liberal democratic society?

Perhaps the democratic principle which derives the authority of government from the "consent of the governed" and exalts the "sovereign people" as the source of all authority, is not so simple a rational principle as Locke and his disciples assumed. The explicit consent which is given or withheld from particular parliamentary governments, expressing the will of a people at a given moment, may be rational. But the authority and majesty of a government which allows this alteration of particular governments is not so simply rational. Its authority rests upon habits of loyalty and confidence in its stability; in short, upon an implicit consent derived not so much from rational calculations as from habits and traditions, analogous to the habits of loyalty in traditional communities.

Such questions suggest that an inquiry into the nature of community on all levels can be valid only if it follows rigorous empirical procedures in distinguishing the contingent and the novel from the permanent and the perennial in history.

The inquiry must disclose both the differences and the similarities between traditional communities and modern democracies. Further, it must note the character of political life when oriented by a culture which is religious, or by one which is modern, secular, and scientific. On the surface the differences are so great that they suggest a veritable chasm of history, dividing the ancient and medieval from the modern era. The chasm can be variously defined, but the history from the sixteenth to the eighteenth centuries roughly gives the outline of the chasm. The differences between the medieval and the modern types of political organization are very great. The question is whether there are any similarities, provisionally obscured by the radical differences, which a closer scrutiny will disclose.

Superficially considered, traditional communities emphasize order, not only as the primary but usually as the sole end of political life, while modern communities pursue justice. Is this difference due to the greater sensitivity of modern man to the moral character of the community? Is there significance in the fact that both Plato and Aristotle seem to equate order and justice, and that both ancient and medieval society followed Aristotle's definition that "Justice exists only among men whose mutual relations are governed by law" [1] and Plato's scheme of values, contained in the question: "Can there be any greater evil than discord, plurality and distraction where unity ought to reign, and a greater good than the bond of unity?" [2] And is it significant that Stoic equalitarianism and the Christian ethic of love had little influence on the hierarchically ordered society of both pagan and Christian Rome? Perhaps this proves the validity of Aristotle's idea that justice consists in "treating unequal things unequally." But it is more likely that traditional communities, whether pagan or Christian, insisted on paying an excessive price in justice for the sake of order, because their order was never secure in the internal cohesions of the community and therefore depended upon an undue emphasis upon the authority of the ruler and upon the value of the boon of order which his authority maintained.

The obvious difference of modern democratic communities is that they insist on justice, rather than order. Nobody has ever been able to define how Aristotle's prescription of justice, as giving each man his due, can be fulfilled, or rather how each man's due is to be defined. But modern democracies universally have thought the price in justice for the boon of order to be too high and have engaged in progressively equalitarian tendencies. They discovered

[1] Aristotle, *Nichomachean Ethics*, V, Chap. 6.   [2] Plato, *The Republic* V.

in the process that the French and the communist revolutions were wrong in regarding equality as a simple possibility for communities, for they cannot be integrated without a hierarchy of authority; but modern democracies have, within this reservation, certainly made equality the regulative principle of justice.

Did they do this because the religious spirits of the seventeenth century England and the rational idealists of eighteenth century France revolted against the monstrous injustices which were the price of social cohesion in all traditional communities, from the dawn of civilization to the dawn of the modern era? Or is it possible to find more economic causes for the democratic development, and establish that the difference between traditional and modern communities was created by the rise of an independent commercial class, which had sufficient independent power to defy both the power and the ideology of the political oligarchs, ecclesiastical, monarchial, and feudal, who dominated the political order of the Middle Ages? This explanation points to at least one aspect of the radical distinction between the old and the new society, though one must hasten to add that the commercial classes were so effective in laying the foundation of a new society because they were unable to guard their economic power and extend their political liberty without creating political standards which could be appropriated later by the industrial classes, who pressed so closely on the heels of the middle classes in democratic history.

Whether one stresses the moral-religious foundation of democracy or the economic causes, the emphasis would still lie on the differences, rather than the similarities, between traditional and modern political organization. But if it should be established that modern societies did not, could not, tolerate those hazards of anarchy, which are immanent in a pluralistic culture, a competitive economic life, and a fluid system of political authority, until various forms of economic and other cohesion had given the community sufficient solidity to afford these risks of disorder with impunity, then perhaps some similarities under the differences between ancient and modern societies would be disclosed. The similarity proving that order must always remain the first value of any community, (because chaos is tantamount to nonexistence), establishes a constant which transcends the most radical change in history. It also gives us a helpful clue in our relations with the non-technical nations of Asia and Africa, striving for both technical competence and national independence and stability. It may prove to us that "free elections" are not the simple boon of community which we assumed them to be.

The radical difference between traditional and modern cultures partly coincides with the differences between religious and secular-scientific ones, but not altogether. Traditional communities used both religious pieties and metaphysical speculations to maintain their order; and modern democracy owes much to both the religious and the rational protests against traditional injustice. It is nevertheless generally true that modern culture is secular and scientific, being thus distinguished from the religious culture of all traditional communities, whether pagan, Christian, or Islamic. The question is whether this difference can hide certain similarities between religious and secular cultures. In the opinion of the Enlightenment, "priestly superstition" was the chief bulwark of the traditional order. This was a natural reaction to the religious sanctification of the feudal order. But the Jacobins soon proved (and were followed by the communists of our day) that fanaticism can speak in the name of "reason" or "Marxist-Leninist Science" as easily as in the name of God. And Napoleon and Stalin proved that despotism could avail itself of secular as well as of religious ideological support.

An analysis of these facts may reveal a constant tendency in human nature which transcends the distinctions between religious and secular manifestations of that tendency. It is the inclination on the one hand to seek a norm, transcending the ideological taints of interest observable in all historical norms, but then promptly to claim some special affinity with the transcendant norm.

The inquiry, which seeks to distinguish the permanent from the novel and historically contingent factors of community, must confine itself to historically and empirically established patterns and forces. It must eschew metaphysical speculations which seek to discern, in the wide drama of history, ontological essences which merely wait upon history for the actualization of potency into reality. History is a realm in which human freedom and natural necessity are curiously intermingled. Man's freedom constantly creates the most curious and unexpected and unpredictable emergences and emergencies in history. All efforts to discern patterns of recurrence, after the manner of Spengler and Toynbee, or patterns of development, in the fashion of Hegel, Spencer, or Comte, must do violence to the infinite variety in the strange configurations of history. But without an empirical inquiry into the relation between the contingent and the permanent forces of community each generation is tempted to exalt some particular instrument of justice, which has succeeded in a given instance, as the absolutely essential instrument of justice; or to attribute injustice to some particular institution or policy which has been the particular cause of particular evils but is falsely understood if interpreted as the final cause of all social evil.

It is important for us to gain some historical perspective on our contemporary problems lest we regard a new manifestation of an old imperial configuration, as we have it in Communism, as a completely new and unheard-of display of imperial power projected by evil men. Such a view will not do justice to the problem we face in Communism.

We must also examine what is modern and what is perennial in the autonomous nation; and what is abiding in what seems to be the abandoned structure of the imperial community and power structure. For the autonomy of the modern nation may be new, but the integral parochial community is as old as history. Furthermore the imperial power structure, as it existed in one form in the classical empires of antiquity and in the Middle Ages and in another form in the national empires of the sixteenth to the nineteenth centuries, may seem to be an outmoded structure of power and community; but many forms of supra-national communities persist and must persist until the present day. Their persistence refutes any simple political philosophy which makes the autonomous nation the only valid structure of community and authority on the one hand, and on the other hand refers all supra-national problems to the principle of "collective security."

Historical perspective is also needed to refute the idea, popular since the rise of liberal democracy in the West, that the authority of government is supplied in the civilized, or at least modern, world purely by rational consent. It is possible to show that democratic governments derive their authority from majesty or prestige on the one hand, and from force on the other. Naturally the majesty of a democratic government is no other than the majesty of the community itself, which is why force plays only a minimal role in its authority. But, as we shall see, it has always had a subordinate role in well-established traditional forms of dominion, and those who derived prestige from the relative justice of their rule.

For the traditional "majesty," a word which described the authority of the state in traditional governments, we have substituted the more inclusive but weaker concept of "prestige" in order to include the reality in foreign relations as well as in domestic national life. We have assumed that "power" and "authority" are in essence synonymous because they both describe the capacity of a government or state to gain obedience or compliance. The two sources of this power or authority are "prestige" or "majesty"— which includes all the forces of tradition and history which induce obedience and compliance—and "force," the capacity to coerce. Usually the "majesty" of a state is the very source of its authority to use force, for the sake of coercing recalcitrants. But force, while always minimal in a well-established state, in comparison with "prestige" or "majesty," may itself be a source of authority, at the beginning of a reign or after a revolution. Coercion enforces obedience until the authority of the government has been established, when it may win uncoerced consent by its prestige.

This study covers political life and thought, particularly of western history, but is not meant to be primarily an historical study, which would be beyond the competence of the author. It is designed to describe the historical constants and variables in the dominion of nations and empires in order to put the struggle between two nations, both with power of imperial proportions, in its proper setting. Of these two nations the one tries desperately not to be an empire, while the other claims not to be, but is in fact a secular reincarnation of the classical quasi-universal empires which existed until the dawn of the modern day.

Both nations are for different reasons "anti-imperialistic," which must prompt us to include in our study the realities of the national imperialisms which engaged the western nations from the sixteenth to the nineteenth centuries. A study of dominion and community in nations and empires in the whole of history is justified as relevant to our present perplexities, if the assumption is correct that present political realities can be fully understood only in the light of historical comparisons, which may discover what is new and what is old in a contemporary configuration of community or structure of political power.

Historical perspective may be particularly valuable for our own nation. We are fated to exercise great power and responsibility in the democratic alliance of nations. Our apprenticeship for this task of leadership has been brief; and our thought has been informed by the political ideals of the past two centuries, rather than by the experience of past ages. Furthermore, the novelties and striking historical emergents of a nuclear age threaten to obscure the lessons drawn from the constant factors in history, not only in our nation but in the whole of our generation.

CHAPTER II

The Two Imperial Nations
of Today

THE modern world is divided by two opposing alliances of nations. Each is under the hegemony of a nation which has the economic and military strength to determine independent policy. The leadership is partly ideological because the two dominant nations are informed by the two contrasting creeds of politics which determine the loyalties of the alliance. The Russian leadership is more obviously ideological because it is, according to the unifying dogma, the "fatherland" of Communism and is destined to come to the support of any communist country. Our hegemony is not as consistently ideological because the noncommunist nations include not only the western democracies but many nations of East and West who are not communist. Among the western nations there would be few who would regard us as the perfect exemplars of the democratic creed. We are merely the strongest of these nations. In that curious mixture of force and prestige which establishes authority in both domestic and international relations prestige is more important than force in the domestic organization of the community, but force is more important in situations of international conflict. The two nations with power of imperial proportions are in their positions because they alone have the capacity to organize a great continental economy which surpasses the economic resources of any other nation.

The contest of power between the two alliances and their respective hegemonic powers is involved in an unprecedented situation: the nuclear stalemate. Each nation has the fairly equal capacity to destroy the other through nuclear weapons, which, together with ever more ingenious guided missiles as instruments of delivery, have radically altered the whole military situation in such a way as to make a large-scale war as calculated policy for either side impossible. Although there may be stages of weapon development at which a great premium will rest temporarily on the element of surprise, the tendency is toward a situation in which even a surprise attack would not guarantee victory and would expose the aggressor to a level of destruction which would make the difference between victory and defeat irrelevant. A disarmament agreement which would eliminate the nuclear level of destruction is possible but unlikely, since no such agreements have ever been reached in a situation of tension. But a war is also unlikely, though always possible by miscalculation or misadventure. The world may live for a long time in this fateful and possibly tragic tension. If the tension should finally result in a war of mutual annihilation, the shape of the world would be so radically altered that all efforts to learn lessons from the perennial factors in human communities would become irrelevant.

But assuming that each side will have both the wisdom and the good fortune to avoid the ultimate conflict it is safe to assume that the two alliances and their hegemonous powers will engage in the inevitable rivalries of power, which are possible, and indeed unavoidable, even in what is known as "peaceful co-existence." If mankind should have the good fortune to avoid the ultimate and suicidal holocaust, it will be necessary to turn from the unprecedented factors of our situation, which have naturally preoccupied us, to the perennial and constant factors, which have emerged in all imperial and national rivalries through the ages. This change of interest is the more necessary because both the imperial nations, possessing power which dwarfs the power of ancient empires, are informed by creeds that are contradictory in many respects but are identical in one respect: they both believe that imperialism is an outmoded form of political organization. The one believes this by virtue of a democratic creed, which persists in America in its pristine purity. The history of the birth of the nation in a revolutionary war against an imperial power gave us the anti-imperial animus; and the continental expanse of the nation had made imperial ventures, at least of the overt variety, unnecessary. The ironic circumstance of our wielding imperial power, though informed by an anti-imperial ideology, places considerable strain on the "democratic" alliance of nations which includes for instance Great Britain, who, despite her democratic heritage, has been involved in the imperial ventures, which characterized the impingement of western nations upon Asia and Africa throughout the eighteenth and nineteenth centuries. Western imperialism, indeed, had its inception in the sixteenth century so that western civilization must bear the odium of imperialism of four centuries, an odium which the communist adversary carefully exploits. The ironic fact is that the Marxist and liberal democratic theories of power relations are very similar in obscuring the perennial factors, though Marxism attributes imperialism to the very form of liberal political organization (capitalism) which liberalism believes to be a force of emancipation from imperialism.

It is, strictly considered, inaccurate to speak of a "democratic alliance." The non-communist world is organized in various ways. It contains various defensive alliances, such as NATO and SEATO and the now partly defunct Baghdad pact. Of these only NATO represents the hard core of Western democracy, organized for Europe's defence against Communism. SEATO contains nations such as Pakistan, which are now military dictatorships. It does not contain India, a democratic nation, but uncommitted with reference to the two power blocs and as critical of us as of Russia. The so-called "uncommitted" nations are, in fact, in various degrees either uncommitted or partially committed either to the Russian or to the western power center. There is a certain "democratic" majority operating in the United Nations. But this contains the military dictatorships of South America, and the nations of the Asian and Arab bloc are now more likely to vote against us than with us.

This confused situation is a perfect illustration of the fact that there are no exact constitutional norms or forms to contain or

to regularize precisely the power relations in any bloc of nations.
Nor can any international constitution prevent the gradations of
power among the nations from creating some kind of hierarchy
of authority, more inexact than, but nevertheless analogous to,
the hierarchy of authority in any national community. Such hierarchies of authority are never as ideal as the holders of great power
profess to believe. But they are usually not as nefarious as the
critics of these hierarchies of power and authority pretend.

We must study more carefully the history of western imperialism, which Communism attacks so consistently. A moral odium
attaches to it in the thought of both liberal democracy and of
Marxism. But the creative factors in this imperialism which are
usually obscured are validated by the fact that none of the recently emancipated nations could have achieved integral nationhood without drawing upon instruments of cohesion supplied by
its former masters.

The ideological system of democratic liberalism has no room
for the expression of any power or the formation of any community above the level of the nation and below the level of the universal community. But democratic liberalism is in conflict with
a Marxist imperialism which is anti-imperialistic for very different reasons. It is in fact a modern version of the classical imperialisms, much older than the national imperialism of the
sixteenth to nineteenth centuries; of the imperialisms which existed from the dawn of history to the end of the Middle Ages. All
of these imperial structures, as we shall see, combined force with
prestige drawn from the claim of having achieved, or being
about to achieve, universal community and ideal justice. Marxism
is the only version of the universal empire which could achieve
relevance in a secular age. For the traditional empires made their
ultimate and universal claims in religious terms. Marxism makes
them in pseudo-scientific terms, presenting an old religious
apocalypse in terms of a materialism which pretends to have
found the "laws of motion" in history, laws which, if properly
understood and manipulated, can lead humanity from the "realm
of necessity to the realm of freedom." The theory implies, as

does the French physiocratic theory, that nature and history are equally subject to absolute laws; but the Marxist theory assumes that a particular class, the "proletariat," is destined to become the manipulator and beneficiary of the laws which work for the ultimate abolition of both injustice and national particularism; in short, for the creation of an ideal and universal society. This scheme of universal redemption is a pseudo-scientific version of the religious absolute. Like all religious visions of a redeemed society, it has the provisional merit of being a source of criticism of established forms of injustice and of particular communities; but it has the defect of easily becoming a screen for new power structures, both national and imperial. Thus the Marxist scheme of redemption distinguishes itself from the original liberal scheme. The latter hoped to abolish force in communities progressively, as human intelligence developed. Marxism intends to make one final use of force in a revolution. There it will play the part of a "midwife" helping the new society, with which the old is pregnant, to come to birth.

In the original apocalypse it is only a class which is destined to play this redemptive role. But in the amended version of the apocalypse, that is, amended by Stalin, the nation which first established the new society, i.e., Russia, is destined to play a leading role in guiding the oppressed classes of every nation to the ultimate triumph of socialism. Thus the universalism of the communist slogan, "Workers of the World, Unite," is easily transmuted into a new imperial universalism in which Russia is called upon to be the "vanguard" of the revolution for the whole world. After Stalin's death and Khrushchev's assurance to the banned heretic, Tito—that there were many paths to socialism—the intimate relation between the imperial and the universal impulse seemed to be dissolved. But this judgment proved to be premature. Khrushchev, probably forced by the remaining Stalinists in the communist oligarchy but more probably by the inner logic of an international dictatorship, reneged on his promise of independence to Tito, and of course brutally suppressed the Hungarian rebellion and left Poland only a tenuous freedom. All this was done with the connivance of the junior partner in the dictatorship, China. This nation seems to follow the logic of the amended Marxism which assigns to Russia a preponderant power for the sake of preserving the unity of the "socialist camp." The whole policy of imperialistic universalism has its difficulties with the European satellites, that is, with the historic national communities; but it admirably fits the conditions of the Asian nations, where the combination of internationalism and the pretended emancipation from European "imperialism," and in addition technical aid for negotiating the gateway to technical competence and economic well-being, offer Russia many advantages over the western or democratic alliance.

There is vivid contrast between a policy of a hegemonous nation speaking for a whole empire in the name of anti-imperialism, and our own policy of frantically avoiding recognition of the imperialism which we in fact exercise, or ought to exercise if imperialism means the exercise of the responsibilities of power. We regard the United Nations as the true organ of the universal community to which all nations must be subject. This point of view is illustrated in President Eisenhower's policy in the Suez crisis and his subsequent suppression of the Israeli defiance of the United Nations edict to leave the territory which had been captured from Egypt. Eisenhower declared in a television address to the nation on February 20, 1957, "When I talked on October last I pointed out that the United States fully realized that the military action against Egypt resulted from grave and repeated provocations; but I also said that the use of military force to solve international disputes could not be reconciled with the principles and purposes of the United Nations, to which we have all subscribed. I added that our country could not believe that resort to force and war would for long serve the permanent interests of the attacking nations, Britain, France and Israel." The President then paid tribute to Britain and France for heeding the resolution of the United Nations to quit Egypt "forthwith." They made, he said, "an immense contribution to world order." But he failed to record that they left Egypt because we, with our superior power, sided with

Russia in ordering them out; and that their desperate venture was understandable only because we failed to understand their predicament under the pressure of a hitherto "colonial" nation, Egypt, which had taken hold of the life-line of European economy in the name of its emancipation from "colonialism." We declared ourselves sufficiently "anti-colonial" to understand the motives of Egypt. The essential pacifism of the President's policy was expressed in the words, "If the United Nations once admits that international disputes can be settled by force then we will have destroyed the very foundation of the organization and our best hope of establishing a real world order. That would be a disaster for us all." [1]

These eloquent words in favor of the United Nations and world peace manage to obscure the real character of that necessary organization which is not so much a super-government as a forum organ for international diplomacy. If regarded as the former, the hegemonic responsibility of our own nation is obscured. It will be remembered that all these events took place while Russia was suppressing the Hungarian nation. The President took cognizance of this fact in the words: "I do not believe that Israel's default should be ignored because the United Nations has been unable effectively to carry out its resolutions, condemning the Soviet Union for its armed suppression of the people of Hungary. Perhaps this is the case where the proverb applies that two wrongs do not make a right."

The proverb also obscures the fact that Russia was powerful enough to defy the United Nations and that Israel was not. His analysis of the Suez crisis, in short, places the whole emphasis on the moral and political prestige of the United Nations, and obscures the power factors which are bound to be operative in any situation but particularly in one in which the international organization has no power except that with which it is endowed by the concurrence of the powerful nations. This concurrence was lacking in this instance. The theory of the United Nations presup-

[1] *New York Times*, February 21, 1958.

posed such concurrence. Since it has been lacking from the beginning it obviously does not promise the kind of world order which the President assumes to be its function.

Mr. Eisenhower's mistake was not a unique but a typical one, that is, a typical American mistake. As president after the Second World War, though an ex-general, he revealed an almost identical approach to world order as Woodrow Wilson in and after the First World War. The fact that meanwhile the nation had been endowed with unmistakable hegemonic power, and should have been ready to assume the responsibilities of leadership, made little difference in the guiding conception. One must draw the conclusion that some deep stream in American life and thought is responsible for reactions which are so at variance with the realities. This stream of liberal democratic theory of foreign relations is wider and deeper than American thought and life. We must analyze its dominant characteristics presently, but record that the universal characteristic of the liberal democratic theory of international relations seems to have two emphases: (1) an emphasis on the integrity and autonomy of the nation, and (2) a vague universalism or consideration of the "community of mankind" which leaves little room for the configurations of power and authority which develop in history between the nation and the universal community. The liberal theory gives constitutional embodiment to its universalism only at one point: it insists on collective security whether through the League of Nations or the United Nations.

The American espousal of this abstract universalism is significant, and possibly dangerous, because it has become the official or semi-official theory of one of the two great hegemonic powers of the world. Woodrow Wilson intended to use it to beguile the growing nation from its isolationism into an attitude of world responsibility. But unfortunately the idealistic color which he gave the conception corresponded neither to the inevitable—and justified—instincts of self-interest of the nation, nor to the power realities of the world. Wilson, in the year before the American entry into the First World War, discussed not the specific

questions which concerned the nation, which was darkly conscious of the fact that events in Europe had destroyed both the
illusion and the reality of American continental security. He
talked abstractly of America's mission in the world. Speaking on
October 5, 1916, he said,

> We have never yet sufficiently formulated our program for Amer-
> ica with regard to the part she is going to play in the world, and
> it is imperative that we should formulate it at once. ... We are
> holding off, not because we do not feel concerned but because
> when we exert the force of this Nation we want to know what
> we are exerting it for. We ought to have a touchstone. We want
> to have a test. We ought to know, whenever we act, what the
> purpose is, what the ultimate goal is. Now the touchstone is this:
> On our own part absolute singleness of heart and purpose in our
> allegiance to America ... by holding the doctrine that it is truly
> American that the States of America were set up to vindicate the
> rights of man and not the rights of property or the rights of self-
> aggrandizement and aggression. ... When you are asked 'Aren't
> you willing to fight?' reply yes you are waiting for something
> worth fighting for, you are not looking for petty quarrels, but you
> are looking about for that sort of quarrel within whose intricacies
> are written all the texts of the rights of man, you are looking for
> some cause which will elevate your spirit, ... some cause in which
> it seems a glory to shed human blood, if it be necessary, so that
> all the common compacts of liberty will be sealed with the blood
> of free men.[2]

We all know the story of Wilson's tragic effort, once having
been drawn into the war for less than idealistic reasons, to give
the struggle this "ultimate goal" by insisting that the League of
Nations should be made a part of the treaty; how his devotion to
the League obscured in his own eyes the significance of some of
the unsavory and vindictive portions of the treaty, which, incidentally, he hoped the League would in time correct; and how the
very nation, of whom he expected "single-minded" devotion to
ultimate principles of right, rejected his League because it was
presented to the nation in purely idealistic terms and seemed to

[2] Edward Buehrig, *Woodrow Wilson and the Balance of Power*, Bloomington:
Indiana University Press, 1956, pp. 247–48.

neglect the nation's vital interests. This pathetic effort to obscure the moral ambiguities of any political order, but particularly of an international order, may have been necessary to beguile the idealistic portions of the nation into world responsibilities. It will be remembered that his Secretary of State, Mr. Bryan, resigned on our declaration of war and that "seven willful senators," mostly drawn from the progressive camp, resisted the war effort. Wilson's politics seemed an artful compromise between the bellicosity of Theodore Roosevelt and the liberal opinion of the nation. For Roosevelt was conscious of American power and lusted for the glory of the nation in world affairs in a different context than Wilson's moral glory. The main body of liberal opinion still preserved Wilson's original position that the war was a sordid commercial quarrel between European nations, in which a righteous nation could have no part.

The episode of Wilsonian idealism in our history is indicative of the power of the liberal-democratic tradition in our nation. It was powerful enough to persist even after Wilson's sentimentalities resulted in the defeat of his idealistic program. It may be worth observing that the League might have failed even if our own nation had joined it. It is, after all, not certain that the much more realistically conceived United Nations will ultimately succeed; and it is quite certain that it will not heal the breach between the two great alliances of nations.

The liberal tradition persisted even after America emerged from the Second World War incontestably the strongest nation in the democratic alliance, and with a sense of power which cured her of her previous isolationism. Professor Buehrig in his study, *Wilson and the Balance of Power*, presents the thesis that Lord Grey, the British Foreign Secretary, wanted the League to beguile America into specific responsibilities in the world, while Wilson desired it to express vague, but not specific, responsibility toward the world order. Wilson could hardly have foreseen the degree of our present power. The possession of this power has fortunately made the old impulses toward irresponsibiilty obsolete and we have certainly assumed specific responsibilities in every part of the

world. But the abstract universalism continues as a subterranean
force, as the similarities between Eisenhower's and Wilson's conceptions suggest. We still regard the United Nations as the source
of policy, when its very constitution prevents it from being more
than a clearing house for the policies of the nations. Occasionally,
despite our effort to assume specific responsibilities, we revert to
vague and abstract solutions for specific problems. Thus when
the failure of co-ordination between British and American policy
resulted in the Suez crisis and the consequent "power vacuum"
in the Middle East because of the destruction of British influence, we proclaimed the "Eisenhower Doctrine" which promised aid to nations of the Middle East if they desired it and were
threatened with communist aggression. Overt communist aggression was the most improbable possibility since the Russians could
gain every triumph by infiltrating their influence in Egypt and
Syria.

The curious fact that the two nations which have achieved imperial power condemn imperialism for different reasons has led
to some serious confusions. We have previously alluded to the
strong aversion of Americans to British imperialism. It was obvious in the First World War in many Wilsonian attitudes, including his emphasis on the freedom of the seas. In the Second
World War, despite the strong friendship between Roosevelt
and Churchill, it was a fixed prejudice of American policy-makers
that we must prevent the British from using the war for their imperial purposes. Suspicion of Britain as an imperialistic nation
was in fact a consistent note in American policy throughout our
history which the intimate partnership of two world wars, in
which common interests and common ideals cemented the
partnership, did little to qualify. Illusions about ourselves and
Britain were partly responsible for Roosevelt's effort to act as
mediator between Churchill and Stalin. These efforts are only
explicable against the background of conceptions which obscured
both the basic affinities of interest and ideals between us and

Britain and the basic contradiction between the policies of western democracies and the Russian hegemony in an utopian imperialism.[3]

President Eisenhower expressed not a unique, but a typical American viewpoint when he sought to emphasize the affinity between ourselves and the Russians with an implied barb at our British ally. In expressing the hope of an accord with Russia despite the ideological chasm which divided the two nations, Eisenhower wrote: "The past relations between America and Russia were no cause to regard the future with pessimism. Historically the two nations had preserved an unbroken friendship, dating back to the birth of the United States as an independent Republic. ...Both were free of the stigma of empire building by force." [4]

The judgment obscured the fact that we were dealing, not with traditional Russia but with a new Russia, the holy nation of the communist creed. If we were dealing with the old Russia, the judgment that it was free of "empire building by force" was fantastically false. In the case of the new Russia the judgment was both false and ironic, as subsequent events proved.

While the misunderstandings between Britain and America are serious, as recent events in the Suez crisis proved, it is not our present purpose to clarify these misunderstandings but to point to them as symptoms of the failure of modern men, but particularly Americans, to distinguish between the perennial and the contingent and ephemeral in the political communities of mankind. We are now in a situation in which a new imperialism namely, that of the Russian Communists, has effectively reconstructed in utopian terms the oldest imperialism of human history. The characteristic of this form of imperialism was to use an ideological universalism as the chief source of its prestige. The utopian form of the imperialism is the more effective because it

---

[3] See Herbert Feis, *Roosevelt, Churchill, Stalin; The War they Waged and the Peace they Sought*, Princeton: Princeton University Press, 1957, p. 574.
[4] Dwight D. Eisenhower, *Crusade in Europe*, New York: Doubleday & Company, Inc., 1948, p. 457.

pretends that its power structures are merely provisional, because its purpose is to eliminate force from human life. These pretensions obscure, more or less effectively, the power impulses which express themselves in the Russian communist structure both in its domestic and in its imperial relations. Mr. Khrushchev never tires of insisting that Russian help to satellite peoples is "without strings" and that the relations between Russia and the weaker peoples is purely "fraternal." This is a new form of an old moral pretension, which, as we shall see, the stoic idealist claimed for pagan Rome and the Christian historian Eusebius claimed for the Constantinian regime of Rome. The question which must be raised is not whether the communist method of obscuring the power impulses of empire are valid, but why they are so plausible. The communist pretensions face us with one of the interesting aspects of human history. This is that the structure of political organization on both the parochial and the imperial level is fairly constant—while the ideological pretensions, which furnish the prestige which is one part of the structure, vary endlessly.

An additional note of irony is added to present confusions because, superficially considered, the nationalistic form of imperialism, in which the western nations engaged from the sixteenth to the nineteenth centuries, seems morally inferior to this new imperialism, in which the dominant nations claim to be merely the servant to the universal community. These earlier nationalistic imperialisms represented the domination over a weaker people by a stronger one. We are living in a period in which the decay of these nineteenth century empires—occasioned by the war and by the extension of technical competence from the West to the agrarian East—has freed many nations and prompted many still dominated nations to long for their freedom. This means that residual and present resentments against imperialism are bound to color the political thought of the colonial and ex-colonial nations. The western nations seem therefore to be at a great moral disadvantage. The disadvantage is so great that, as we have seen, the hegemonic nation of the democratic alliance is tempted again and again to share the indictment of its allies which the communist foes make against the West. This is the more pathetic because the communist dogma does not exclude us from the indictment; for the dogma insists that capitalism is the final cause of imperialism. The facts are at variance with this dogma, for if imperialism had any political form it was the pre-capitalistic mercantilism in which political authority, primarily the monarchy, tried to gain advantage by extending its dominion. Schumpeter declares that the communist theory "seems to follow beautifully from two premises, which are embodied in the system: the theory of classes and the theory of accumulation. A series of vital facts seems perfectly to be accounted for. The whole maze of international politics seems perfectly cleared up by one stroke of analysis. ...At first sight the theory seems to fit the facts tolerably well. The most important instances are the Dutch and English conquest of the tropics. But other cases such as the colonization of New England, it does not fit at all." [5] Schumpeter proceeds to prove that the theory of the class struggle is as irrelevant to the facts of capital accumulation as to the facts of imperial expansion, which, like all political phenomena, is the product of a complex of causes.

The communist charge of "capitalist aggressiveness" is refuted by the essential pacifism of the bourgeois classes in the nineteenth century, though this essential pacifism does not of course prevent them from seeking economic advantages from any extant imperial enterprise. "Far from being the instigators of imperialistic policies," declares Hans Morgenthau, "capitalists as a group—aside from certain individual capitalists—were not even enthusiastic supporters. The literature and policies of the groups and political parties representing the capitalist element in modern societies are a testimony to the traditional opposition of the merchant and manufacturing classes to any foreign policy that, like imperialism, might lead to war." [6]

The refutation of the communist effort to make capitalism the

---

[5] J. A. Schumpeter, *Capitalism, Socialism and Democracy*, 2nd ed., New York: Harper & Brothers, 1941, pp. 50–51.
[6] Hans Morgenthau, *Politics Among the Nations*, 2nd ed., New York: Alfred A. Knopf, Inc., 1956, p. 48.

final and most virulent form of imperialism does not, of course, efface the deleterious effects of western imperial expansion on the weaker peoples, though it serves to prove that economic exploitation is not the sole motive or consequence of the impingement of strength upon weakness. In the light of nineteenth and early twentieth century history, one is inclined to hazard the judgment that the expression of ethnic and cultural arrogance left a mark upon subject people much more than economic exploitation. But the primary mistake in the liberal and Marxist indictment of imperialism is the failure to recognize the creative as well as baneful effects of the impingement of strong nations upon weak ones, particularly if the strong nations have some cultural, political, or technical resource which the weaker nation can use for its communal integration, for lifting the standards of its economy, or for enriching its cultural life. When, as in the case of the western impingement on China, the weaker nation is informed by an ancient and high culture, the resources for preserving political order may have been so weak as to invite imperialism. The order created by the western nations in China's "treaty ports" was an achievement, though the wounding of Chinese pride was a high price for the boon.

India, too, is informed by an ancient culture, but it lacked means of national cohesion in terms of a common language, a common legal tradition, and means of communication. Despite the resentments against British rule and despite the necessity of winning independence against the reluctant British master, it is obvious that India could become a nation only by the force of a common resentment against the imperial master on the one hand, and by the instruments of community which the master furnished on the other. The Indonesian relationship to the Netherlands is almost identical in illustrating the moral ambiguity of the imperial connection. In the case of the two nations which were briefly under our tutelage in our brief excursion into traditional imperialism, the Philippines and Cuba, it is clear that the Philippines profited greatly from our tutelage but it is not clear whether the average Cuban would not be better served by our continued sovereignty over the island than under the military dictatorships which have ruled that island since its independence. Autonomous nationalism is certainly no clear guarantee of domestic justice. It is difficult to measure the value of the independence of a parochial community against the value of justice in the arrangements of that local community. But the fact that many emancipated nations have not been able to establish either stability and order, and that the free Liberia, in which descendants of American Negro slaves have become an uncreative aristocracy in an African nation with lower standards of justice than other nations graduated from the tutelage of colonialism, is proof of the moral ambiguity, rather than the moral evil, of the imperial enterprise in which the western nations have been engaged.

The fact is that imperialism participates in the moral ambiguity of all community as it is related to dominion. We shall have opportunity of studying the unvarying factors in the relation of dominion to community. The most unambiguous relation of dominion to community is established in a free integral community in which checks are placed upon the dominion within the community, and in which every subordinate power is balanced by some other power. This approaches the ideal of order through a central power, and of justice through an equilibrium of subordinate powers.

We shall see that the price of larger, that is, of imperial community, was excessively high in ancient and medieval times because justice—the rightful relation of the various vitalities and forces in the community—was rigorously subordinated to the principle of order, the very basis of existence in the community, whether parochial or imperial. From the modern perspective, therefore, community was sacrificed too much to dominion, because it could not exist without dominion. Therefore all classical and medieval communities, whether parochial (national) or imperial, heightened the moral ambiguity of community and obscured the high price paid for order by excessive moral pretensions.

In the gradation of moral ambiguity we must place next in line the nationalistic imperialisms of the sixteenth to the nineteenth centuries. They developed when the old vision of a universal community had perished. The vision perished, rightfully in modern eyes, because no historic agent could justly claim the right to organize such a community or to give it a tolerable justice. These nationalistic communities which developed after the old sense of a world order, centered in Europe, had disintegrated were fractional efforts to extend that order to the outer or larger world. But they did it from the real center of their national life. Imperial urges were always compounded of missionary, political, and economic motives. But the power of the missionary motive did not necessarily give validity to the imperialism. Thus the Spanish Conquistadors both "saved" and enslaved the Latin American Indians; and from Columbus to Cortes the Christian missionary impulse was powerful. Spanish imperialism was actually the residual product of Spain's Christian encounter with the Moslems who had for so long occupied a portion of the Spanish soil. Their defeat being accomplished, the impulse directed itself to the virgin land of America, which Spanish and Italian love of adventure had opened up to Europeans.

The French missionary impulse to "civilize" was less powerful, and the French dominions were mostly lost in the eighteenth and nineteenth centuries, partly to the English and also through Napoleon's sale of Louisiana to America. The English missionary impulse was compounded of the desire to spread the gospel and to extend the institutions of democracy, which did not of course prevent a certain tardiness—in the nineteenth century—in granting the freedom for which the imperial enterprise was ostensibly the tutelage. In every case the universal value ostensibly propagated was transmitted through a national culture and lost some of its moral prestige by that transmittal. Clearly nationalistic imperialism was morally too ambiguous to be a lasting form of dominion and community. But this does not obscure the creative elements in such imperialism. The transmission of whatever virtues western political life possessed and of whatever skills western technology developed prevented these nationalistic imperialisms from being the unalloyed evils, which are now asserted by communist propaganda and also frequently felt by the victims and beneficiaries of this imperialism. Their reactions are for the moment politically very potent and very embarrassing to the western world. But the sober judgments of history will be less charged with the emotions of the hour.

Among the various forms of dominion and community we must regard as most dubious the modern form of universal imperialism, elaborated from a utopian vision. It is morally dubious precisely because it contains ingredients which make for its present success. It builds a tremendous power apparatus by the prestige of a creed which promises the elimination of all force from human society. It is universal in claims because it pretends to have a cure for universal evils. It is the character of utopianism to promise redemption not from some evils but from all evil. Imperialism in the name of universal values was, as we shall see, a characteristic mark of dominion for many millenia. The claims were always dubious because no value embodied was as universal as claimed, and the community which was organized by and for the prestige of the ideological scheme was not as universal as intended.

The modern Marxist form of this compound of universalism and imperialism is particularly dangerous, partly because of the spuriousness of the utopian claims and partly because a monopoly of power has been built upon the basis of the ideological claims. This monopoly operates in both national and international relations. The proletarian class in theory possesses the monopoly of power because it has a monopoly of disinterested virtue. The party is surrogate for the class and speaks for it. The nation which first achieved socialism claims the same monopoly internationally as the party claims nationally.

No more implausible scheme of power and utopia could have been presented. Yet this pseudo-universalism, which is bound to come in conflict with the developed national communities of Europe, has a certain plausibility in Asia and Africa where its utopianism is attractive to nations immersed in poverty; and where its universalism seems compatible with the desire for national independence which it promises to fulfill. The western democracies have probably not fully appreciated as yet how great the ideological advantages of the communist imperialism are, particularly since it has proved itself technically efficient and has thus offered the non-technical world a key to the gateway of technical civilization, which does not require the price of democratic freedom. This price is very high and seems beyond the competence of nations which are just emerging from pastoral and agrarian economies. After all, the development of democracy in the West was a long and tortuous process. It required both a religiously motivated defiance of political authority and an independent middle class which had sources of power in the economic life and not in the state machine.

The final question is where the empire of the American superstate fits into this gradation of value; and where the empire which is so desperately anxious not to be an empire stands. The immediate answer must be that it may fit into the gradations on a high level in terms of abstract morals but politically its position is dubious. We must examine presently the cause for the vague and politically unimplemented universalism and aversion to imperialism of liberal democracy. We can only say provisionally that liberal democracy is vague on levels of community above that of the nation because its characteristic policies of assuring both order and justice by a check upon power and by an equilibrium of power do not apply except in a highly integrated parochial or national community. Nations have of course striven for both justice and an uneasy peace by the principle of the balance of power, which guaranteed justice in the national community. But the lack of a single organ of dominion and authority made it impossible to achieve a stable peace.

The exertion of our power corresponds to the liberal democratic standards in two ways: (1) Our power is checked by many independent centers of national power. We hold no monopoly of power as do the Russians. The equilibrium of power is in fact great enough to raise the question, not about the adequacy of justice, but about the adequacy of the center of power for order. The Russian bloc is certainly more cohesive than our own.

(2) Our power is subject to constitutional checks in so far as it submits to the disciplines of the United Nations. But the United Nations is not, and cannot be, a constitutional world order. To be so, the responsibilities of the nations would have to be measured more in terms of their power. Such a constitutional system is impossible on the present level of integration of the world community. For constitutions which perfect the equilibria of a community must also presuppose a measure of integration, which the world community lacks, and presumably will lack for decades to come, to the despair of those who think it easy to "put teeth" into the United Nations and to transform that organization into a constitutional world government. If we have made a mistake at all, in our abhorrence of empire, it was to treat the United Nations too much as if it were a world government.

There is, in short, no way of applying the liberal democratic standards to the expression of our power in world affairs. Our power is too great to conform to absolute or even to relative standards of justice, though the checks are sufficient to prevent arbitrariness. We may claim that we use our power in the interest of the total community with as much justice as is possible for nations, when all nations are instinctively prompted to consider their own interest, and the interests of others only as these are compatible with their own. But our moral claims ought not to go beyond this limit. We are not a sanctified nation and we must not assume that all our actions are dictated by considerations of disinterested justice. If we fall into this error the natural resentments against our power on the part of the weaker nations will be compounded with resentments against our pretensions of a superior virtue. These resentments are indeed a part of the animus of anti-Americanism throughout the world. They may be said to be the fruits of our efforts to govern an empire in terms of the ethos of liberal democratic idealism. We must analyze the permanent and unvarying factors and forces in the anatomy of communities, nations, and empires for many reasons, but chiefly to correct mistakes which the liberal democratic creed was bound to make from the limited perspective of advanced national communities, when it tried to come to terms with the problem of the community on the imperial level.

Both the liberal and the Christian conscience are frequently appalled by the factors of interest and power with which they must come to terms in dealing with community in larger dimensions. They do not want to come to terms with what seems to be the immoral conduct of the larger communities. It is frequently insisted that there is only one moral law for individuals and for nations. It is possible to accept this dictum only if it is understood that a valid moral outlook discerns the similarities in the conduct of individuals and communities. In both cases an action motivated solely by self-concern is immoral. In both cases the self-concern (or, in the case of the nation, sole concern for the national interest) is more powerful than the individual or the nation is inclined to admit. A valid moral outlook must be based upon an honest regard for the facts in the human situation, and must not construct norms which are impossible to achieve in view of the persistence and the power of man's self-concern, and more particularly of his collective self-concern. It is obviously wrong for either the individual or the group to pursue its interests consistently without regard for the interest of other individuals or groups who are bound to it in the bundle of life. It is also wrong to claim a larger measure of disinterestedness than is possible for either individuals or groups. But it is possible for both individuals and groups to relate concern for the other with interest and concern for the self. There are endless varieties of creativity in community; for neither the individual nor the community can realize itself except in relation to, and in encounter with, other individuals and groups.

It is interesting that a valid psychiatry has come to the same conclusions with respect to the individual as those at which a valid political science has arrived in regard to communities. This conclusion is that it is not possible permanently to suppress, by either internal or external pressure, the concern of the self for itself. The most loving parent combines with "sacrifice" for the children a healthy pride in perpetuating himself or herself in the other generation. Even the most loving parent may insinuate the love of power with concern for the child. A valid moral outlook for both individuals and for groups, therefore, sets no limits to the creative possibility of concern for others, and makes no claims that such creativity ever annuls the power of self-concern or removes the peril of pretension if the force of residual egotism is not acknowledged.

In individual as in collective life a tolerable harmony of competing and co-operating life impulses is reached, if the individual or the group recognizes the possibilities of creative relation to other life, and guards against excessive assertions of interest by moral and communal restraints, and balances competing vitalities as much as possible so that no force or vitality will be able to express itself unduly. All these forms of restraint do of course presuppose a central authority, which manages the whole competitive and co-operative enterprise. It has this authority by reason of the possession of both prestige and force. Only integral communities have been able to create stable authority through the prestige of the authority speaking for the community. In international life there is no stable source of prestige for the whole community. Efforts to create such an authority by purely constitutional means must confront the fact that the prestige of authority is necessarily the product of historical forms of community, which legal and constitutional means can perfect and redirect, but which they cannot create out of whole cloth. It is probable, therefore, that the world will live, if it does not destroy itself, for a long time in a state of semi-anarchy in which certain centers of authority, power and prestige will mitigate the anarchy much as anarchy was mitigated in nineteenth century Europe by a balance of power.

But despite these limitations on the principle of order for the community of mankind, the peril of mutual annihilation by the two blocs of power has reintroduced concern for mankind in such a way as would have surprised the idealists of the past centuries. The peril of nuclear war is so great that it may bridge the great ideological chasm between the two blocs and make them conscious of having one thing in common: preference for life over death. It is too early to predict in what form and by what arrangements this sense of a common humanity may be institutionalized. But if it is institutionalized and the enemies achieve some kind of accord on the edge of the abyss of mutual annihilation, it will once more be proved that history is as full of unpredictable developments as of recurring patterns of community.

CHAPTER III

Community and Dominion in Nation and Empire

ALL communities of mankind, from the most primordial, the family, to the larger communities of nation and empire, are dependent on the one hand upon some internal force of cohesion and on the other hand upon the unifying power of a central authority. The internal force of cohesion is not necessarily a "common love" or interest as Augustine assumed. The family and the larger family of the primitive community are bound together by the attractive power of consanguinity. The sense of kinship is the first, and the most persistent, force of community. Economic and political mutualities, that is, mutualities of trade, and the binding force of common political obligations, are later forces of communal cohesion.

But none of these cohesive forces, which may be described as "horizontal," obviate the necessity of the vertical force of cohesion inherent in a central authority. Dominion is a necessity of community from the lowest to the highest, from the most primordial to the latest forms of communal life. This dominion validates itself to the community as a prerequisite of its order; but every form of dominion, except possibly the first dominion of fatherhood, contains an embarrassment to the moral consciousness of man. That embarrassment consists in the fact that the dominion and authority are established from motives of self-interest. The integral and parochial communities are organized and ordered by the classes in the community which hold the most significant social power.

The fact of dominion in all communities, whether national or imperial, is a continuing factor in man's communal existence, though it is a factor which is easily obscured in modern culture.

33

Does not the democratic principle of "the consent of the governed" eliminate dominion and establish self-rule? And has not a democratic society eliminated force as an instrument of dominion since voluntary consent obviates the necessity of force? And has not the elimination of force also eliminated empire, the cohesion of which rested primarily upon force?

But despite the seeming chasm between traditional communities existing from the dawn of civilization to the end of the Middle Ages and the modern democratic communities, there is a constant factor in the need of a community for government. The fact that the authority of all governments rests upon both force and prestige also belies the theory of a radical difference between new and old forms of nations and empires. The cohesion of the American national community presumably was established by the rational consent of the thirteen colonies, who wisely formed a single nation. But while the Civil War is studied in all our history books it has not struck the imagination of the nation that in a crisis force was necessary, and was used, to preserve the unity of the nation. A war solved the unanswered question about the Constitution: whether it established a confederation of states or an integral nation. Yet it must be observed that not merely the force of arms but the rapidly developing means of community on the level of communications, trade, and geographic integrity were potent in establishing the unity of the nation and the prestige of the federal government. When, in 1957, the governor of a state sought to defy the Supreme Court of the United States, federal troops were ordered into the state to quell the defiance. It is significant that they were used not so much as instruments of force as of symbols of majesty, and if the federal government had been quick enough to assert the majesty of the law it might have dispensed with force as the symbol of that majesty. The final majesty was the general recognition, even by a recalcitrant minority, that the nation was in fact united and that its conception of justice ultimately would prevail over all parochial conceptions.

The majesty of a democratic national government is simply the majesty of its obvious right to speak for the community. It is the mouthpiece of the community. But the majesty also includes another more transcendent element. It is derived from the belief that it elaborates a "justice" which the community recognizes as a norm, more authoritative than any given law. In short, on the national level dominion is obscured in democratic communities, both because the force is used only in crises and in subjecting recalcitrant minorities, and because the majesty of government is the majesty of the community itself, plus the majesty of justice, which transcends any parochial conception of justice.

We have stumbled in our national life upon some of the constant factors of man's communal and political existence. It is obvious that the anatomy of community and dominion is clearer in traditional than in democratic societies and we must therefore turn to traditional societies to study the anatomy. The anatomy is clearer partly because the component of force is more obvious, since traditional societies have, on the whole, been integrated by military power. The interested nature of the rulers is also more obvious since it was usually their ambition which served as the motive for integrating both the parochial and the imperial community. The moral embarrassment both about the factor of force and the motive of its use is the same in both traditional and modern societies, but the strategies of obscuring both the factor of force and the interested motive of its use are different. And the difference makes for a clearer outline of the relation of prestige or majesty to force than in the modern situation. For in all traditional societies religious and philosophical claims are used much more obviously to increase the prestige of the ruler.

It is significant that priests and soldiers were partners in both primitive and civilized traditional societies. The soldiers were the obvious wielders of force, but the priests or priest-kings were more potent in the partnership for they organized and manipulated the ideological system which gives the soldier the right to use force in the interest and in behalf of the community. It must be understood that the term "priests" is used symbolically. It includes the political oligarchs of an atheist communist state, who have recently given abundant proof that they can maintain ascendancy over the soldier (the discomfiture of General Zhukov comes to mind) even in a dictatorship in which force is so important that few dictatorships escape the dominance of the military man. But the priests who are the first and last agents of the "organization of consent" can maintain their dominance if the community lives within a general ideological framework in which prestige rather than pure force operates in giving the ruler authority, because they are the creatures and manipulators of the ideological frame which gives the community its final cohesion.

If the integral parochial community is organized by the class possessing the most significant power the larger imperial community is organized by some dominant parochial community. The various city-states of Egypt and Babylon succeeded in giving unity to these first great nation-empires, partly by the imposition of superior force and partly by the manipulation of the ideological factors which gave the rulers of the particular dominant city-state the right to rule over the vast dominion. Thus the priests of the Egyptian city-states of Memphis, Abydos, and Heliopolis constructed and reconstructed the texts of the solar monotheism or henotheism of Egypt to present the ruler, the Pharaoh, as the instrument of Re, Osiris, or Amon. In the same way, though not so expertly, the Babylonian Empire, which was variously ruled by the kings of Sumeria, Akkad, Babylonia, and Assyria, constructed the religious pantheon to give the god and the ruler of the particular city-state the prestige of an intimate relation with, or being the manifestation of, Marduk and Shamash. It was in the name of the latter god of justice that the greatest lawgiver of ancient times, Hammurabi, claimed to present his code of laws. These religious pretensions, which are the very stuff of the ideological framework of prestige, are not to be thought of as pure fraud. The priests of the city-states certainly manipulated the sacred texts, but they did not create the religious dimension out of whole cloth. The idea that the king was the nexus between the cosmic and the social order, and the instrument of the conformity of the one to the other, springs naturally in the human heart not only among primitive people but also in ancient civilizations whenever men are

impressed by the stability of a political order which their generation did not create and therefore recognize as the fruit of "providential" factors.

The religious factor in the prestige of authority may be manipulated by the conqueror himself in co-operation with a captive
priesthood. When the Persians, who preceded Alexander and the
Romans in world conquest and the establishment of "universal"
dominion over both Mesopotamia and Egypt, sought to stabilize
their rule, Cyrus, the first Persian conqueror, and his son Cambyses claimed not identity but affinity with the gods of both Babylon and Egypt without renouncing their relation to Ahuramazda,
the great Persian god. Cyrus announced his rule in the following
fashion in Babylon:

> I am Cyrus, king of the universe, great king, mighty king, king
> of Babylon, king of Sumer and Akkad, king of the world quarters,
> ... seed of royalty from of old, whose rule Bel and Nabu love,
> over whose sovereignty they rejoice in their heart.[1]

Cyrus claimed the favor of the Babylonian god Marduk specifically in this way:

> When I made my gracious entry in Babylon, ... I took up my
> lordly residence in the royal palace. Marduk, the great lord, turned
> the noble race of the Babylonians toward me, and I gave daily
> care to his worship. My numerous troops marched peacefully into
> Babylon. In all Sumer and Akkad I permitted no unfriendly treat-
> ment. The dishonoring yoke was removed from them. Their fallen
> dwellings I restored; ...
>
> Marduk, the great lord, rejoiced in my pious deeds, and gra-
> ciously blessed me, Cyrus, the king who worships him, and
> Cambyses, my own son, and all my soldiers, while we, in sin-
> cerity and with joy praised his exalted godhead. ...[2]

Cyrus' son Cambyses, in a monument in the other great land
of Egypt, was equally pious in claiming the favor of the Egyptian
pantheon. The monument bears the inscription

---

[1] Albert Ten Eyck Olmstead, *History of the Persian Empire, Achaemenid
Period*, University of Chicago Press, 1948, p. 51, cites Cyrus *Cyl*, II, 20ff.
[2] *Ibid.*, p. 53.

Horus, Samtowi, king of Upper and Lower Egypt, Metsiu-re, son of Re, Cambyses, may he live forever. He made as his monument to his father, Apis-Osiris, a great sarcophagus of granite, which the king of Upper and Lower Egypt, Metsiu-re, son of Re, Cambyses, dedicated, who is given all life, all stability and good fortune, all health, all gladness, appearing as king of Upper and Lower Egypt, forever.[3]

After the death of Cambyses, Darius, the usurper, claimed the Persian throne and made shrewd contact with the Persian, the Babylonian, and the Egyptian pantheon of the gods. To the Satrap Aryandes he wrote of his desire to cultivate the priesthood of Egypt:

Let them bring to me the wise men among the warriors, priests, and scribes of Egypt, who have assembled from the temples, and let them write down the former laws of Egypt until year XLIV of Pharaoh Amasis. The law of Pharaoh, temple, and people let them bring here.[4]

In his relation to Babylon Darius was more pretentious for he tried to appear as the new lawgiver, after the fashion of the famed Hammurabi. Darius' laws were explicit imitations of the code of Hammurabi but the code was promulgated in the name of the Persian god Ahuramazda:

O man, what is the command of Ahuramazda, let this not seem repugnant to you; do not depart from righteousness, do not revolt.[5]

On a much more primitive and purer level we see the anatomy of sovereignty, particularly the relation of the religious and the martial factors, in the Saul and David legends in the books of Samuel. Here the primitive priest-elder, Samuel, is being replaced by tribal warriors, whose prestige derives partly from his anointing of them and partly from their military prowess. "Saul slew a thousand, but David ten thousand," chanted the women of Israel. The embarrassment of later generations about the martial basis for kingship is charmingly betrayed in the story of the build-

---

[3] *Ibid.*, p. 90.   [4] *Ibid.*, p. 142.   [5] *Ibid.*, p. 123.

ing of the temple by Solomon, the son of David.[6] According to
the story, David confesses:

> As for me, I had in mine heart to build an house of rest for
> the ark of the covenant of the Lord, and for the footstool of our
> God, and had made ready for the building. But God said unto
> me, Thou shalt not build an house for my name, because thou
> hast been a man of war, and hast shed blood. Howbeit the Lord
> God of Israel chose me before all the house of my father to be
> king over Israel for ever: ... And he said unto me, Solomon thy
> son, he shall build my house and my courts; for I have chosen him
> to be my son, and I will be his father.

The religious prestige of the dynasty both obscures the force
which established it and makes force less necessary in preserving
its authority. But it is wrong to assume that religion is the only
source of prestige for the authority of government. Aristotle manages to veil both the factor of force and the interested nature
of dominion in his study of politics. This indifference to the facts
of dominion is the more remarkable because Aristotle initiates
his study of the community by pointing to the most primordial
and persistent of all communities, the family, and observing the
dominion of the father in this community. "There must be a
union," he observes

> of those who cannot exist without each other, namely male and
> female, that the race may continue. This union is formed, not
> of deliberate purpose but because in common with other animals
> and plants, mankind have a natural desire to leave behind an
> image of themselves.[7]

In this community, in which nature and history are not yet clearly
distinguished, as Aristotle rightly observes, the binding force of
community is not merely kinship but the dominion of the father.
Aristotle quotes Homer to the effect that "each one gives law to
his children and to his wives." [8] This dominion is important for
Aristotle and he introduces not only the male dominion but the
fact of slavery by the dubious expedient of terming the ox, which

[6] I Chronicles, 28; 2–6.   [7] Aristotle, *Politics* I, Chap. 2, sec. 2.
[8] *Ibid.*, I, Chap. 2, sec. 7.

Hesiod regarded as necessary for the household, as "the poor man's slave." For had not Hesiod said, "First house and wife and then ox for the plow"? The authority of the father as the primary source of all dominion has been a perennial theme in the political theories of the West. These theories are always logically dubious but correct historically. They are dubious logically if they assume that the endless contrivances of force and prestige, by which political authority is maintained, is justified as inherently right because they are historically related to the most primordial of dominion, the authority of the father. For the authority of the father is so imbedded in the community of the family; and, despite the incidence of wicked fathers, the relation of power to justice and love is very intimate. But the legitimacy of the primordial dominion does not prove the legitimacy of any dominion historically derived from it. This fault in logic is clearly seen in Luther's effort to derive the authority of government from the authority of the father in the "order of creation." Nothing in history, except perhaps the authority of the father, belongs to the "order of creation." For in history human contrivance is always mixed with nature; and human contrivance always has the twofold effect of creatively enlarging the purposes of pure nature and of corrupting her innocence. John Locke devoted the first of his *Two Treatises on Government* to a refutation of Sir Robert Fillmer's defense of the royal power as being derived from the authority of the first father, namely Adam.

While the relation of the father's authority to all subsequent forms of dominion does not morally legitimatize them the proposition is historically correct, with the exception that male authority is probably itself an historical contrivance and that a purer nature, or history closer to nature, had evolved matriarchy rather than patriarchy. For the mother is the more obvious parent of the two; and in kinship groups it is the mother's—rather than the father's —authority in which dominion first expresses itself in community. Bachhofen in *Das Mutterecht* suggests that the plays of Aeschylus and Sophocles echoed the struggle between patriarchal and matriarchal forms of government, which preceded the flowering of Athenian culture; and Aristotle may have been as unhistorical as

Luther in assuming that the father's authority belonged to the "order of creation." Perhaps the father's authority is established at the historical moment when human contrivance first interferes with pure nature.

What is more significant is that when Aristotle moves rather quickly from the most primordial community of the family to the more advanced community of the Greek *polis* he obscures the factor of dominion, which he had illumined in dealing with the family. "A social instinct is implanted by nature in all men," he writes; "yet he who founded the *polis* is the greatest of all benefactors." [9] The *polis* was not so simply founded as these words imply. It was the product of a more tortuous history than is implied in Aristotle's theory that the benefactor who founded the *polis* was the one who gave the city its constitution. Aristotle is not unmindful of the tortuous history of the Athenian state nor of the rival lusts for dominion which resulted in anarchy before a precarious order was established. The historian Thucydides, who described this history very well, came to the conclusion:

> Of the gods we know, and of men we believe, that it is a necessary law of their nature that they rule wherever they can.[10]

Community or the enlargement of community is thus a by-product of the lust for dominion.

In Aristotle's mind the authority of the *polis* was derived from its constitution, and the constitution was not conceived as the product of vital historical forces but as a product of pure reason. Hence the "inventor" of the *polis* was regarded as a "benefactor." Plato, in distinction from Aristotle, sought disinterestedness, not in the law but in the philosopher king, whose knowledge of the eternal ideas and love of truth would make him transcendent to the play of passion and interest in the community. Plato had, of course, some awareness of the temptation of the corruption of interest, in the thought of the rulers, for he seeks to protect the "guardians" from this corruption by ordaining that

[9] *Ibid.*, I, Chap. 2, sec. 15.
[10] Thucydides, *History of the Peloponnesian War* V, Chap. 105.

> None of them should have any property of his own beyond what is absolutely necessary. Neither should they have a private house or store, closed against anyone who has a mind to enter. ... They should agree to receive from the citizen a fixed rate of pay, enough to meet the expenses of the year and no more, ... Gold and silver we will tell them, they have from God. The diviner metal is within them, and they therefore have no need for the dross which is current among men, and ought not to pollute the divine with any such earthly admixture.[11]

Aristotle does not expect this transcendent disinterestedness from the rulers. He places the transcendence over interest in the law. The "statesman," rather than philosopher-king, must deal with a realm of contingency, which is not to be mastered by pure reason (*nous*) but by practical wisdom (*phronesis*). The exercise of pure reason is limited to the contemplation of the pure forms of reality.

> Now if you take away from a living being action, and still more production, what is left but contemplation? Therefore the activity of god which surpasses all others in blessedness is contemplative; and of human activities, therefore, that which is most akin to this must be most of the nature of happiness.[12]

Clearly rational disinterestedness for Aristotle is not possible for the statesman but only for the scientist and philosopher-mystic. The relation between the political order and the cosmic order is established by a rational law which imitates the reason of the cosmos. It will be seen that the metaphysical method of obscuring the factors of interest and power in the dominion of the community differs from the religious approach. Yet from Plato to Hegel the philosophical identification of some contingent establishment of political order with the cosmic order is not as different from the religious sanctification of dominion as it may at first appear. It is surely significant that both Plato and Aristotle took the Athenian city-state for granted as the final form of political organization,

---

[11] Plato, *The Republic* III.
[12] Aristotle, *Nichomachean Ethics* X, Chap. 8, 1178b.

thus betraying that the purest reason must begin with some historical presuppositions. It is also significant that Aristotle's pupil,
Alexander, annulled the power of the city-states and incorporated
them into his empire, availing himself of Stoic universalism, rather
than the particularism of his tutor. Furthermore it was not the
philosophical preference for universalism over particularism which
motivated him but the impulse to imperial dominion.

It was a constant debate in the early days of imperial Rome and
throughout the Middle Ages whether the law stood above the king
or whether the king embodied the law. Thus Plutarch (*circa* A.D.
50–120) asked,

> Who, then, shall rule the ruler? We may answer, with Pindar,
> "Law, the king of us all, both mortals and immortals"—not the
> external law which is written in books or on tablets of wood, but
> the law which is Animate Reason (*empsychos logos*) embodied
> in him [i.e. the ruler]; the law which always lives with him and
> watches over him, and never leaves his soul destitute of the gift
> of leadership.[13]

Plutarch's confusion about whether the law is over the king or
embodied in the king may be said to mirror accurately the confusion between the sense of the supremacy of the law, which is said
to be one of the sources of the Roman political genius, and the
adoration of the emperor in religious terms, which was a consequence and presupposition of the immense authority of the emperor in imperial Rome.

In any case traditional communities, whether city-state or empire, were as interested in proving that the ruler used his power
disinterestedly because he had contact with or embodied the cosmic, divine order as modern liberalism is concerned to prove that
dominion is responsive to the public interest, empirically determined.

In either case the prestige of the ruler, and his consequent right

[13] Ernest Barker, *From Alexander to Constantine, Passages and Documents
Illustrating the History of Social and Political Ideas*, 336 B.C.–A.D. 337,
Clarendon Press, Oxford, 1956, p. 309.

to use force, depends upon his ability to persuade the community that he speaks and acts not by motives of dominion but in behalf of the community and for the community.

If the prestige of the rulers of an integral community derives from the claim that they speak for the community and in the interest of the community, the prestige of an integral community, whether city-state or nation in an imperial community, derives from the claim that the ruling state speaks in the name of or is the instrument of a cosmic or universal purpose. In rational terms the claim is that the law established by the dominant state is identical with the cosmic order. In religious terms the claim is that the ruler of the dominant state is ordained by God to establish the universal order. All traditional empires from that of Alexander to the eastern Christian, the western Christian, and the Islamic empires have an ideological framework of quasi- or pseudo-universalism.

The claim of universality began with Alexander who used Stoic universalism to overcome the division between Greeks and Persians in his empire, which was actually unified by the force of arms. It is significant that the imperial community which Alexander built actually influenced the universalism of Stoic thought and that Zeno's thought was more universalistic after Alexander's triumphs than before. The history of empire and universalism or pseudo-universalism reveals Bergson's theory in his *Two Sources of Religion and Morality* to be quite abstract, for it does not deal relevantly with the actual course of history. According to Bergson, the two sources of religion and morality are the "static" religion operating in a closed (i.e., primitive) community in which "religion is a defensive reaction of nature against the dissolvent power of intelligence." It gives sanctity to the community against the interests established by rational egotism. Bergson's view of the relation of self-interest to reason is quite similar to that of Thomas Hobbes. The second form of religion is "dynamic" and it operates to "open" the society by creating a sense of universal community. Bergson rightly emphasizes the universalistic tendency in Stoic and Christian thought but is quite oblivious to the actual history of imperial communities and the relation of the prestige of imperial dominion to the claims that the imperial community is in fact the universal community; and that the ruler of the imperial community is sacred because he is the instrument of ultimate values. The facts of history contradict this thesis of Bergson. Instead, they support the contention of Denison that the empires formed at the dawn of civilization substituted loyalty to the "sacred ruler" for loyalty to the "sacred brotherhood." Loyalty to the ruler became a more inclusive force of cohesion than loyalty to the community because the imagination is unable to comprehend the total larger community with which it has no direct contact, except through the symbol of the sacred ruler who embodies the order and justice of the larger community.[14]

A distinction must be made between the claims of the royal dynasts, who ruled by "the Grace of God," and the emperors, who claimed both divine favor and universal authority for their rule. Both types of religious prestige must be studied more closely as a prelude to the question whether there are any modern secular analogies in either the communist culture or the liberal democratic culture. In studying the rise of the modern nation, which preceded by no more than a century or two the development of democratic institutions, it is obvious that the authority of the king was used by the national communities and by other opponents of the imperial community or universal community of church and empire. Thus the Reformation's anti-papalism became involved in Luther's and Calvin's rather extravagant protagonism of the divine authority of the royal or princely ruler of the parochial, chiefly national, community.

The substance of the prestige of the national king is on the legitimacy of his rule, and that legitimacy is established by dynastic succession. Kings of the Christian nations were never thought to be divine, yet they still claimed to rule by "divine right." The right was inherited from their fathers. The principle of dynastic legitimacy is so absurd a principle of selection of men fit to rule

[14] Cf. John Hopkins Denison, *Emotion as the Basis of Civilization*, New York: Chas. Scribner's Sons, 1928.

that its persistence throughout all history, despite the weight of injustice which absolute monarchy created, must have some fairly obvious cause. That cause is the prevention of anarchy, the avoidance of competing claims to the throne upon the death of the monarch. Dynastic legitimacy from the Egyptian Pharaohs to the kings of contemporary nations was a fairly simple way of preventing competition for the right to exercise power in the name of the community. If that right was undisputed the royal government was "legitimate," in the sense that it could count on the implicit consent of the subjects and did not have to use force to gain their explicit, though unwilling, consent. The explicit consent by which authority is transmitted in a democracy is obviously a more rational method when a society has become mature enough to submit the problem of succession to explicit choice without running the danger of civil strife. In Latin American republics the community is not mature enough to have very much success in averting such strife.

The legitimate governments of traditional societies availed themselves almost universally of the institution of monarchy to integrate the community and furnish it with a single organ of will. The monarchs of the nations were more universally hereditary than those of the empires, for in both the western and eastern Christian empires the principle of adoption or election was frequently used, primarily because the empire possessed some select electoral body which could insure the succession. It was not necessary that the emperor should be the legitimate heir of his father; it was only necessary that it appear so. The Japanese nation boasts of one royal house from the beginning of its history to the present time; but in many periods of its history, particularly during the Shogunate of the Tokugawa family in the late eighteenth century, surreptitious adoption of an infant was resorted to. There may be some question whether any of the Tsars of Russia possessed Romanov blood after Catherine the Great. She certainly had no Romanov blood and was so promiscuous that her son Paul may not have been of royal blood.[15] The fact that the semblance of legitimacy was more im-

[15] Cf. Richard Charques, *A Short History of Russia*, Dutton, New York, 1956, p. 103.

portant than the fact proves that the important function of legitimacy was to insure implicit consent of the rule and thus to dispense with the necessity of a clash of force to determine the right to rule. The monarchs naturally took seriously the idea of legitimacy as an inheritance of a right divinely ordained for their family. The Pharaonic monarchy of Egypt, for example, insured the succession by elaborate rites in which the new Pharaoh was liturgically celebrated as the embodiment of the divinity of the deceased father. In his study of Egyptian political life, Henri Frankfort reports:

> The danger of chaos also existed in the political sphere, even though the nature of kingship in Egypt excluded the rise of pretenders that marked almost every interregnum in the Assyrian and Roman Empires. Those who were of the blood royal could assert their claims to the throne, though normally the eldest son was expected to succeed. Tuthmosis III reports how he was chosen as the next ruler by an unsolicited oracle of Amon. But the gods were not always so obliging, and there are indications that even in the early Fourth Dynasty princes contended among themselves. Then chaos engulfed the state.
>
> The Egyptians had evolved a scheme which mitigated the risks of the succession and had the further advantage of conforming to the mythological pattern of "Horus appearing in the arms of his father Osiris." This scheme consisted in appointing the heir-apparent co-regent with his father. The transition at the death of the old king would then, it was hoped, be entirely smooth. . . .[16]

In Ernst H. Kantorowicz' comprehensive study of the religious pretensions of medieval monarchs, *The King's Two Bodies*, all the various elaborations of the idea of divine calling and divine infusion are presented. The idea of the king's divinity is most succinctly stated by the anonymous Norman author in the late Middle Ages:

> We have to recognize [in the king] a twin person, one descending from nature, the other from grace . . . ; one through which, by

[16] Henri Frankfort, *Kingship and the Gods: A Study of Ancient Near Eastern Religion as the Integration of Society and Nature,* University of Chicago Press, 1948, p. 101.

the condition of nature, he conformed with other men: another through which by the eminence of [his] deification and by the power of the sacrament [of consecration], he excelled all others.[17]

Kantorowicz' analysis reveals the great similarity in the religious doctrines of royal absolutism in the late Middle Ages, with the general tendency toward the divinization of the monarch in all cultures. The similarity includes preoccupation with the idea that royal dignity does not perish with the death of the king, an insistence which is liturgically symbolized by the phrase, "Le roi est mort! ...Vive le roi!", which made its first appearance in the the interment of Louis XII in 1515, but which expressed a traditional insistence of the medieval culture, acknowledged by innumerable papal decretals that *dignitas non moritur*.[18]

It must be noted that these religious interpretations of royal authority were expressed within terms of the Christian faith, ostensibly abhorring all idolatrous worship of the creature, rather than the creator; and that religiously justified royalism outlasted the Middle Ages by centuries. Royal absolutism was indeed, in some respects, accentuated by the Reformation and Renaissance.[19]

Whether anything in the rational and sober age of democracy corresponds to this dimension of authority in the religious age, is a question to which we must now address ourselves.

---

[17] Quoted in Ernst H. Kantorowicz, *The King's Two Bodies: A Study in Mediaeval Political Theology*, Princeton University Press, 1957, p. 500.
[18] *Ibid.*, p. 411.
[19] It was not only Luther and Calvin who were extravagant in their support of royal or other princely authority, as distinguished from Papal and imperial authority. Tyndale, the early English Reformer and translator of the Bible, had this to say about royal authority: "The King is in the world without law, and may, at his lust, do right or wrong and shall give accounts to God only. ...God hath in all lands put kings, governors and rulers in his own stead. ...whosoever, therefore resisteth them, resisteth God...and they that resist shall receive their damnation."

CHAPTER IV

Democracy and Authority

THE prestige of political authority in traditional communities, whether of empire or nation, or whether drawn from philosophical or religious presuppositions, seems so absurd to the modern mind that a great chasm would seem to exist between democratic governments deriving the authority of the "ruler" from "the consent of the governed" and the traditional rulers who derive their prestige from the claim of incorporating the cosmic order. But while the chasm is great it is not as great as the modern imagination assumes. A careful scrutiny establishes the fact that the religious claims of the kings and emperors was an indirect expression of the passion for the peace of the community, and "the king's second body" is but the established order of the community which is guaranteed to be without interruption of rule by the insistence that the heirs of his "natural body" have a right to succeed to his rule. Kantorowicz sums up the matter in the words:

> It was indeed the amalgamation of the dynastic continuity of the natural body with the perpetuality of the Crown as a political body in the person of the ruling king which accounts for many ambiguities and inconsistencies in late-mediaeval English political theory.[1]

The thought of Thomas Hobbes, a true "modern" though not a democrat, furnishes the bridge between the medieval and the modern world. For Hobbes' protagonism of royal absolutism for the sake of preserving the peace of the national community betrays at once the utilitarian motive in the royal absolutism of traditional communities and the modern empiricism and voluntarism, which insists that historic communities are the artifacts of human reason

[1] Kantorowicz, op. cit., p. 381.

and imagination and not the products either of a cosmic reason or of a divine will. Hobbes is a rigorous anti-Aristotelian both in his empiricism and in his voluntarism. "It is manifest," declares Hobbes,

> that during the time men live without a common power to keep them all in awe, they are in that condition which is called warre, and such a warre, as is of every man, against every man.[2]

This state of nature is as mythical as Aristotle's "benefactor" who first "founded the *polis*"; for history is not as sharply divided from nature as the Hobbesian theory of the social compact assumes, but it is also not as identical with a cosmic rational and natural order as classical philosophy assumes. The social compact in which men exchange the insecurity of the state of nature for the security of an ordered community is in fact the product of slow accretions of habits of loyalty and community; and therefore historical community is built on natural community by imperceptible stages, which makes the war of all against all an unhistorical concept.

But a very significant realism is hidden in this myth, which partly explains the fact that, once conceived, John Locke could build a democratic conception of government on the idea of the social contract which Hobbes had used in the service of political absolutism. That realism consisted in the fact that he recognized that the rational faculties of men did not, as the classical or medieval political theory assumed, inevitably guide man to the common or the general good. Reason was in fact the servant of interest and passion. It was precisely man's rational capacity which created a disharmony between a private and a common good. For, declared Hobbes, in marking the distinction between animal and human communities:

> ... these creatures, having not (as man) the use of reason, do not see, nor think they see any fault, in the administration of their common business: whereas amongst men, there are very many,

[2] Thomas Hobbes, *Leviathan, or The Matter, Forme & Power of A Commonwealth, Ecclesiasticall and Civil*, ed. with introduction by Michael Oahshott, Oxford, Basil Blackwell, 1955, Pt. I, Chap. 13, p. 82.

that think themselves wiser, and abler to govern the public, better than the rest; and these strive to reform and innovate, one this way, another that way; and thereby bring it to distraction and civil war.[3]

Hobbes' description of the political realities is remarkably similar to Augustine's conception of the uneasy armistice of contending forces in the *civitas terrena* caused not by the love of war, but by everyone altering the peace according to his lights and interests. Both Augustine and Hobbes may express an extravagant realism and fail to do justice to the moderating influences upon human ambitions exercised by the traditional restraints, mutualities, and loyalties of the community. But in Hobbes' case these restraints are all comprehended in the order of civil society, as distinguished from the state of nature. In his case the mistake in his realism consisted mainly in making too sharp a distinction between nature and history and fixing the covenant of civil society with too great a precision. Thus the gradual development from primitive to civilized community is obscured.

But whatever the defects of the Hobbesian realism, we have in his thought a thoroughly empirical and utilitarian conception of dominion which gives a very modern justification for a traditional institution, so modern in fact that it was embarrassing to the royalists of Hobbes' day. Hobbes' thesis is that the ruler's majesty is the majesty of the community itself and his authority must be absolute in order to preserve the peace and order of the community against the peril of anarchy, arising from competing factions and interests. Hobbes' political absolutism had only a brief day in the history of English thought for revoltuion and restoration soon gave way at the end of the century to the constitutional monarchy of William and Mary established by Parliament, and laid the foundation for that curious partnership between monarchical and parliamentary legitimacy which has been the achievement of English political life.

Since the theories of both Hobbes and Locke rested upon the

[3] *Ibid.*, p. 117 (Pt. II, Chap. 17).

conception of the social contract, and since both appealed to the courts of "nature" and "reason," we obviously confront two contradictory revisions of the classical and medieval conception of natural law. An analysis of this contradiction may prove that the testimony of reason is not as immune from the traditions and habits of history as each of these exponents of rationalism believed, or, for that matter, not as free from historical conditioning as the classical and medieval exponents of natural law assumed.

In the thought of Hobbes men were "rational" when they pursued their own ends without restraint, and rational in another sense when they entered into a social contract which abolished war of all against all by the imposition of a superior authority. From the standpoint of Locke men were rational in guarding their "natural" rights and in setting up a government which drew its authority from the "consent of the governed." The natural right which men do not sacrifice in civil society is their "freedom from absolute arbitrary power." For, argues Locke,

> This . . . is so necessary to and closely joined with a man's preservation that he cannot part with it but by what forfeits his preservation and life together; . . .[4]

The government which Hobbes regarded as necessarily absolute for the sake of preventing anarchy, Locke regarded as dangerous because "absolute arbitrary power" imperiled the life and liberty which Hobbes intended to preserve. This contradictory attitude toward the state can be explained only in terms of history. Behind Locke's reasoning is the whole history of the Puritan radicalism which inspired or informed the Cromwellian revolution. According to the radical Puritans,

> The continual oppressors of the nations have been kings, which is so evident that you cannot deny it; and ye yourselves have told the king (whom yet you owne) that his whole sixteen year reign was one continued act of breach of the law.[5]

[4] John Locke, *Two Treatises of Government*, ed. with intro. J. W. Gough, Oxford, Basil Blackwell, 1946 *Second Treatise*, Chap. IV, par. 23, p. 13.
[5] Quoted from Don M. Wolfe, *Leveller Manifestoes of the Puritan Revolution*, Thomas Nelson Sons, 1944, p. 115 (1646 Leveller tract "Remonstrance of Many Thousand Citizens").

The great watershed of history was not in Locke but in the Puritan messianism of the revolution, which regarded royal authority not as the guarantee of order but as the source of injustice and oppression. Since traditional governments are productive of both order and injustice, the turning point in history comes when the emphasis lies upon the fruit of injustice rather than the fruit of order. This change could only come when a new class had entered society which felt the weight of injustice and also had the capacity to resist it. But that class would also have to be armed with the conviction that it could create a system of justice and order which would avoid the anarchy against which Hobbes warned. The democratic radicals both in England and France had this confidence, but England eventually avoided anarchy while France did not. Both appealed to "reason" and "nature." The difference was that the English radicals were operating against an historical background in which the principle of "the consent of the governed" was already validated by the power of Parliament and by a conception of "reason" as expressed in Sir Edward Coke's *Institutes of the Laws of England*. Coke had been the champion of Parliament against the royal prerogative in the reigns of Elizabeth and James I. A part of his work was suppressed by King James and was only published in 1642. His *Institutes* consistently appealed to the established historical rights of Englishmen, beginning with Magna Carta, and supplied "incontrovertible proof that the laws to which Parliament appealed sprang from the mind of God and were revealed in the life and history of men." [6]

The confidence that the welfare of the community could be maintained on the principle of the "consent of the governed" was justified by the long history of parliamentary power, at least sharing the authority of the king in representing the community. It was justified "rationally" by the idea that the king ruled only as long as he obeyed the covenant of justice, which presupposes a previous covenant between the community and the king. In the words of a Puritan preacher, Andrew Perne,

---

[6] William Haller, *Liberty and Reformation in the Puritan Revolution*, Columbia University Press, 1955, p. 71.

> If a nation consent together and choose a king to reign over them, the people will fight for him as long as he keeps the agreement between them. But God is above kings and religion above civil laws.[7]

The concept of a mutual covenant between king and people was almost universal in the radical protestantism of the seventeenth century. It is classically expressed in the anonymous (Huguenot?) tract "*Vindiciae contra Tyrannos*":

> It is certain that the people require the performance of covenants. The people ask the king whether he will rule justly. He promises he will. Then the people answer, and not before, that they will obey faithfully. The king promises, the which failing to be accomplished, the people are quit of their promises.

This myth of a mutual covenant is probably the source of the myth of the social contract as propounded by Hobbes and Locke. It expresses succinctly the element of human decision in history, even as the myth of the reason and the will of God having been revealed in the parliamentary history of England symbolizes the factors in history which are there "providentially" and not by the conscious contrivance of any generation. Taken together these two strains of thought give Locke the assurance, not only to rest government's authority on the "consent of the governed," but to trust that the governed will organize their government through the will of the majority. So Locke argues,

> ... when any number of men have, by the consent of every individual, made a community, they have thereby made that community one body, with a power to act as one body, which is only by the will and determination of the majority; ...[8]

To give the community an organ of will through a majority of the representatives of the citizens was by no means an obviously "rational" way of supplanting the royal organ of communal will. It became rational only against the background of the traditional procedures of parliament, which incidentally also gave some se-

---

[7] Quoted in Haller, *op. cit.*, p. 76.
[8] Locke, *op. cit.*, p. 169 (*Second Treatise*, Chap. VIII, par. 96).

curity to the minorities, which was lacking in the French Revolution.

Whether through the confusion of Rousseau's conception of the "general will," which would fulfill and annul the particular wills of individuals, or through the physiocratic conception of the "laws of nature," which must be obeyed though tyranny is necessary to enforce obedience, or whether in Condorcet's vague conception of free men having no sovereign "other than their reason," the confidence in reason and in liberty based on reason bred tyranny and anarchy in France. On the other hand the Lockean theories of consent of the governed, combined with the idea of this consent being expressed through the rule of majorities, made for ordered government in both Britain and America. "Rational" procedures, relying on the wisdom of historic traditions and experience, proved more reasonable than the procedures dreamed up by abstract reason.

Locke's theory evidently rested upon historic traditions which it did not adequately explicate. The idea that government derives its authority from its prestige—and its prestige from the fact that it speaks for the community—was expressed by implication. But the fact that even such a government must avail itself of force and could not have been established except by the revolutionary force which first annulled the right of King Charles I to rule, is not expressed at all. The radical Puritans who first announced the theory of the consent of the governed were quite conscious of the fact that they were establishing that right of democracy in a civil war against the king. Therefore they always united their protagonism of the principle of consent with that of the right of resistance to tyranny. But in Locke's more peaceful era even this echo of the clash of forces disappears and Locke merely contents himself with blandly proving that tyrants and conquerors have no "right" to rule over the conquered. Locke's confidence that a purely rational democratic process would correct injustice is stated as follows:

> ... Whensoever, ... the legislative shall transgress this fundamental rule of society, and either by ambition, fear, folly, or corruption, endeavour to grasp themselves, or put into the hands

of any other, an absolute power over the lives, liberties, and estates of the people, by this breach of trust they forfeit the power the people had put into their hands, for quite contrary ends, and it devolves to the people, who have a right to resume their original liberty, and by the establishment of a new legislative, such as they shall think fit, provide for their own safety and security, which is the end for which they are in society. ...[9]

The people may have "a right to resume their original liberty"; but a simple theory which makes the principle of consent both a right and a power obscures the components of authority, both force and prestige, which implement the right in specific instances. Fortunately the Anglo-Saxon democratic tradition, in both England and America, was not limited to a theory which only implied, but did not explicate, the actual experience by which the people achieved their rights, while the prestige and power of government remained in its traditional position.

David Hume drew upon the empirical tradition of British philosophy and the empirical political tradition in challenging both the concept of the state of nature and the idea of imprescriptible rights. Hume believed that

... 'tis utterly impossible for men to remain any considerable time in that savage condition, which precedes society; ...[10]

and he denied that the "state of nature" had ever existed. It was a "mere philosophical fiction, which never had, and never cou'd have any reality." [11] He gave a more accurate historical account of the rise of civil government, declaring that the first rudiments of government "arise not from the quarrels, not from men of the same society, but among those of different societies." [12] Communities were in short integrated by the increase of the power and the prestige of its leaders, enhanced by the crisis of conflict with

[9] *Ibid.*, Chap. XIX, par. 222, p. 108.
[10] David Hume, A *Treatise of Human Nature*, ed. L. A. Selby-Bigge, Oxford, Clarendon Press, 1951, Vol. III, Pt. III, p. 493.
[11] *Ibid.*, p. 493.
[12] *Ibid.*, p. 540. Compare Essay V "Of the Origin of Government," *Essays Moral, Political, and Literary*, 2 vols., ed. T. H. Green and T. H. Grose, London, Longmans, Green & Co., 1898.

other communities. This was a description of the historical process of integration, in which the modern principle of the consent of the governed was not read back into the foundation of communities and the creation of government.

Edmund Burke, emphasizing the historical processes in the creation and preservation of authority in modern governments, was even more specific in supplementing the democratic theory, if it placed too great reliance on the principle of explicit consent as the source of the state's authority. The authority of the government to speak for the community is derived both from tradition and from its ability to harmonize and express the multifarious interests and passions of the various groups. The prestige of government therefore depends partly upon its unbroken rule. For a good government

... moves on through the varied tenor of perpetual decay, full renovation, and progression. Thus, by following the method of Nature in the conduct of the state, in what we improve we are never wholly new, in what we retain we are never wholly obsolete.[13]

The emphasis upon historical tradition as the source of authority is balanced by the emphasis upon the prestige of the state which is derived from its ability to harmonize and give expression to the greatest variety of interests. "The British State," he declares,

... is without question, that which pursues the greatest variety of ends and is the least disposed to sacrifice any one of them to another or to the whole. It aims at taking in the entire circle of human desires, and securing for them their fair enjoyment. Our legislature has been ever closely connected, in its most efficient part, with individual feeling and individual interest.[14]

In the thought of Burke both Hobbes' passion for the harmony of the whole and Locke's passion for freedom are fused in the conception of a state which draws its authority and its capacity to preserve peace both from an unbroken tradition and from its

---

[13] Edmund Burke, "Reflections on the Revolution in France" in *Works of the Right Honourable Edmund Burke*, rev. ed., 12 vols., Boston, Little, Brown & Co., 1865–7, Vol. III, p. 275.
[14] *Ibid.*, "Regicide Peace," Vol. 5, p. 374.

ability to harmonize, without annulling, the variegated interests and passions of a modern community. In his theory the place of the throne in the structure of the state was rather more important than it proved to be in subsequent history. But its power was eroded by precisely those historical processes which Burke regarded as superior to the inclination of the French Revolution to reform the state according to a logical design. The French revolutionary state, he declares, "is systematic. It is simple in principle; it has unity and consistency in perfection" but "the design is wicked, immoral, impious and oppressive" because the pretentious wisdom of a generation has forced an arbitrary order upon the complex historical unity of the community without regard to the historical factors.[15] Burke's "Reflections on the Revolution in France" may not have done full justice to the differences between a political order in which modern liberties were gradually insinuated into ancient unities, and one in which the old degenerated into an oppressive unity until new forces in society became so obsessed with the oppression that they were blind to the wisdom expressed in the historical process. But he did give a most impressive account of the way that historical growth could adjust the new to the old in such a way that the legitimacy of government, drawn both from its historic right to speak for the community and from its ability to satisfy its varied interests, could be seen to be something more complex than the prestige drawn from explicit consent.

Our founding fathers, having established a new republican government, were naturally not intent on proving the traditional sources of authority. The union through a constitution gave the principle of explicit consent an immediate relevance. But they agreed with Burke in deriving the prestige of government not merely from its "right" to speak for the community in terms of its original charter but in terms of its ability to give the community a tolerable harmony of interests under conditions of freedom. James Madison, as conscious as Hume and Burke that reason could not simply arbitrate conflicting interests since it was the servant

[15] *Loc. cit.*

rather than the master of interest, contended in his defense of the federal constitution that a wider community of the federal union would be most likely to prevent any interest from becoming oppressive. He wrote:

> As long as the reason of man continues fallible and he is at liberty to exercise it, different opinions will be formed. As long as the connection subsists between his reason and his self-love, his opinions and his passions will have a reciprocal influence upon each other. ... The diversity of faculties in men, from which the rights of property originate is no less an insuperable obstacle to the uniformity of interest. The protection of these faculties is the first object of government.[16]

Madison's opinion that the wider federal union would create a realm of harmony and competition in which no sectional or sectarian influence would become oppressive to other interests, his effort to render "faction" harmless by enclosing it in a wider competition of interests, hardly anticipated the development of the two-party system in Anglo-Saxon democracy or its superiority over multi-party systems of continental democracies. But it did foreshadow the non-ideological character of the American parties and their tendency to become alliances of local interests.

The integrity of government rested upon the fortuitous circumstances that the right of suffrage, demanded by the commercial middle classes to gain political power commensurate with their growing economic power, was something more than a middle-class ideology. That was proved by the fact that the industrial workers could use the vote as an instrument of their interests as they pressed hard upon the heels of the middle classes in entering the arena of the struggle for rights in the modern industrial state. The use of this wider political power led to policies of which the modern "welfare state" is the end product. But it is significant that this equalization of political power could not validate itself as an instrument of justice until the middle classes projected the economic policies of classical economics as the fruit of a disinterested science when it was in fact, or proved to be, an ideological

[16] James Madison, et al., Federalist Papers, No. X.

weapon for middle-class interests in their contest with the industrial proletariat. The prestige of modern democracies could not be vindicated until bitter experience refuted this error. It could not be corrected in time to prevent the Marxist challenge of democratic society from gaining a degree of plausibility in some western democracies.

Adam Smith, author of "The Wealth of Nations," was certainly no bourgeois ideologue; but he made the honest mistake upon which classical economic theory is founded. He equated the self-interest of men with their economic interests and assumed that if the irrelevancy of political power in economic life were removed the free market would ultimately harmonize all competing interests, including those of labor and capital. Unfortunately the worker was not as free to follow the market as Smith assumed. He was restricted by his craft and his locality. He was subject to ethnic loyalties, traditional ties, and other than economic interests which gave him as an individual a great disadvantage in bargaining with the ever-growing aggregates of industry. The injustices of early industrialism were the consequence.[17] It is important to realize that the error embodied in classical economy, which may have been "honest" in its inception, became nevertheless an ideological weapon of the classes of industrial owners. It continues to be such a weapon, long after common experience has refuted the error and modern democracies have vindicated the prestige of democratic government by allowing the organized power of the industrial worker to enter the arena of communal competition for the purpose of gaining the equilibrium of power which is the perennial prerequisite of justice. Only by establishing this new equilibrium under the conditions of modern industrialism were western democracies rendered immune to the virus of Marxist rebellion. The moral prestige of democratic government slowly weaned the industrial workers from their devotion to the revolutionary apocalypse and drew them back into the give and take of the democratic equilibrium of social forces. In the process some hitherto unknown

[17] See Karl Polanyi, *The Great Transformation*, New York, Rinehart and Co., 1944.

quasi-sovereignties of management and labor union were developed which would have surprised, and probably outraged, both John Locke and Adam Smith.

The prestige of a democratic government is clearly only partly derived from the idea that it speaks with the "consent of the governed." It must fashion equilibria of social and political power which will impress the people with its capacity to preserve order and to extend justice. If it fails in this purpose generally, if it operates only with the confused notion of Rousseau's "general will," it will either lose the tacit consent of the whole people, haunted by the fear of anarchy, or it will lose the confidence of a section of the people, which feels itself particularly defrauded of justice. In that case it must meet rebellion with force. Montesquieu was quite right in pointing to the difficulty of achieving this balance. He attributed the prevalence of "despotic" governments to the failure of nations to create the balance which would create both order and justice, though he thought of the balances in purely political terms and neglected the social vitalities beneath the level of government but subject to its regulation which are the problem of all democratic governments. "After what has been said," wrote Montesquieu,

> one would imagine that human nature should perpetually rise against despotism. But notwithstanding the love of liberty, so natural to mankind, notwithstanding their innate detestation of force and violence, most nations are subject to this very government. This is easily accounted for. To form a moderate government it is necessary to combine the several powers; to regulate, temper and set them in motion; to give, as it were, ballast to one, in order to enable it to counterpoise the other. This is a masterpiece of legislation, rarely produced by hazard, and seldom attained by prudence.[18]

Montesquieu was speaking of separation of political powers which the various efforts at constitutional monarchy after the

---

[18] Baron (Charles de) S. Montesquieu, *The Spirit of the Laws*, Book V, Chap. 13, p. 76, translated: T. Nugent, rev. J. V. Prichard. Intro. O. W. Holmes, 2 vols. New York, D. Appleton & Co., 1900.

French Revolution tried vainly to achieve. They failed because the divided and balanced authorities of king and parliament had different sources of prestige, the one in a decaying monarchical tradition and the other in the suffrage of the people. The confusion of the people in failing to give their representatives a clear mandate for the principles of democracy added to the stalemate of the contest of the two powers of government.

Montesquieu's analysis of the necessary balance in government for the sake of moderation and justice is much more valid when applied to the social and economic forces which democratic governments partly express and partly manipulate. Their prestige and the tacit loyalty of the community depends partly upon their reputation for accomplishing this difficult task with success. They need not gain the explicit consent of all elements in the population for every measure they take as long as they have the implicit trust of the people that the system will make for order and justice in the long run.

If the sources of authority of democratic governments are fully measured, it will be clear that the prestige of a state which allows the hazardous alternation of particular governments by explicit consent rests upon this implicit trust of the people. This confidence is necessary to overcome disappointments in the preservation of what they conceive to be their vital interests in the short run. Implicit consent is, in short, not the fruit of a purely rational process or calculation. It is informed by emotions and attitudes which are not quickly formed or re-formed. In that respect democratic legitimacy and traditional legitimacy are similar despite the chasm which separates them.[19]

The fact that habits of loyalty are only slowly changed is attested by the tardiness with which the parliamentary democracies which have retained the symbol of the crown have shifted authority from the monarch to parliament until the monarch becomes merely the mouthpiece of parliament.

In England, where Parliament proved its supremacy, not only

[19] See Guglielmo Ferrero, *Principles of Power*, G. P. Putnam's Sons, New York, 1942.

in the settlement of 1688, which was so significant to Locke's democratic thesis, but again when the Hanoverians were brought to the throne, this obvious supremacy of Parliament did not prevent the King from having considerable authority. His authority was so great, in fact, that our founding fathers could cast George III in the role of a despot, though their conflict was obviously with King and Parliament and not with an absolute monarch. The authority of the king gradually evaporated, decade by decade and century by century, until the crown has attained the status of symbol in the modern day. The crown is the symbol of the authority of government as it has been bequeathed to one generation by history and tradition. It has the authority of the community which knows itself the heir of the ages, and is, in Hooker's phrase, a "corporation immortal." The government constructed through parliamentary majority, upon the basis of suffrage, meanwhile wields the actual power. But even in a contemporary instance the Crown becomes an important symbol. For when a party government speaks through the mouth of the monarch the authority of the majority becomes the authority of the community by the alchemy and poetry of a tradition which has given the present not merely a relic of the past but a symbol capable of expressing both the fluid balances of democracy and the perennial habits of loyalty toward traditional authority, which represented the one virtue of traditional government.

The very fact that this conflation of two philosophies of authority exceeded the wisdom of both the monarchists and the anti-monarchists is a revelation of an historical wisdom which is derived not from the conscious calculations of men but from their gradual adjustments to each other in new situations.

It is significant that all monarchies based upon the principle of the "separation of powers," beginning in revolutionary France and comprising the so-called constitutional monarchies of Russia, Spain, Italy, and Prussia, perished, some of them not until the two world wars. They perished for many reasons, some of them irrelevant to our present interest. But they were all defective in that they tried to balance traditional authority against parliamentary authority. They tried to follow Montesquieu's prescription for a separation of powers. But that prescription succeeded only in America where the executive and the legislative, with their separate powers, both derived their authority from the suffrage of the people.

Thus through long and tortuous decades modern men have learned that the absolute and irresponsible power of traditional monarchs is dangerous to the justice of the community, tending to sacrifice it so much to the boon of order that the order becomes more and more oppressive in a community of varying vitalities and awakening and growing interests. But they have also learned that the majesty of government is not simply derived from the rational and explicit consent of the people; and that the order and justice, necessary for the preservation of its prestige, are not simply the fruits of freedom or of reason. They are difficult products of a free expression and manipulation of social forces. The art by which they are achieved was not anticipated in the simpler democratic theories of the eighteenth and nineteenth centuries. Modern democracies confound the Marxist strictures against democracy which assume that present practice corresponds to past theories.

The most interesting aspect of this development is that wherever practice forced amendment to the original theory it also recovered some of the values which were implicit in the traditional conceptions of the prestige and majesty of government, but which were discredited by their involvement in a system of irresponsible power. Fortunately the freedom permitted and enjoined in the pure democratic theory gave democratic communities the opportunity to correct the theories in the practical experiences of their statecraft. Thus this freedom was justified even when, and precisely when, it permitted the correction of the original theory that there was a simple step from the realm of tyranny to the realm of freedom. The competitive Marxist culture, lacking this basic freedom, cannot easily make the corresponding corrections in its presuppositions. It is important to remember that modern democratic theories, almost without exception, assume the autonomy of the national state. Modern nationalism usually availed itself first of the instrument of royal absolutism and, in the second stage, of democracy. This nationalism was in sharp contrast to the universalistic conceptions of dominion which dominated western history from antiquity until the end of the Middle Ages. This universalism, in practical political terms, created the empires which we are about to analyze more thoroughly.

The similar nationalism of the royal absolutists on the one hand and the liberal democrats on the other is obvious if the thought of Milton and Locke is compared with that of Hobbes and Jean Bodin. Both schools of thought assume devotion to the national community as man's ultimate loyalty. But the liberal democrats have one distinguishing mark. It consists in the expression of a vague universalism as a kind of vestigial remnant of the more precise universalism of Dante, for example. The modern concepts are vague because no one proposed to organize the universal community, at least not until the twentieth century liberals came upon the principle of "collective security."

John Locke expresses the vague sentiments of good will toward the community of mankind admirably when he writes:

> The end of government is the good of mankind, and which is best for mankind that the people should be always exposed to the boundless will of tyranny, or that the rulers should be sometimes liable to be opposed when they grow exorbitant in the use of their power, and employ it for the destruction and not the preservation of the properties of their people? [20]

In the mind of Locke and his disciples the "good of mankind" was served very simply by the abolition of tyranny. The organization of any supra-national community did not engage him as a significant problem.

We must make a more thorough study of this vague universalism of liberal democracy, presently; and must analyze its embarrassments as it comes into conflict with an organized pseudo-universalism as we have it in modern Communism. For this form of universalism seeks to reconstruct in modern terms a structure of power which dominated western history until the rise of the modern nation.

[20] John Locke, *op. cit., Second Treatise*, Chap. XIX, par. 229, p. 112.

CHAPTER V

The Anatomy of Empire

EMPIRES, since the dawn of civilization, have been the fruit of an expansive parochial community, either city-state or nation. These parochial communities have, by superior military prowess, usually established dominion over other parochial communities, sometimes annulling their sovereignty and sometimes only abridging it by subordinating the subject community to the dominant power.

The inevitable result of imperial domination has been the enlargement of community, but usually only on the level of the expansion of trade. (In the construction of modern empires it was indeed the necessities of trade which prompted the gradual expansion of sovereignty by military means in the case of British and Dutch imperialism in Asia.) The other instruments of community, in addition to a dominant military power and trade, were added in varying proportions: common laws and a common language for the élite in the conquered dominion. But neither in the ancient empires before Rome nor in the modern empires since the fall of the Christian Roman Empire has a cohesive community been established on the imperial dimension. Hence the word "imperialism" to the modern mind connotes aggressive expansion. The connotation remains correct in the sense that empire, in its inclusive sense, is the fruit of the impingement of strength upon weakness. But the power need not be expressed in military terms. It may be simply the power of a superior organization or culture. The desire to expand the superior culture is one of the motives of imperial expansion.

The usual course of empire in the west has been that of a city-state creating a larger dominion by forcibly bringing other city-states under its control. (There were, of course, empires built by nomadic tribes; those of Genghis Khan and the Moslems, for instance.) The nation as we know it did not exist in this early history. The Roman empire was gradually formed by the military and political genius of the Roman city-state. Its first victories resulted in the unification of the Italian peninsula, in the course of which it used the policies of both federation and annexation.[1]

There is little to distinguish imperial structure and imperial nations in ancient history, for both are unified by a superior power; and the factors of cohesion, other than force, are minimal. But there is a slight difference which is symbolized by the first two civilizations of Egypt and Babylon or Mesopotamia. Egypt was a geographically and ethnically homogeneous region, alternately unified and broken up by the various city-states but always exhibiting a basic geographic integrity and ethnic homogeneity, even in the periods of its decay. China, from ancient to modern times, exhibits the same characteristics of an imperial nation in which military and bureaucratic organization furnished the principal force of cohesion, but in which a sense of ethnic kinship prevented the structure from being "imperial" in the conventional use of the word.

Mesopotamia, the other great early civilization, growing in the river valleys of the Tigris and Euphrates, had a different history. The foundations for the civilization were laid by the Sumerians. The kings of Akkad built upon Sumerian foundations and Hammurabi furthered the unification of the community by the first written code of law known to history. The region was subsequently overrun by various peoples, Hittites and Kassites, but the first imperial conquerors were the Assyrians, for their dominion extended beyond the boundaries of the integrated Mesopotamian culture. The Assyrians have become historic symbols of aggressive imperialism. They had not the art of subjugating without annihilating their foes. They razed the cities which they conquered, murdered the kings and magnates, and ruled by terror.

Therefore one must give the Persians the honor of being the first successful imperialists, for they not only conquered both

[1] Cf. Leon Homo, *Primitive Italy: The Beginnings of Roman Imperialism*, Routledge and Kegan Paul Ltd., 1927.

Egypt and Mesopotamia, but federated and subordinated subject peoples, artfully constructing the religious myths of the subject peoples so as to give the Persian emperors the prestige of being the instruments of the "great god." We have previously noted that the ultimacy of the claim of dominion does not necessarily connote a claim to the universality of the dominion. As late as the nineteenth century the emperor of China addressed Queen Victoria in a fashion which denoted the ultimacy of the claim without connoting universality of dominion. The famous imperial commissioner, Lin Tse-hasü, wrote to the government of Queen Victoria in this fashion:

> Magnificently our great Emperor soothes and pacifies China and the foreign countries, regarding all with the same kindness. If there is profit, then he shares it with the peoples of the world; if there is harm, he removes it on behalf of the world. This is because he takes the mind of heaven and earth as his mind.[2]

The vertical claim of the ultimacy of the emperor's sovereignty almost, but not quite, implies the universality of his dominion and reveals the structure of political-poetic imagination very similar to the claim of the Persian emperors, expressed for instance in the words:

> I am Cyrus, king of the universe, great king, mighty king, king of Babylon, king of Sumer and Akkad, king of the world quarters . . .[3]

Perhaps the conclusion is permissible that the universality of sovereignty is always implicit in the ultimacy of the sovereign's claim. But it does not become explicit in the ancient empires, where there was no strong consciousness of a larger community beyond the sovereignty of the ruler.

It is important to note that when unqualified ultimacy is ascribed to the god from whom sovereignty is derived, as was the case in the prophetic interpretation of Yahweh, the God of Israel,

---

[2] John K. Fairbank and Ssu-yü Teng, *China's Response to the West*, Harvard University Press, Cambridge, 1954, p. 24.
[3] Quoted by Olmstead, *op. cit.*, p. 51.

the universality of his rule is not identified with the nation's rule. The God of Israel becomes the lord of all the nations, who uses the great empires of Babylon as his "battle axe" and Cyrus of Persia as his "anointed." [4] We must postpone consideration of this dimension of community until we study the problem of the universal and the imperial community.

THE CITY-STATE, NATION, AND EMPIRE

A striking fact in the history of community is that the parochial community, which becomes the organ and core of empire, is not the nation but the city-state. The step from city-state to empire makes the integral and autonomous nation a late arrival in history.

Among the many causes for this development, which must be examined with greater care, presently, it is necessary only to point out that the first techniques of civilization, particularly those of war and trade, were the instruments of power rather than of integral cohesion. Therefore the integral community, which was bound together not only by dominion but by the sense of kind and the habits of co-operation, could not be enlarged until the invention of printing increased the range of communication for the integral community.

While the Greek city-states were conscious of a common nationality, yet the varying dialects prevented a common language from becoming a force of cohesion. Even the prestige of the Athenian dialect was not able to overcome this divisive element to which, of course, lack of geographic contiguity contributed. In the same fashion the sense of a common German nationality in the Middle Ages was obscured by the multiplicity of dialects until Luther's translation of the Bible gave the German people a common tongue. Linguistic homogeneity added to the sense of ethnic kinship are two of the most powerful agents of integral parochial communities, which in these latter times are identified with the modern nation-state. Whether the nation-state is really the absolute norm for a parochial community we shall have reason to inquire presently.

[4] Cf. Sigmund Mowinckel, *He that Cometh*, Oxford, Basil Blackwell, 1956.

EMPIRE AND UNIVERSAL COMMUNITY

We have noted the various expansive and aggressive developments of early civilization which resulted in the creation of larger—that is, imperial—units of community. But in these developments community was obviously subordinated to dominion. Empires did not become unified communities until they were invested with the sense of being a universal community, or at least a community comprising the civilized world. Alexander the Great took the first steps in this direction by using Stoic universalism as a cohesive power which would bind Greeks and Persians into a common community. The Alexandrian empire did not outlast the life of its founder, but the Roman Empire increasingly availed itself of Stoic universalism as an ideological cement of cohesion, to supplement the force which was the final source of its unity.

Beginning tentatively with Alexander and more positively in pre-Christian Rome, particularly in the late stages of the Republic, we have the gradual elaboration of an interesting conjunction in history, which was fully developed in the three religiously oriented empires of the Middle Ages. This is the conjunction of the imperial impulse with the religious and philosophical idea of the ideal community, as it was first presented by Stoicism and Hebraic prophetism and fully developed by Christianity, the heir of both prophetism and Stoicism. The Islamic Empire must be regarded as a vulgarized version of this conjunction. It had the same sense of universality as the two Christian empires, but its sense of the identity between the ideal and the actual was more complete and without the reservations which both prophetism and Stoicism had bequeathed to Christianity.

The conjunction between the idea of an ideal community and the large community which military prowess had established contains almost all the problems of the relation of morals to politics which have engaged, and sometimes tortured, the conscience of civilized man. For the ideal community must be at once more uni-

versal and more just than any actual community. The consciousness of a hiatus between the justice of the historic community and
the justice of the ideal community reveals the fact that men of the
earliest civilizations were conscious of the tremendous price which
had to be paid for the boon of order. The Messianic visions in the
cultures of both Egypt and Babylon prove the presence of this
uneasy consciousness even before the rise of the high religions of
Stoicism and Hebraic prophetism.

The uneasy conscience of the first two great civilizations, expressed primarily in various Messianic hopes and pretensions, significantly shows concern about the price of injustice which the
imperial order exacted, though the form of that order was taken
for granted and though there was no social force to give relevance
to the moral sentiments. Thus an Egyptian baron in the old kingdom, second union (twenty-seventh century B.C.), testifies in a
pyramid text:

> I gave bread to all the hungry [in his domain]. I clothed him
> that was naked therein. ... I never oppressed one in possession
> of his property. ...

A court physician of the same period wants it known, according to
this pyramid text, that

> I never used violence against anyone. Never have I taken the
> property of another by violence.[5]

In the subsequent feudal age some priestly courtier produced the
first document of social protest, since given the title of "The Eloquent Peasant," in which an unjustly accused peasant brings the
significant charge against his judge, which could be made with
equal validity against other courts and governments:

> Thou art set for a dam for the poor man to save him from
> drowning, but behold thou art his moving flood.[6]

[5] Charles Breasted, *Dawn of Conscience*, New York, Charles Scribner's Sons,
1933, pp. 124–25.
[6] *Ibid.*, p. 189.

The "Admonitions of Ipuver" give the first Messianic vision of the future reign of an ideal king, who is indeed the god Re himself. It is promised that

> ... he brings cooling to the flame [of social confusion]. It is said that he is a shepherd of all men. There is no evil in his heart. When the herds are few, he passes the day to gather them together. ... Where is he today? Does he sleep perchance? Behold, his might is not seen.[7]

The Messianism of Babylonia was retrospective, rather than proleptic, referring back to the Sumerian kings, particularly the reformer king, Urukagina, "Who righted the wrongs of the poor," and the king Gudea, who disciplined the priests and brought it about that "the strong did not oppress the weak."

The ethical rigor, manifested in both the hope of a universal community and in the establishment of justice within the community, expressed in both Hebrew prophetism and Greek and Roman Stoicism, thus had faint, though perceptible, anticipations in the oldest empires.

Hebraic prophetism was more rigorous in its demands because it spoke in the name of the transcendent creator God, and against the background of a pastoral equalitarianism, which a growing agrarian civilization was destroying. The rigorous justice which both Amos and the first Isaiah demand in the name of God is certainly beyond the reach of the great empires, with their hierarchy of power and privilege.[8] While the nation of Israel is constantly reproved for the failure of the elders and rulers to establish an equal justice, the Messianic vision of prophetism envisages the establishment of a Messianic universal community, which will realize the universality of the divine sovereignty of the God of Israel, whose power and glory transcend the vicissitudes of the nation. Of the universalistic content of the Messianic vision of the second Isaiah, Mowinckel declares:

---

[7] *Ibid.*, p. 198.
[8] Amos, Chaps. 6 and 8:4; Isaiah, 5:8–22.

... Yahweh has become king of the world, because He Himself has created this kingdom of His: As He was 'the first,' who created in the primordial age, so now He is 'the last,' who now creates anew. ... In the end Yahweh will receive homage from the whole world and be recognized as the supreme, the secret, the saving God. The honouring of Yahweh is the final goal of history.[9]

The rigor of this ethical perfectionism and universalism is expressed in the context of an eschatological hope. These are norms which transcend the possibilities of history. Even in the first Isaiah the vision of a perfect community presupposes the redemption of nature as the basis for a history in the Messianic age in which the rule of the Messiah will be characterized by perfect justice, for

... righteousness shall be the girdle of his loins, and faithfulness the girdle of his reins.

But this justice is possible only in a transformed nature,

... For the wolf ... shall dwell with the lamb, and the leopard shall lie down with the kid; ... and a little child shall lead them.[10]

Though the theological and philosophical presuppositions of Stoicism are quite different from those of prophetism the ethical rigor is remarkably similar. The one is rooted in a rational pantheism, in which god and nature, or the cosmic order, are identified. The other is informed by a theism which posits a personal God whose righteous and holy will created the world, and is sovereign over history, and who demands justice in all human relations. Yet the similarity in the ethical norms is striking. The divine justice defined by the prophets redresses the disbalances of history, demands special concern for the poor and needy, and pleads for the "widow and orphan." The Stoic rigor is expressed in its equalitarianism and universalism. Both these are, as in the case of prophetism, regarded as a primordial norm, from which men have strayed in historic existence. The "Golden Age" of Stoicism was rightly regarded by Christianity as analogous to its conception of "*justitia originalis*" or "perfection before the fall."

[9] Mowinckel, *op. cit.*, p. 144.   [10] Isaiah, 11:1–8.

There is even an inchoate eschatology in Stoicism faintly analogous to prophetic Messianism, though the perfection of the new age is not so clearly outlined.

> ... When the annihilation of the human race has been completed, and the wild beasts ... have likewise been destroyed,

writes Seneca,

> ... every species of animal will be created afresh, and the earth will once more be inhabited by men,—men born under happier auspices, knowing naught of evil. But their innocence will endure only so long as they are new. Wickedness creeps in swiftly.[11]

While the similarities of Stoic and Prophetic ethical rigorism are striking, the differences in their historical engagement are significant. The prophetic ethic never came in contact with the centralizations of power of a large empire, nor was there any temptation to identify its eschatological universalism with an imperial community. Stoicism, on the other hand, became culturally and religiously involved in two imperial ventures, those of Alexander and Rome. In both cases a pattern was laid which became the pattern of the mutual support between high religion and the imperial community. That pattern was to claim some identity between the universal community of religious vision and the actually established imperial community, and to subordinate the equalitarianism to the hierarchical necessities of imperial rule. Roman Stoicism made much of the difference between the *jus naturale*, which stated the ideal requirements of justice, and the *jus gentium*, the law of nations, which allowed, or even enjoined, the institutions of property, slavery, and government as requirements of relative justice.

The conjunction of Stoic idealism with empire is first observed, and in clearest outline, in the empire of Alexander. What was striking is that Stoic universalism was substituted for the parochialism of Aristotle, the tutor of Alexander. Aristotle had said, quoting Euripides,

---

[11] Seneca, *Questiones Naturales*, III, xxx, 7–8.

...Among barbarians there is no natural distinction between women and slaves because there is no natural ruler among them. They are a community of slaves, male and female. Therefore the poets say 'it is meet that Hellenes should rule over barbarians' as if they thought that barbarians were slaves by nature.[12]

It was not idealism but the practical demands of imperial state-craft which persuaded Alexander to abandon the apology for slavery and the parochialism of his distinguished tutor and to adopt some of the teachings of the Stoic philosopher, Zeno. The Persians whom he had conquered were obviously not the slave people with whom Aristotle identified the barbarians. Moreover, it was necessary to unite Greeks and Persians into a wider *homonoia* than hitherto had been envisaged. Before Alexander's imperial success,

> The business of a Macedonian king was...to promote Homonoia among the Greeks and utilise their enmity to barbarians as a bond of union; but barbarians themselves were still enemies and slaves by nature, a view which Aristotle emphasised when he advised his pupil to treat Greeks as free men, but barbarians as slaves.[13]

This mutual interaction between Stoic idealism and Alexandrian imperialism may be symbolic of the mutual relations between the impulse to dominion and the impulse to community, which we shall have the opportunity to view again and again, in the history of western politics. It may reveal that thought follows action as frequently as it prepares for new action. "The foundation of Zeno's World-State," declares Tarn,

> was Alexander's declaration that all men are brothers, a declaration which transcended all differences of race.[14]

[12] Aristotle, *Politics*, Bk. I, Chap. 2, 1252b.
[13] W. W. Tarn, *Alexander the Great*, New York, Cambridge University Press, 1948, Vol. II, *Sources and Studies*, Appendix 25 I, p. 404. In this Appendix Tarn traces the influence of Alexander's imperialism upon Stoic and Cynic universalism.
[14] *Ibid.*, Appendix 25 IV, 423.

In contrast to Alexander's universalism it is significant that the impulse to increase the religious prestige of his rule probably persuaded him to accept the title "the son of Zeus," a policy which was not popular among his Greek supporters.[15]

THE ROMAN EMPIRE

Of all the political achievements of western civilization the gradual extension of the dominion of the Roman city-state, first over the Italian Peninsula, then over the Mediterranean world, and finally over Europe and Asia Minor, had the most lasting effect upon the political life and thought of the West.

The Roman Empire began more modestly and proved to be more lasting than the imperial venture of Alexander, which disintegrated into the three succession states dominated by dynasties founded by his three generals, Ptolemy, Seleucus, and Antigonas. The Roman imperium began as a pure venture in military consolidation and lacked both the dynastic and the religious forces of cohesion in its inception. The Roman city-state was, in fact, under the rule of a republican government; and the senatorial oligarchy, which controlled both the army and the civil policy, made no pretensions about the universality of its rule or the ultimacy of its authority. It abolished the royal authority of the Etruscan city-state, which it had defeated, and maintained the supremacy of the senatorial oligarchy until the prestige of its army commanders surpassed the prestige of the senate. Beginning with Julius Caesar and ending with Augustus, the republic was transmuted into an imperial structure in which the Caesars were given the supreme authority in the empire and (though usually after their deaths) were worshipped as gods.

The conflict between the moral and religious legitimacy of dominion on the one hand and the pretensions of universal community on the other hand were evident in the encounter between Stoicism and Roman imperialism from the days of the younger Scipio to the Stoic emperor Marcus Aurelius. Stoic equalitari-

---

[15] *Ibid.*, Appendix 22 III, pp. 370–73. On Alexander's reservations see page 358.

anism was in conflict with the necessities of imperial dominion; it adjusted itself to the realities of power by advocating a mixed constitution, in which the king, the aristocracy, and the people divided the power. There was of course no dynast in republican Rome, but Scipio was cast into the role of the supreme ruler whom the Stoic philosopher was glad to guide. The other side of Stoic idealism, the universalism, was more compatible with Roman dominion and thus Stoicism became the ideological instrument for the Roman claim of being a "city composed of all the Nations" (Cicero). The exact relation between Rome and the universal community was of course not completely clear, even as Cicero's conception of the *jus naturale* and the *jus gentium*, the universal law of nature and the common law of all the nations in the Roman imperium, was somewhat confused. Cicero believed that the natural law was the law of a universal nature. It enjoined not only absolute equality, as in the primitivism of Seneca, but also justice in which liberty and order (*imperium et libertas*) were both secured. And one of the facets of liberty was the security of property. Thus Cicero became the father of the democratic theory which emerged in the English seventeenth century, for he believed both in the consent of the people as the basis of sovereignty and in the rights of property as the basis of any civil order.[16] Cicero's measured idealism, in which the equalitarianism of Stoicism was related to the idea of a mixed constitution, harking back not so much to a golden age as to the early Rome which he idealized, anticipated the theories of Montesquieu on the separation of powers, even as his theories of the purpose of government being to secure the rights of property anticipated John Locke. Cicero's idea of a balance of political powers, anticipating (or inspiring) the thought of Montesquieu, is expressed in *De Republica*:

> ...But all three [forms of government] have defects: in monarchies, persons other than kings have not sufficient rights under the system of civil law, or enough of a voice in deliberation; in

[16] Charles Norris Cochrane, *Christianity and Classical Culture: A Study of Thought and Action from Augustus to Augustine*, Oxford, Clarendon Press, 1940, p. 45.

an aristocratic system of government, the masses can hardly share in liberty, being destitute of any voice in common counsel and of all power; where everything is managed by the people, the government may indeed be just and moderate, but the uniformity of equality is itself inequitable since it leaves no room for any grading of degrees of worth.[17]

This modified equalitarianism is an admirable adjustment of the ethical ideal to the realities of the hierarchical structure of any community which both the liberal democrats and the Marxists of the eighteenth and nineteenth centuries neglected to their confusion.

Cicero's justification of property in which he anticipated (or inspired) John Locke is given in his *De Officiis*:

> The primary concern for those responsible for public affairs will be to make certain that every man is secure in his possessions and that there is no invasion of private right on the part of government. ... This indeed is the reason why states and republics have been created. For though nature herself prompts men to congregate together, nevertheless it is in the hope of protecting what they have that they seek the protection of cities.[18]

Cicero is commonly held to have been an unoriginal thinker who borrowed rather confusedly from his Greek sources. But he has the great merit of relating the ethical rigorism and universalism of Stoic idealism to the necessities of the Roman imperium in such a way that he created a moral frame of reference for Roman politics which even the Augustan age could not afford to disregard. Hence Augustus' elaborate recognition of the authority of the senate whose real power his own omnipotent power had in effect annulled.

On occasion Cicero stooped to sentimentality; for instance, when he criticized both Caesar and Pompey, "for both of them make power, rather than welfare their aim." [19] His mistake was no more grievous than that of the moralists of all the ages who failed to measure the intricate interaction between the impulse

[17] *De Republica*, I, xxvii, 43.   [18] *De Officiis*, II. c. 21, § 7.3.
[19] *Epistolae ad Atticum*, VIII, xi, 1–2.

to dominion and the impulse to justice. Furthermore, he must be credited with more circumspection than the liberal thinkers of the modern age which drew so heavily upon his thought.

Cicero's confusion in regard to the *jus naturale* and the *jus gentium*, the law given in nature and the law common to all nations, continues to plague natural law theorists throughout western history. In medieval Catholic theory it becomes the distinction between relative and absolute natural law, the latter consigned to man's "original perfection" (the Stoic "golden age") and the former permitting and enjoining the institutions of property, slavery, and government, which are the necessities of relative justice in the historic, that is, sinful world. Translated into modern terms, a rigorous ethical idealism does not permit the hierarchies of power and the harnessing of self-interest which all human communities find necessary. These necessities of communal integration are comprehended in post-Ciceronian theories under the concept of *jus gentium*, which the Roman jurist Hermogenianus (circa A.D. 300) defines:

> It is from this law of nations that there have been introduced among us wars; the separation of nations; the foundation of kingdoms; the distinction of properties; the setting of boundaries to estates; the grouping of buildings together; commerce; buying and selling; letting and hiring; and the creation of obligations —except for some which have been introduced by civil law.[20]

This distinction marks the basic difference between nature and history, between the forms of life which are given in natural necessity and those which contain human and historical contrivances, particularly the contrivances by which the community guards its order and the liberty of its citizens against the expansive desires of men. It is a distinction which classical idealism found difficult to make because it was not in accord with the basic presupposition of classical ontology, which regarded history, as well as nature, as subject to the eternal forms of reality. Nevertheless it is significant that Cicero came to terms with this distinction more

[20] Quoted in Barker, *op. cit.*, p. 261.

adequately than the modern idealists who were inspired by his thought.

It is not quite fair to Roman stoicism to present Seneca's less successful effort to relate Stoic idealism to Roman imperialism; for Seneca was a rhetorician, rather than philosopher, and the tension between morals and politics turns into sentimentality in his thought. It is nevertheless worth noting that Seneca's primitivistic equalitarianism and universalism could be expressed by one who tutored the young man who was to rule Rome as the Emperor Nero:

> It was greed which begot need, and by craving much, lost all. And so, though she [avarice] now tries to recover what she has lost, though she adds field to field, evicting neighbors either by purchase or by violence, though she extends her country-seats to the size of provinces and calls walking through her vast estates possessing them—in spite of all this, no enlargement of our boundaries can bring us back to the state from which we have departed. When we have done all we can, we shall possess much; but once we possessed the whole world.[21]

Seneca was able to brush aside the class distinctions of the Roman state with the observation:

> Do not all men spring from the same origin and breathe the same air? What is a Roman knight, what is a freeman, and what is a slave? These are but names springing from ambition and injury.

Yet Seneca could adjust himself to these distinctions to the point of glorifying the emperor's power in the name of the moral ideal of clemency and of the universality of his rule. Roman dominion is equated with the community of mankind with less reservation than in the thought of any other Stoic. In *De Clementia* Seneca addresses the young Emperor Nero on the significance of his dominion and declares:

> Just as the whole of the body is the servant of the mind . . . so this innumerable multitude [of all the human race], which sur-

---

[21] Seneca, *Epistolae Morales* XC, 34, quoted by Arthur O. Lovejoy and George Boas, *Documentary History of Primitivism and Related Ideas*, Baltimore, Johns Hopkins University Press, 1935, Vol. I, p. 273.

rounds the life of one man, is ruled by his breath and swayed by his reason, and would crush and break itself, by its own force, if it were not sustained by his counsel.[22]

* * *

I have just made mention of the gods; and that reminds me that I shall do well to set up this rule as a standard to which the prince should conform—he should wish so to do to his subjects as he would that the gods should do to him. ... Herein consists the servitude of supreme greatness, that it can never become any less; but this inescapable lot is one which you [Nero] share with the gods. The gods, too, are kept in bondage by the heaven which is their abode; ...[23]

It will be seen how easily the equalitarianism is qualified by the religious respect for the imperial power and how Roman imperialism is equated with the community of mankind. The fantasies of Seneca are not of course as important as the interpretations of the founder of the empire himself, Augustus, who interpreted his supreme power constitutionally in such a way as to appear comparable with the republican constitution. In his *Res Gestae* he declares:

In my sixth and seventh consulships (28–27 B.C.), when I had extinguished the fires of civil war after receiving by common consent absolute control of affairs, I handed the commonwealth over from my own control to the free disposal of the Senate and the people of Rome. For this service done by me I received the title of Augustus by decree of the Senate...[24]

The power realities were of course quite different from the version Augustus suggests. The emperor had the supreme power and he allowed the senate to function for the purpose of enlisting the traditional loyalties of the republican period and appeasing the senatorial aristocracy, which incidentally was radically changed in the imperial period. This justification of imperial power in the name of the "consent of the governed" did not of course preclude

---

[22] *De Clementia*, I. iii § 5. Quoted in Barker, *op. cit.*, pp. 236–37.
[23] *De Clementia*, I. vii § 1 and viii § 3. Quoted in Barker, *op. cit.*, p. 237.
[24] *Ibid.*, p. 229.

religious justification in the spirit in which Seneca venerated the later Emperor Nero. Thus the proconsular preface to a decree of the Greeks in the province of Asia, ordaining the celebration of Caesar's birthday, observes:

> Whether the birthday of the most divine Caesar be more a matter of pleasure, or more a matter of profit, it is a day which we may justly count as equivalent to the beginning of everything ... inasmuch as it has restored the shape of everything that was failing and turning into misfortune, and has given a new look to the Universe at a time when it would gladly have welcomed destruction if Caesar had not been born to be the common blessing of all men. ... [25]

The course of the encounter between the power realities and the ideological system of Roman imperialism may be briefly summarized. Republican Rome had already justified its system of order by imposing the *pax Romana* on the anarchy of the Mediterranean world. But as the military exploit became more and more important in the preservation and extension of this order the senatorial aristocracy was unable to prevent civil war from breaking out between its various ambitious commanders.

The prestige of the senatorial oligarchy was not sufficient to control the military leaders, armored with both power and prestige. The victory of Julius Caesar gave a momentary peace but at the price of the annulment of traditional liberties. Caesar having been assassinated by the senatorial conspirators, fresh wars broke out among his heirs and collaborators and peace was finally restored by Octavius' victory over Anthony at Actium. Obviously the power realities in Rome were never quite what either Cicero or Seneca pictured them to be. But a republican façade of government maintained itself for centuries despite the greater and greater prominence of military power. The victory of Augustus made military power supreme in the Roman structure but not without some of his authority being derived from the prestige of one who had restored peace to the vast domain. This prestige was translated into

[25] *Ibid.*, p. 211.

religious veneration, partly by the influence of oriental and Hellenistic ideas but partly by the spontaneous reaction of a people to the blessings of a stabilized social order, somewhat akin to the stability of the cosmic order to which every successful social order is bound to display some similarities. The identication of the Roman community with the universal community of mankind was perhaps the most inevitable and pardonable form of ideology, for Rome did seem to comprise the sum of the civilized world.

Naturally the peace of the Augustan Principate was not as lasting as Virgil and other appreciators of the new day hoped. The history of the Roman Empire still had centuries to run and it would be filled with wars and tumults of every kind. Some aspects of its life would conform to Augustine's critical description of the *civitas terrena*. But Augustine could hardly foresee that many of the agonies of pagan Rome would be repeated in Christian Rome, reminding us that there are some aspects of man's search for community, particularly for community on wider levels, which are unvarying in all climes and cultures. The order and peace of a community is always precarious; and the order of a heterogeneous imperial community is particularly precarious. The centers of authority must be high and mighty enough to overcome chaos, particularly when cohesive forces of community are lacking. The price which men pay for the boon of order is always great. It is significant that Stoic equalitarianism gradually adjusted itself to hierarchical inequalities, which were the concomitants of imperial order.

It was natural, too, that the same idealism which adjusted its demand for equality to the hierarchical structure of the Roman Empire should have found the point of relevance between its universalism and the quasi-universal imperial community of Rome. Perhaps the most impressive achievement of Stoicism was that this was not done without reservation, certainly with more reservation than in subsequent forms of imperialism, which used some conception of the universal community as the ideological framework for the prestige of the imperial community.

A Stoic Roman emperor, Marcus Aurelius (A.D. 161–180), presiding over the destinies of an empire which exhibited the first marks of the final decay of its order, recreated by Augustus, could still make a radical distinction between Rome and the universal community of mankind. In his *Meditations* Aurelius confesses:

> Every man's interest consists in following the lead of his own constitution and nature. Now my nature is a rational and civic nature; my city and my country, so far as I am Antoninus, is Rome; but so far as I am a man, it is the universe. Whatever therefore is to the advantage of these two cities, and that only, is good for me.[26]

The concept of the two cities was one of the several images of classical thought which was to inspire Augustine in his projection of the two cities, the *civitas dei* and the *civitas terrena*, in which he tried to come to terms with the tension between universalism and imperialism. Augustine thought them to be the more incompatible than Aurelius did. The subsequent ages changed the images sufficiently to make one of the cities into an historical force, the Church rather than Aurelius' cosmic order. In this way Augustine's rigorous separation of the two cities became the basis for a more confusing identification of the two. Thus the persistence of the human tendency to claim ultimate validity for fragmentary human and historical values was exhibited. We must study this strange development further in dealing with Christianity's encounter with empire.

THE CHINESE EMPIRE

If the history of western empire reveals a perpetual tension between the universalism of high philosophy and religion and the contingent historical character of the actual empire, an analysis of the ideology and the structure of Chinese Confucian imperialism proves that universality can be derived simply from the ultimacy of the emperor's claim. "The Confucian monarchy," writes John K. Fairbank,

---

[26] Marcus Aurelius, *Meditations*, vi, 44, quoted in Barker, *op. cit.*, p. 320.

exercised the universal rule of the Son of Heaven, who in theory represented all mankind, and set no territorial limits to his sway. The Chinese Emperor's role may be better described by simply calling him the Son of Heaven, rather than emperor of any kind. His influence according to the Confucian-Mencian theory of government was held to emanate from the fact of his virtuous conduct. While his semireligious functions, signalized in the state cult of Confucius of which the emperor was the head, were centered in China, they were held to be valid also for the surrounding peoples. Whenever occasion offered, it was therefore appropriate in theory that the moral supremacy and as far as possible the actual rule of the Son of Heaven should spread over the barbarians of Inner Asia. ...

The idea of a universal rule was in fact a help for the barbarian rulers who periodically gained supremacy over the Chinese state. For, as Fairbank continues,

> ... The example of the universal and inclusive Confucian monarchy seems to have set the political style for the barbarian rulers, from the Shan-yü of the Huns down to the unlimited sway of Chingis Khan himself. ...[27]

The vague idea of a universal monarchy played the same role in extending the rule of the emperor over the barbarians and in allowing barbarian rulers to assume control over China which Stoic and Christian universalism played in the west. In the words of Fairbank:

> The imperial institutions of China and Inner Asia tended to coalesce—despite the continuing differences in social base, economy, and culture, barbarian Sons of Heaven came to look very much like Chinese Sons of Heaven both in their administrative functions and in their theoretical position in the political order in East Asia. Thus by early modern times the Manchu rulers of Mongolia and China were able to use, over Mongolia, devices of divide-and-rule administration which they had inherited from the Ming, and, over China, devices of centralized control which the Ming had originally inherited from the Mongols. ...[28]

[27] John K. Fairbank (ed.), *Chinese Thought and Institutions*, University of Chicago Press, 1957, p. 208.
[28] *Ibid.*, p. 209.

In short, the Chinese empire, with an ethnically homogeneous core, could transcend the Chinese limits, rule over the barbarians, and be subjected to the rule of barbarian emperors, not by the force of a universal ideology but merely by the prestige of a religiously sanctified imperial institution in which the claim of universality was derived from the claim of ultimacy. That this could be achieved within the framework of a humanistic culture in which the realm of transcendence was sceptically defined a "heaven," or "Tien," shows that there is an inner logic in imperial pretension which does not have to borrow from explicit religious reverence. The Chinese emperors gained power, like all ancient rulers, through force or chicane. But having possessed themselves of the imperial institution, they could add its prestige to the original force as the source of their authority.

The long history of China reveals the difficulty of holding a vast realm under social and political control when the sole organ of community is the centralized political power, with its obedient bureaucracy. Wittfogel attributes the consistency of the despotism in this and in other oriental empires to the fact that the fertility of the agriculture depends upon an irrigation system, which both demands a centralized authority and places all power over economic life in the hands of the state. Its bureaucratic agents have no independence in the economic life, and hence there is no countervailing power to check either the despot or his agents. The rulers of an "hydraulic state," according to Wittfogel, have absolute power primarily because they control the Corvee labor upon which the irrigation system depends.[29]

Whether the irrigation system aggravates, or is basic to, the despotism, the plain fact is that Chinese politics was consistently concerned with the problem of maintaining order in the vast realm and of protesting against the injustice which resulted from the monopoly of power. Chinese history represents regular cycles of integration and feudal disintegration, in which the former periods under strong emperors and dynasties achieved order but

[29] Karl Wittfogel, *Oriental Despotism*, New Haven, Yale University Press, 1957. (See particularly Chapter 4.)

at a great price; while the latter periods of feudalism suffered so much from political chaos that a new period of centralization was welcomed. Confucianism made a purely moralistic approach to the problems of justice even more consistent than in the west. It was consistent that one could hazard the opinion that until the modern period an analysis of the power realities in empire were universally neglected even by the reformers and protesters against injustice. These contented themselves either with offering moralistic advice to the emperor, imploring him to be just, or in proposing minor changes in the pyramid of power in the imperial hierarchy, either the creation or the abolition of a prime minister, or a change in the examination system of the scholar-bureaucrats, or some minor change in the administrative mechanism of the court.

Despite the great differences between Chinese and western forms of imperial ideology, the similarities are striking. No similarity is more striking than the idealization of the past as a point of departure for criticism of the present injustices of a despotic regime. The idealization of the past under the sage philosophers, clearly analogous to similar Stoic (particularly Ciceronian) attempts, is most clearly developed by Huang Tsung-hsi, famous scholar of the late Ming period (1610–1695), who gave this ideal picture of an early order which had overcome a primitive chaos:

> At the beginning of creation every man was selfish and every man was self-seeking. There was public good in the empire but probably no man cared to promote it. There was public evil in the empire but probably no one cared to get rid of it. Then there appeared a man who did not consider his personal interests as the object of benefit, but made it possible for the people to share the empire's benefit. ... The assiduous toil of this man must have been a thousand or myriad times more than the people of the empire. ... Rulers of later ages were different. They considered that the authority to bestow benefit or harm was entirely in their own hands; the benefit of empire was entirely received by them while the harm of the empire was entirely given to others. ... In ancient times the people were the primary interest, the ruler secondary. Now the ruler has the primary interest and the people

are secondary, and the one who does great harm to the empire is the ruler. In ancient times the people loved their ruler, comparing him with their parents and respecting him in heaven. Now the people hate their ruler, looking upon him as an enemy and calling him dictator. . . .[30]

This poignant analysis of the moral ambiguity of political order states an almost universal theme of human history. Perhaps it is an interesting coincidence that it was uttered in the same seventeenth century when the English Puritans came to their conclusions in regard to the nature of royal authority, its price in injustice, and the contrast between its then present state and an ideal state before the Norman Conquest.

[30] Fairbank and Ssu-yü Teng, *op. cit.*, p. 8.

CHAPTER VI

The Encounter
between Christianity and Empire

THE long history of the dialogue between the Christian faith and
the political communities of the western world began significantly
in a period in which one political community had achieved an order so comprehensive as to include what seemed to be the whole
civilized world. We have noted that religious faith was powerful in all ancient empires in attributing ultimate significance to
the contingent political order which soldiers and rulers were able
to establish. This was done partly by the kings and priests; but
they could not have done it if the imagination of men had not
encouraged it. The worship of the Gods of city-states and empires
was in essence the fruit of a basic fact of human spirituality. Men
are contingent creatures, whose ideas and ideals are the products
of time and place. But they have a residual transcendence over the
temporal flux in which they are involved, and seek for a point of
reference and an authority which is higher than their own interest and opinion. Even Heraclitus, the philosopher of flux,
affirmed that "The customs of men possess no wisdom, those of
the gods do." [1]

Inevitably the social and political order in which men find security is given a higher sanctity than their own interests and opinions. It is derived from the divine *logos* or reason and attributed
to the divine will. We have noted that the Roman state, originally
free of the oriental or even Hellenistic religious overtones, was
progressively involved in emperor worship as the empire of Augustus and his successors gave peace to the civilized world after a
spate of civil wars.

[1] Heraclitus, *Fragments*, No. 78.

89

Before the advent of Christianity, as we have previously observed, two forms of ethically rigorous religion were known in the civilized world: Stoicism and Hebraic prophetism. Prophetism did not enter into dialogue with imperialism, except defensively. Thus the God of Israel, who, according to the prophets was the creator God, transcending the vicissitudes of nations, was inevitably engaged in the struggle for national liberation against Seleucid imperialism, for example, even as he was the ally to the nation in its earlier wars with the Philistines.

But Stoicism had come into creative contact with Roman imperialism. Since Stoicism made a necessary distinction between the meaning of human existence, which men had by virtue of the social order in which they lived—and the meaning of life which they were able to discern by virtue of the transcendent freedom of the individual over all social orders—the question is what did the Christian faith add to this form of idealism? One can answer that the Christian faith had a theory of salvation according to which the primal predicament of man was derived from "the fall" in which the self-contradiction of human freedom began. Man was fated to use his freedom both creatively and destructively because he used it both for the sake of others, and also for the purpose of subordinating all interests to his own aggrandizement.

The message of salvation in the Christian faith would seem directed primarily to individuals, as they survey their precarious freedom and become conscious of the predicament of the brevity of their lives, threatening the meaning of their existence; and of their abortive efforts to hide their insignificance by various forms of self-worship. They were to be redeemed from this pride if they became aware of this predicament and repented. The Christian gospel seemed only negatively relevant to the community. This was the conclusion at which the reformer Martin Luther arrived and which he expressed in his doctrine of the "two realms, the heavenly and the earthly realm." In the heavenly realm men experienced forgiveness and the power of a new life as individuals; but in the "earthly realm" they were under the power of "Caesar," which means, in the political realm, the primary purpose of God and of Christians was to preserve order against the perils of chaos created by human sin.

It is not possible to carry through such a rigorous individualistic interpretation of the Christian faith for at least two reasons. One was that the gospel contained a vision of an ideal universal community. In this vision of the New Testament the universalism of the prophets would seem to have been carried to its logical conclusion. The law would no longer be given "from Zion." The last remnants of Hebraic particularism were overcome in Paul, the champion of Christian universalism, who proclaimed that "there is neither Jew nor Greek, ... neither bond nor free ... in Christ." [2] The Pauline universalism drew on both Hebraic prophetic sources and upon Stoic universalism. The new Christian community, the "Israel of God," was not a natural community of history. It was a redeemed community in which redeemed individuals from all the nations drawn into the *koinonia* became the witness of the universal redeemed community, which Christ would establish on his *parousia*, the triumphant return of the "Son of Man."

The rigor of this universalism and its eschatological character, that is, the hope of its possibility only at the end of history and not within history, would seem to make it only critically relevant to the task of organizing either a universal community in history —or any community at all. The eschatological character of the vision of a perfect and universal community is consistent in both the Old and the New Testaments. From Isaiah, who hoped for a peace in which men "would beat their swords into ploughshares" but under conditions of a transmuted nature in which the "wolf and the lamb will lie down together," to the vision in the last book of the New Testament, the Book of Revelation, in which the seer proclaims:

> ... I saw a new heaven and a new earth: for the first heaven and the first earth were passed away; and there was no more sea,[3]

---

[2] Galatians 3:28.   [3] Revelation 21:1.

the faith of the Bible looks to a final redemption of all communities, a redemption exceeding the possibilities of history, that is, as grounded in nature. These visions prove that *"Ah, but a man's reach should exceed his grasp, Or what's a heaven for?"* (Browning); only it is not Plato's heaven but that unique Hebraic transcendent vision, "The Kingdom of God," which does not annul but transmutes all the fragmentary achievements of human history.

The negative relevance of such a vision is of course obvious. It is a source of criticism for all the kingdoms of the world in which

> ... The kings of the Gentiles exercise lordship over them; and they that exercise authority upon them are called benefactors. But ye shall not be so: but he that is greatest among you, let him be as the younger; ...[4]

This critical note was elaborated in the apocalypse of St. John the Divine, when the early persecution of the church prompted the seer to pronounce this judgment upon Rome, the very Rome which was ultimately to make use of the Christian faith as a cement of cohesion for a decaying empire:

> ... for he hath judged the great whore, which did corrupt the earth with her fornication, and hath avenged the blood of his servants at her hand.[5]

This critical perspective upon the empires of the world would seem to refute the hesitancy of Pilate, who was reluctant to crucify Jesus because presumably he saw no danger in the kind of kingdom which Jesus proclaimed despite the warning of the elders, "... whosoever maketh himself a king speaketh against Caesar." [6]

But a second fact of history refuted both Pilate and the elders and made the new religion relevant to the empire of the Caesars, not as a source of criticism of its moral ambiguities, but as a support of its authority. That fact was the powerful impulse in imperial communities to bend any historic religion to its purposes, even a religion whose absolute universalism and ethical rigor would

---

‘ Luke 22:25–26.　　⁵ Rev. 19:2.　　⁶ John 19:12.

seem to guarantee a tension between the faith and the empire.

The empire was able to use Christianity as it had used Stoicism. It equated Christian universalism with its own quasi-universalism, and it quieted the Christian fear of idolatry (which had persuaded early Christians to die rather than to worship Caesar) by presenting the Christian emperor as a servant of the true God.

The history of the Christian empires contains two chapters. In the first chapter the emperor of Rome claims to have achieved a Christian millennium in which the desire of the ages has been fulfilled. When the empire continued to decay and the barbarians wrecked the ancient imperial structure, the church began the second chapter of Christian imperialism by supervising the reconstruction of a Germanic Roman empire in which the Pope, combining the genius of the Caesars with the spirit of Christ, preserved a precarious imperial or international unity in the feudal chaos of the new European civilization.

The first chapter begins with the establishment of Christianity in the Roman empire under the Emperor Constantine. It is not relevant here to trace the history of the little eschatological sect which was the Christian church and which had grown to such proportions that it became politically relevant to the empire. It is enough to recall that the last persecutions of Christians under the Emperor Diocletian were not popular even among the pagans, and that various edicts of toleration had preceded the Constantinian adoption of Christianity. It is more to the point to trace the devious and tortuous path by which Constantine, though only the son of the concubine of his father Constantius, made himself the sole master of the Roman *imperium*, becoming in effect a second Augustus. His rise to power included victories over his fellow rulers, the murder of his former ally Licinius, and the murder of his wife Fausta, the daughter of Maximinian. The political motives which persuaded him to embrace the Christian faith were involved in the tortuous politics and warfare which led him to the pinnacle of power. They were not unconnected with the politics of his final struggle with Licinius and probably prompted by the latter's espousal of the cause of paganism.[7]

The methods of Constantine's rise to sole power were not unique in the annals of Roman power politics; but they were certainly not calculated to commend the Christian faith as a new source of moral power in a dying imperium. What interests us in the context of this study is the way in which Constantine, and his apologists, the church historian Eusebius and the Stoic Christian philosopher Lactantius, used the Christian faith to cover Constantine's crimes and to exalt his rule as the agent of a Christian millennium.

> The pagan emperors had been traditionally devoted to self-advertisement [so writes Cochrane], but it remained for the first Christian sovereign to discover a more effective instrument of propaganda than any hitherto devised. As the emperor himself became more and more the tool of designing churchmen, the pulpits of the empire resounded with fulsome adulation of the political saint whom it was not considered impious to designate as "equal to the Apostles." [8]

His chief apologist, Eusebius of Caesarea, whom Burckhardt has defined as "the most consistently dishonest historian of antiquity," quoted Constantine with approval, interpreting the significance of his defeat of Licinius, his last formidable enemy:

> ...it appears that those who faithfully discharge God's holy laws and shrink from the transgression of His commandments are rewarded with abundant blessings and endued with well-grounded hope as well as ample power for the accomplishment of their undertakings. On the other hand, those who have cherished impiety have experienced consequences in keeping with their evil choice. ...I myself was the agent whose services God deemed suitable for the accomplishment of His will. Accordingly...with the aid of divine power, I banished and destroyed every form of evil which prevailed, in the hope that the human race, enlightened through my instrumentality, might be recalled to a due observance

---

[7] For a detailed portrayal of these complicated events, see Jacob Burckhardt, *The Age of Constantine the Great* (tr. Moses Hadas), New York, Pantheon Books, 1949, Chap. VIII, pp. 244ff.
[8] Cochrane, *op. cit.*, pp. 207–08.

of God's holy laws and, at the same time, our most blessed faith might prosper under the guidance of the almighty hand. ...[9]

This venture in self-appreciation and self-exculpation shows how easily success can be made the proof of virtue, using a religious faith which denies the compatibility between them. But politically it was more important that it proved that the veneration of the emperor, as an instrument of God, could be even more efficacious than the worship of the emperor as God.

Self-appreciation remains impotent, however, if it be not echoed and supported by the culture. The Christian courtiers were not remiss in supplying the monarch with the support for his extravagant pride, which courtiers of every culture have given their sovereigns. Thus the ineffable Eusebius estimated the reign of Constantine:

> He frames his earthly government according to the pattern of the divine original, feeling strength in its conformity with the monarchy of God ... for surely monarchy far transcends every other constitution and form of government, since its opposite, democratic equality of power, may rather be described as anarchy and disorder.

> Our emperor derives the sources of his authority from above, and is strong in the power of his sacred title. Bringing those whom he rules on earth to the only-begotten Word or Saviour, he renders them fit subjects for His kingdom. ... He subdues and chastens the adversaries of the truth according to the usages of war. ...[10]

The enemies of Constantine have conveniently become "enemies of truth" and his ruthless elimination of them is justified by the "usages of war."

The important point is that without explicit idolatry the Christian emperor is invested with a divine aura which was for countless Christian centuries appropriated by Christian sovereigns who claimed to rule by divine right. Eusebius is quite explicit in the claim of a divine appointment for Constantine:

[9] Eusebius? *Vita Constantini*, II.24 and 28; quoted by Cochrane, *op. cit.*, p. 184.
[10] Eusebius, *Panegyrici*, 2., quoted by Cochrane, *op. cit.*, 3. § 4–5, pp. 185–86.

> The God of all, the supreme governor of the whole universe,
> by His own will appointed Constantine, the descendant of so
> renowed a parent, to be prince and sovereign; so that, while others
> have been raised to this distinction by the choice of their fellows,
> he is unique as the one man to whose elevation no mortal may
> boast of having contributed.[11]

Naturally the complexities of historical causation were obscured in
this pious interpretation of the rise of Constantine to power. But
the argument leaves Constantine not wanting any degree of religious prestige which Augustus once had by the poetic grace of
Vergil.

The other outstanding courtier, the Stoic-Christian philosopher
Lactantius, was equally extravagant in his pious appreciation. He
addresses Constantine in this wise:

> The providence of the supreme deity has elevated you to the
> dignity of prince, enabling you with true devotion to reverse the
> evil policies of others, to repair their errors and, in a spirit of
> fatherly mildness, to take measures for the safety of men, re-
> moving from the commonwealth the malefactors whom the Lord
> has delivered into your hands, ... By an inborn sanctity of char-
> acter and with a recognition of truth and God, in everything you
> consummate the works of justice. It was fitting, therefore, that,
> in the task of ordering human affairs, divine power should have
> employed you as its agent and minister.[12]

Evidently there is a psychological force in impressive sovereignty
which even the most equalitarian religions and philosophies find
difficulty in negating. Lactantius' appreciation of Constantine is
analogous to Seneca's appreciation of Nero, though the latter's
De Clementia had the moral advantage in being composed in
the youth of Nero, before his outrages were committed.

If Constantinian Christianity emulated Stoicism in coming to
terms with the divine pretensions of the emperor, it also betrayed a significant similarity in relating its own universalism confusedly to the quasi-universalism of Rome which, according to
Cicero, was "a city composed of all the nations." Eusebius inter-

[11] Eusebius(?) *Vita Constantini*, I.24; quoted by Cochrane, *op. cit.*, p. 186.
[12] Lactantius, *Divine Institutions*, VII.26; quoted by Cochrane, *op. cit.*, p. 186.

preted the Constantine sovereignty as nothing less than the realization of the hope of a perpetual and universal peace. Christianity, he declared, provided the basis for the universal community because it had substituted for all the local and national deities the revelation through Christ of the one true God, creator and preserver of mankind.[13] The identification of religious universalism with Roman imperialism is more unqualified than it was in the thought of Cicero and certainly more explicit than in the thought of the Stoic emperor Marcus Aurelius.

In fairness to early Christianity, it must be recorded that others in the church would not have followed Eusebius and Lactantius in their uncritical devotion to the Constantinian Christian empire. In the second century Tertullian, who tried to preserve the values of the old eschatological tension of early Christianity, anticipated Augustine in his estimate of the power realities which the loyal Constantinians later obscured. He rejected the idealization of the Roman dominion after the manner of Vergil and Cicero, and declared:

> Unless I am mistaken all kingdoms and empires owe their existence to the sword, their expansion to success on the battlefield.

The Romans, he declared, far from growing great by subduing the proud, wax proud by slaughtering the saints.[14] Tertullian, in fact, anticipated Augustine's critical judgment of the *civitas terrena*, availing himself of an ultimate principle of criticism for surveying the moral ambiguities of an imperium built by power. Tertullian likewise, with equal lack of equivocation, rejected the religious veneration of the emperor.

> I refuse to call the Emperor a god [he declares]. If he is human it behooves him as such to bow the knee to God. Augustus, the founder of the Empire, was reluctant to be addressed as Lord (*dominus*), and this, indeed, is an appellation of God. I am willing to call the Emperor Lord but only in the conventional sense, never in the sense in which I accord that title to the Omnipotent and Eternal who is his Lord as well as mine.[15]

[13] *Ibid.*, p. 185.   [14] *Ibid.*, p. 227.
[15] Tertullian, *Apologeticus*, 33-4; quoted by Cochrane, *op. cit.*, p. 227-28.

Anticipating Milton by centuries in making the distinction between political loyalty and ultimate religious commitment, a distinction which made religion into a servant of conscience against the state, Tertullian declared:

> We have, for Caesar, the image of Caesar which is impressed on the coin, for God, the image of God which is impressed on human beings. Give Caesar his money; give yourself to God. ...[16]

Milton's interpretation of the text was, of course, slightly different: "My conscience I have from God and I cannot give it to Caesar," he declared, commenting upon the well-known text about the tribute money which Christ said should be given to Caesar.

Tertullian unfortunately combined his disavowal of imperial Christian politics with an ascetic disavowal of all political responsibilities. His rigorous rejection of the identification of Roman imperialism with Christian universalism also involved a rejection of the duties of citizenship, anticipating the monastic withdrawal from the world which was to become the refuge of sensitive spirits from the days of Constantine throughout the Middle Ages. It may be defined as a negative reaction of the conscience to the ambiguities of politics, whether imperial or national; a method of contracting out of the problems of community for the sake of realizing the ultimate vision of a true community.

> For us [declares Tertullian] nothing is more foreign than the commonwealth. We recognize but one universal commonwealth, viz. the world. ...
>
> I owe no obligation to forum, campus, or senate. I stay awake for no public function, I make no effort to monopolize the platform, I pay no heed to any administrative duty. ...[17]

The irresponsibility toward the political order, which is the unvarying concomitant of a rigorous Christian perfectionism, was thus succinctly expressed by Tertullian.[18]

---

[16] Tertullian, *De Idololatria* 15; quoted by Cochrane, *op. cit.*, p. 228.

[17] *Apologeticus*, 38, and *De Pallio* 5.

[18] In fairness to Tertullian it is necessary to point to his many references to

The criticisms of Athanasius of the empire were more significant than those of Tertullian because they were made in the period of the Constantinian Christian empire. Athanasius, the champion of Christian orthodoxy, had been victor in the theological controversies of the Council of Nicea which was held under Constantine's auspices. He was nevertheless critical of the Caesaropapism which Constantine initiated and which was preserved throughout the ages of the Byzantine empire. "When has an ecclesiastical judgment ever received its validity from the emperor?" he asked. It must be observed that his critical attitude and his championship of an independent church, which contributed so much to the preservation of the church and its capacity to outlast a dying empire, was partially prompted by the filtration with Arianism on the part of Constantius. But we shall have occasion to observe again and again that historically creative positions are taken not from some absolute perspective but under the promptings of very tangential historical causes.

Whether Christianity contributed to the decay of Rome or preserved it for a season, the fact is that "eternal Rome" proved mortal, and that all the hopes of Vergil, expressed in the Augustan period, and of Lactantius, in the Constantinian period, and all the other dreams of the lasting character of the impressive *pax romana*, were disappointed when Alaric sacked Rome.

It was at this point in the catastrophe of a civilization which had seemed able to defy the vicissitudes of history and to extend and preserve a political order, seemingly in accordance with the classical dream of a true political order which would emulate and be incorporated into the permanence of the cosmic order, that the Christian church produced a theologian who seemed to make sense out of this catastrophe and to refute the charge that the Christian faith was responsible for it: the African bishop, Augustine.

---

the responsibility of Christians for the peace and good order of the empire; but this responsibility is expressed chiefly through prayer. See his *Apology*, 30.1.

It is not within our competence or the purpose of this study to estimate the position of Augustine in the history of western Christian culture. His influence was certainly immense for many reasons. His synthesis of biblical and classical modes of thought was new. Christian Platonism, which had prevailed before him, was informed by the classical dualism of body and soul. Classical thought had also identified nature and history and had comprehended the drama of history in terms of the cyclical recurrences which characterize the life of nature—where birth, growth, decay, and death complete the cycle within the limits of one form of life. Augustine used his idea of the radical newness of the Christ event to refute the cyclical theory of history, as he used the Trinitarian formula to provide a structure of meaning in which the divine was conceived as both transcending history (God the father, "all mighty creator of heaven and earth") and being involved in history (Jesus Christ, "His only begotten son"). This formula made it possible to interpret the variegated drama of history without either pressing it into a rational form or regarding the temporal flux as a corruption of the eternal. Augustine artfully combined Hebraic biblical elements with neo-Platonic thought; but in his acceptance of "the goodness of creation" he rejected neo-Platonism and stubbornly accepted the simple biblical dictum that "God saw all that he had made and behold it was very good." It is the dictum which lies at the basis of all life-affirming and history-affirming tendencies in western civilization.

In interpreting the nature of human freedom Augustine again skillfully combined neo-Platonic elements with biblical ones to explicate the Christian doctrine of man as made in the "image of God" and as fallen into sin, i.e. the biblical story of the fall. In short, he sought to interpret both the creative and the destructive possibilities of human freedom, which would furnish a key to the bewildering drama of history, in which events do not follow the pattern of recurrence which Greek rationalism designed for it, nor, for that matter, the pattern of progress which modern culture thought it discerned in it.

The destructive possibilities of human freedom derive, according to Augustine, from the *superbia* of the human spirit and not from the inertia of the flesh warring against the wider purposes of the mind.

> It was not the corruptible flesh that made the soul sinful but the sinful soul which made the flesh corruptible. And, though from this corruption of the flesh there arise certain incitements to vice, and indeed vicious desires, yet we must not attribute to the flesh all the vices of a wicked life.[19]

The conception of the evil in human nature is sufficiently colored by neo-Platonism to define the defect of self-love as primarily the lack of the love of God, "the unchangeable good." The love of the neighbor has no real place in the Augustinian ethic, except as this love leads the neighbor to the love of God.

> ...You love yourself suitably, when you love God better than yourself. What, then, you aim at in yourself, you must aim at in your neighbor, namely that he may love God with a perfect affection. For you do not love him as yourself, unless you try to draw him to that good which you are yourself pursuing.[20]

This Augustinian error in the analysis of man's ethical problem deserves to be mentioned because it is the basis of subsequent errors in his reconstruction of the Christian interpretation of history. Upon the basis of this conception the world is divided between those who seek an immutable good and those who seek a mutable one. The love of the neighbor is equated with *amor mundi*, the love of the world "which passes away." The conception rightly apprehends that the self is so formed that it cannot realize itself within itself but only by constantly going out from itself. But the possibilities of self-realization are only envisaged vertically and religiously and not horizontally in the community. The Augustinian conception of selfhood had the virtue of recognizing a "proper self-love" which Reformation thought later denied.

[19] St. Augustine, *De Civitate Dei*, XIV, iii.
[20] St. Augustine, *Morals of the Catholic Church*, Chap. XXVI.

He who loves God and not himself, loves himself. For he who cannot live of himself will certainly die, if he loves himself.[21]

The thought is a neo-Platonic rendering of the basic paradox that self-realization cannot be the intended end of action but is the inevitable byproduct of any intention of the self beyond itself. But the defect of the conception was that the moral quality of an action was simply determined by the adequacy of the object, whether it be "mutable" or "immutable."

Thus the foundation was laid for the whole architecture of the "two cities," the *civitas dei* and the *civitas terrena:*

> ...two cities have been formed by two loves: the earthly by the love of self, even to the contempt of God; the heavenly by the love of God, even to the contempt of self. The former...glories in itself; the latter in the Lord.[22]

This was the conception which provided the framework upon which medieval Christianity built a new civilization; it was built upon the conception of a "commingling" of the two cities, the heavenly acting as a leaven for the earthly city by drawing it from its proximate ends to the ultimate end.

The heavenly city was the church but with reservations. Augustine had reservations about the church, though he defined it as the only perfect society. While he brought the millennial hopes of the early church to rest by identifying the church with the kingdom of God, he was certain that the historic church included both the redeemed and the unredeemed:

> In this wicked world...when the Church measures her future loftiness by her present humility, and is exercised by goading fears, tormenting sorrows, disquieting labors and dangerous temptations,...there are many reprobate mingled with the good; and both are gathered together by the Gospel as in a drag net; and in this world, as in a sea, both swim enclosed without distinction in the net, until it is brought ashore when the wicked must be separated from the good.[23]

---

[21] In Joannis Evangelium tractabus, cxxiii, 5.
[22] St. Augustine, *De Civitate Dei*, Bk. XIV, Ch. xxviii.
[23] *Ibid.*, Bk. XVIII, Ch. xlix.

In this conception we find the Reformation distinction in embryo between the visible and the invisible church. But the defect in it lies in Augustine's failure to recognize that there can be no clear distinction between the good and the evil. Whether virtue is defined in terms of the love of God or the love of the neighbor, Augustine's confidence in the possibility of unambiguous virtue prepared for the religious politics of the medieval church. In the name of the gospel he satisfied one of the most universal of all human ambitions: the ambition to be clear, or to be thought clear, of the ambiguity of all human achievements. In the long history of the West, various schemes of salvation were offered for the attainment of this ideal state. Piety, reason, science, poverty were presented as instruments for the attainment of this selflessness. In private life the illusions of perfection made for priggish pride. In politics the illusions bore the fruit of political power, derived from the pretensions of sanctity, whether in the "rule of the saints" in our New England Calvinism or in the ecclesiastical imperialism of the medieval period.

The vision of a perfect man and a perfect community in Augustine was the more remarkable because he rejected the classical idea of perfection derived from the rational control of the passions. It was the self and not the body which was the cause of sin.

> The flesh lusteth after nothing save through the soul. It is said to lust against the spirit when the soul, with fleshly lust, wrestles against the spirit.[24]

He comprehends, in short, that the basis of evil in human life is not the vagrant passion of the body but the inordinate desires of the finite and contingent self, seeking to hide its contingency. Significantly, Augustine makes the same point against Platonism which Epicurus had made, earlier, within the frame of classical

---

[24] St. Augustine, *Seventeen Short Treatises* (chiefly on Faith and Works) *De Continentia*, VIII, 19; volume from *A Library of Christian Fathers*, London, 1884.

naturalism. Evil is due not to the inordinate lusts of the flesh but
to the inordinate ambitions of the self. For Epicurus the cure for
this inordinacy is to moderate human ambitions so that they will
conform to the limits of nature. For Augustine the answer is to
find God who alone can satisfy the self, which indeterminately
transcends itself.

Even more remarkable than the perfection of individuals who
have found their *summum bonum* is the perfect society, the
civitas dei. Evidently it is not troubled by collective ambitions
and lusts and the harmony or *concordia* of the community is
achieved because wills which are obedient to God are in concord
with one another. So Augustine declares:

> Peace between man and God is the well-ordered obedience to
> eternal law. Peace between man and man is well-ordered concord.
> ... The peace of the celestial city is the perfectly ordered enjoy-
> ment of God, and of one another in God.[25]

No more utopian perfection could be conceived. The same
theologian who initiated a new chapter in Christian thought by
analyzing the relation of the freedom of the self to the inevitable
inordinacy in the expression of that freedom, has a very simple
answer for the human predicament. Let the self find the ultimate
rather than the immediate end of life. Epicurus and Augustine
are similar in this too, though their answers are contradictory.
They both regard the fear of death as the root of the human
predicament. For Epicurus, Death was "a matter with which we
are not at all concerned." But Augustine explained the fear of
death as the root of sin in this way:

> For men strive to avoid what they cannot avoid, namely the
> death of the flesh, for not to sin is a thing about which men
> take little thought, whereas not to die, which is unattainable, is
> yet eagerly sought after.[26]

Both Epicurus and Augustine take little account of the endless
compounds of ordinate and inordinate ambitions, of creative and

---

[25] St. Augustine, *De Civitate Dei*, Bk. XIX, Ch. xiii.
[26] St. Augustine, *De Trinitate*, IV, xii, 15.

destructive vitalities, of the search for proximate and ultimate ends, which characterize the predicament of man's incongruous position in human history.

If Augustine's description of the *civitas dei* is remarkably "utopian" and bears little relation to any known historic reality, yet it is by the perspective of this illusion that he can give such a realistic account of the *civitas terrena*, or of any community in history. The point is worth mentioning because it is related to the fact that in the long history of the relation of moral and religious idealism to the moral ambiguities of the political order of the community, with its balance of power and interest and its acceptance of dominant power for the sake of order, no idealist, standing historically and ideologically within a given order, has been able to give an unbiased account of its realities. That fact is illustrated by the sentimentalities of Cicero describing the Roman imperium as a *patrocinium*, of Seneca extolling Nero, of Eusebius and Lactantius giving false accounts of the Constantinian empire, and, for that matter, of Thomas Aquinas estimating the moral realities of the papal empire in the thirteenth century.

The truth about a political order is told by those who stand historically and ideologically outside it. Thus Augustine saw the Roman realities starkly after the sack of Rome because he had an ideological vantage point which made it unnecessary to obscure the moral ambiguities of Rome. His realism, like all realism so derived, erred of course in failing to do justice to the moral achievements involved in these balances and disbalances of the Roman state. While both Augustine and Lenin would have been offended by the comparison, it is nevertheless valuable to point out that Lenin's estimate of capitalism is as one-sided as Augustine's estimate of the Roman state. Both discover antinomies which have been hidden through blindness and through propaganda. Both are quite unfair, for they report only the negative aspect of the balances and disbalances of power and competition of interests.

The gravamen of Augustine's indictment of the *civitas terrena* and, by implication, Rome, which was the historical model for all historical communities, contained the important truth that the justice which it was able to achieve was due to an uneasy armistice between contending social forces and that its order was due to the dominance of some superior force.

> Thus the founder of the earthly city was a fratricide. Overcome with envy, he slew his own brother, a citizen of the heavenly city, and a sojourner on earth. So we cannot be surprised that this first specimen, or as the Greeks say, archetype of crime, should, long afterwards, find a corresponding crime at the foundation of that city which was destined to reign over so many nations, and be the head of the earthly city of which we speak. For of that city, also, as one of their poets has mentioned, "the first walls were stained with a brother's blood," or as Roman history records, Remus was slain by his brother Romulus.[27]

The social peace is an uneasy armistice, for:

> Miserable are the people who are alienated from God. Yet even this people have a kind of peace which is not to be lightly esteemed, though it will not have it long for it used it not well while it had it.[28]

They will not have it long because the victorious power becomes proud and "lays a yoke upon its fellows which only God can lay." Here Augustine touches upon the idolatrous tendencies in all historic sovereignties. His attitude to government borrows from Stoic equalitarianism and is sharply distinguished from that of the Reformation, with its extravagant appreciation of government as an "Ordinance of God." Augustine takes as his norm the "natural order" which is reminiscent of the Stoic concept of a primitive unspoiled equality. For, declares Augustine, "The holy men of old were shepherds of cattle rather than kings of men." [29] He does not deny the necessity of government as a "remedy for sin," for "it is better to be a slave of men than a slave of sin." The conception not only equates slavery with government, but fails to recognize the danger of the hierarchical structure of society, a failure which Christian thought shared with Augustine, through all the ages until the modern period.

[27] *De Civitate Dei*, Bk. XV, Ch. v.   [28] *Ibid.*, Bk. XIX, Ch. xxvi.
[29] *Ibid.*, Bk. XIX, Ch. xv.

Generations of experience were required before men, reacting against the injustices created by both government and property, which were ostensibly "remedies for sin," that is, instruments of justice and order among self-seeking men, realized that they were necessary instruments, however dangerous. Neither a consistent idealism nor a consistent realism was able to come to terms with the complex realities of the political and economic order; neither had sufficient empirical grasp of the facts to analyze the ambiguities of the instruments of community which were also instruments of dominion. It could be argued that the lack was not only an empirical grasp but an ideological system which would allow men to grasp the facts. Yet we must not put too much emphasis upon the conceptual systems by which facts are analyzed. For the most disparate and contradictory systems of meaning have obscured the facts. Augustine should have been the last man to imagine that any historical person or institution could be free of the ambiguity in all human striving and the consequent ambiguity in every institution, which seeks to bring a tolerable order into the initial chaos of conflicting human impulses which arises when human freedom both extends the simple harmonies of nature and corrupts her innocence.

Yet Augustine gathered the stuff out of which all the ideological instruments of ecclesiastical dominion in the Middle Ages were fashioned. He did not, of course, anticipate this development. His church was not really an historical institution but a vision. When it was fashioned into an historical institution and into an instrument of dominion it suffered the fate of all such visions, and thereby one more strand of consistency in the variegated patterns of history was disclosed.

CHAPTER VII

The Lessons
from the Three Empires

THE period commonly known as the Middle Ages was "Middle" in many senses. In the organization of the community on both the parochial and the imperial level it was intermediary in that it slowly elaborated patterns of community which exhibited two main characteristics. The first of these was that three competitive empires took the place of the classical Roman empire which, alone of all the empires of history, could plausibly regard itself as the community of the civilized world. The second characteristic was the slow emergence of autonomous parochial communities: the nation-states. None of these was fully developed until the close of the period. Indeed, their emergence was one of the many developments which heralded the end of the Middle Ages and the dawn of the modern era. We must postpone, for the present, an analysis of their history until we have examined the structure of the three medieval empires.

The three empires who contended with one another were all religiously oriented. Two of the empires were Christian and the third was formed by the religion of Islam, which arose among the Bedouins of Arabia in the seventh century and within but two centuries had captured parts of the Near East, Europe, and Asia. Though the western part of the old Roman empire was destroyed in the fifth century by the Teutonic tribes pressing against its ramparts and insinuating themselves in its seats of power (Theodoric), it was not until the victories of Islamic power that this part of the empire was definitively separated from the old Roman empire, which, since Constantine had not only become Christian but had its capital transferred from Rome to Constantinople.

108

This severance was the beginning of the western Christian empire, constituted by Charlemagne as emperor but with the pope, who crowned the emperor, the effective center of authority in the West. The Christian church was the agent of transmitting not only the Roman religion but the whole of Roman culture to the barbaric tribes; and the church, under papal authority, became the chief source not only of religious but of political authority in the West.

The German tribes who had conquered the empire made this transition possible because they did not desire to shatter the religious, legal and political foundations of the ancient culture, the military might of which they had conquered. On the contrary they were assiduous in imitating and being formed by the culture, which they recognized as superior to their own. Thus the political and cultural material was ready for the reorganization of an independent western Christian empire which, until the Moslem invasion, had continued to recognize the authority of the emperor in Constantinople.

The Arabs, who were certainly on no higher level of civilization than the Germanic tribes, challenged the Roman civilization instead of becoming absorbed in it.

> While the Germans had nothing with which to oppose the Christianity of the Empire, [so declares Henri Pirenne] the Arabs were exalted by a new faith. It was this, and this alone, which prevented their assimilation. For in other respects they were no more prejudiced than the Germans against the civilization of those whom they had conquered.[1]

Not only the Islamic, but the two Christian empires, give vivid examples of the interplay of historical contingencies and "ultimate" ideas. These ideas and faiths have historical potency beyond the historical situation in which they were generated. Western history was dominated throughout the Middle Ages by a peculiar political construct in which the Pope of the "uni-

[1] Henri Pirenne, *Mohammed and Charlemagne*, New York, W. W. Norton & Company, 1939, p. 150.

versal" church really had a more ultimate authority than the emperor of the empire. The eastern empire, on the other hand, had a religious-political system, usually defined as "Caesaro-papism," because the emperor seemed to be both the religious and political ruler.

Where did the papal supremacy of the West originate? The history of western political thought is full of the controversy between the papal canonists and the anti-papalists, and the history of western political life is filled with the tension between the church and the empire. This tension was due to the uneasy partnership between the priest and the soldier-ruler, in which the two sources of power, the one of religious authority and the other of political force, both supported and also competed with one another. The original structure of authority in the West was given by a historically contingent factor. The Roman emperors in the East proclaimed religious doctrines (iconoclasm) which were not acceptable to the Pope. He had become more and more an independent ruler of the Roman-western state. But he lacked an army; and this want was gradually supplied by the Frankish kingdom, which protected Rome both from the Lombards and from the Arabs. The Pope recognized Pippin, the Carolingian mayor of the palace; and by this recognition put an end to the Merovingian dynasty.[2] Pippin's consecration introduced the idea of royal prestige being derived from the church; and the Carolingian king, unlike the Merovingians, ruled "by the grace of God."

After Charlemagne's success in making himself the master of the West, the Pope went one step farther and crowned him emperor. Pirenne interprets the motives of the Pope in this way:

> In Rome itself, the Pope, although he did not deny the sovereignty of the Emperor of Byzantium, was no longer his subject. Was it not inevitable that the idea should occur to him, recognizing as he did the power and prestige of the King of the Franks, of reconstructing, for the benefit of Charles, the Empire, which, since the fifth century had no longer existed in the West?[3]

---

[2] *Ibid.*, p. 223.   [3] *Ibid.*, p. 231.

From the time the Pope added the imperial dignity to Charlemagne's crown, and throughout the Middle Ages, the Pope was the senior partner in the imperial structure of dominion, however much the emperors, the anti-papalists, and finally Dante might protest against the political authority which he had drawn from his religious majesty. He was the senior partner, for it was the church, rather than the empire, which was the final force of cohesion, because the Christian faith was the cement of community for this super-national sovereignty, and the Pope was the authoritative teacher and interpreter of that faith. Moreover he held the "keys of heaven," the power of interdict and excommunication.

The other two medieval empires, the Byzantine and the Islamic, were also formed partly by political and military power and partly by religious authority, which bound the imperial community into a cohesive whole. An analysis of the similarities and differences of the three empires can be instructive by indicating both the perennial structure of the imperial community and the relation of that structure to some basic characteristics of human nature.

THE SIMILARITIES IN THE EMPIRES

Though two of the empires were Christian and one Islamic, the most obvious similarity between all three is that they built an imperial community upon the basis of a strictly monotheistic faith. The significance of this similarity lies in the fact that, in principle, a strict monotheism would seem to make the religious sanctification of even a large community impossible. But history proves it to be possible. The reason for this is rather simple. The religious consciousness expresses itself in the constant tension between the partial meanings and coherences—which are discerned by the individual and the group—and the sense of a meaning and a purpose which transcends these partial meanings and refutes their ultimacy. The polytheism of the early empires consisted, as we have seen, in ascribing ultimacy, without reservation, to the imperial structure which gave meaning to life. Rigorously applied a strict monotheism makes a complacent ascription of ultimacy to all historically contingent communities and structures impossible.

But we have seen that even the rigorous monotheism of Hebraic prophetism and of Greco-Roman Stoicism and of early Christianity did not make it impossible to identify both the imperial community and the structure of power in the community with divine purpose. It is therefore not surprising that at least two of the empires, the eastern Christian and the Islamic, should make a monotheistic faith into an instrument of imperial community. It is a little more surprising that the western empire should accomplish the same purpose by a more tortuous route. For it was necessary to relate the power realities, for which Charlemagne is a convenient symbol, to the idealistic vision of Augustine's *civitas dei*. In principle, this was not a political vision but a vision of a historical community which transcended, and was critical of, all historic communities. But, though Augustine had many reservations about the identification of the *civitas dei* and the historic church, the identification was made. With that the ideological frame was established by which the mediaeval structure of empire could draw, on the one hand, from the political power of Charlemagne and his successors, and on the other hand, from the spiritual prestige of the church. In the process, the church, which was, in principle, free of the power political realities of empire and which transcended the competition of interests which characterize any community—particularly an imperial one—became, by the very prestige of such disinterestedness, and by the power of "holding the keys of heaven," an imperial power which constantly overshadowed the empire. Thus the community of grace, as envisaged by Augustine, became the real source of power in the western Christian community. It is impossible to trace the complicated historical process by which the idea of two equal realms, coordinated and each serving its distinctive functions—the spiritual and the secular, the *sacerdotium* and the *regnum*, which Pope Gelasius had defined in the fifth century in a letter to the emperor reigning in the East—was transmuted into the theory of the supremacy of the papacy over the empire.

For our purpose it is necessary only to note the final development in this process, beginning with Gregory VII and ending with Pope Innocent IV. The figure of Gregory is significant in the history of the West because his consistent claims to universal dominion sprang from a reforming zeal; and his desire to eliminate the evils of simony and to overcome the divided loyalty of the ecclesiastical princes for the sake of establishing the unity and autonomy of the universal church sprang from a monastic idealism. Hildebrand was a Cluniac monk, and his papal reforms were the final fruits of the Cluniac passion for relating ascetic rigor to papal universalism. His reign may therefore be regarded as a convenient symbol of the genius of Roman Catholicism for recapturing the essentially irresponsible perfectionism of monasticism for the service of the ecclesiastical dominion.

Gregory VII did not initiate radically new policies. He only applied with consistent rigor the ancient policies of the church, which had their origin in the prestige gained by the Roman Pope as the residuary legatee of the empire and as the effective agent of the prestige of the Frankish kings as the emperors of the West. In his well known contest with the Emperor Henry IV, which ended in the emperor's humiliation at Canossa (an experience undertaken to escape the Pope's terrible weapon of excommunication and interdict), the ultimate supremacy of the Pope over the empire was established. It was maintained until the golden age of the Middle Ages, when the implications of the theory of papal supremacy were finally explicated by Innocent IV.

Carlyle records the position of Gregory, as set out by him in a letter to the bishop of Metz in 1076.

> He addressed himself primarily to the contention of those who maintained that it was not proper to excommunicate a king. He cites various authorities and historical precedents to show that this was lawful, and that it had been done; and then argues that the conception that any man could be exempt from ecclesiastical jurisdiction was intrinsically absurd, for it would mean that he was outside the Church, and alien from Christ.[4]

[4] R. W. and J. Carlyle, *History of Mediaeval Political Theory in the West,* London, Blackwood & Sons Ltd., 1950, Vol. IV, Pt. iii, Ch. 1, p. 187.

The theory which brought the emperor to heel was elaborated
for two more centuries and authoritatively stated by Thomas
Aquinas in a letter to the King of Cyprus and published under
the title *De Regimine Principum,* or "Governance of Rulers." In
this letter the logic by which the religious community of grace is
given authority over the secular community of the empire is stated
as follows:

> ...in order that spiritual things might be distinguished from
> earthly things, the ministry of this [Christ's] kingdom has been
> entrusted not to earthly kings, but to priests, and in the highest
> degree to the chief priest, the successor of St. Peter, the Vicar of
> Christ, the Roman Pontiff, to whom all kings of Christian peoples
> are to be subject as to our Lord Jesus Christ Himself.[5]

Any post-medieval judgment upon these papal claims, whether
Protestant or secular, will of course be negative and will be reminiscent of the Reformation indictment of the idolatry of the
church, particularly of the papal claim of being the mouthpiece
of Christ. It is important to recognize that the development of
papal absolutism represents a clear evidence of the perennial nature
of the impulse to dominion and its intimate involvement with the
impulse to community. The impulse is so strong that a community,
which is supposed to mediate grace for man's trans-historical or
supra-political ends, can be used as an engine of authority and
power.

Naturally an historical institution which makes claims of being
trans-historical, a center of power which assumes that its disinterestedness is superior to all centers of historical power will, and
indeed did, prompt reactions of resentment from all competitive
authorities. The historian Henry Hallam's judgment upon Gregory VII may express fittingly the judgment of critical observers
upon every effort to obscure the moral ambiguity of all men of
action, particularly of men of power, who obscure the human mo-

---

[5] St. Thomas Aquinas, *On The Governance of Rulers,* trans. by G. B. Phelan,
published for the Pontifical Institute of Mediaeval Studies by Sheed & Ward,
London & New York, 1938, Ch. 14.

tives which actuate even, or perhaps particularly, dedicated men of power, whether Popes or Calvinist theocrats. Hallam writes:

> The object of Gregory VII, in attempting to redress those more flagrant abuses which for two centuries had deformed the face of the Latin church, is not incapable, perhaps, of vindication, though no sufficient apology can be offered for the means he employed. But the disinterested love of reformation, to which candor might ascribe the contention against investitures, is belied by the general tenor of his conduct, exhibiting an arrogance without parallel, and an ambition that grasped at universal and unlimited monarchy. He may be called the enemy of all sovereigns whose dignity as well as independence mortified his infatuated pride.[6]

We must postpone for a moment any criticism of this ecclesiastical dominion in an empire, and also an appreciation of the beneficent fruits which came to western culture through the rivalry between Pope and emperor, until we examine the similarities between this western Christian empire and the eastern Christian empire and the Islamic one.

The most obvious similarity is that all three derived the ideological frame of empire from a rigorously monotheistic faith. In regard to Islamic universalism, Goldziher reports on the vision of Mohammed:

> At the very beginning of his mission he asserts that Allah had sent him ... 'out of mercy for the world' (Sura 21, v.107). ... [The] *alamun* is constantly used in the Koran in all its various meanings. God is 'lord of the *alamun*'. (Sura 30, v.21.) He has adopted the differences in speech and color amongst men as signs of the *alamun*. This is surely mankind in its widest sense. In the same sense Mohammed extends his mission over the whole area indicated by this word according to his understanding of it. His point of departure is naturally his own people and country. Nevertheless, the connections which, toward the end of his career, he aspired to make with foreign powers ... show a striving toward lands beyond Arabia. ...

---

[6] Henry Hallam, *View of the State of Europe During the Middle Ages*, 3 Vols., London: John Murray Ltd., 1872, II, 192.

Islamic tradition itself, in various utterances of the prophet, indicates that he was convinced of having a mission to all mankind; ...[7]

A religious vision claiming universal validity is, of course, not unique. What was unique in Islam is the creation of a religiously motivated military imperialism, the conquests of which were integrated in a theocratic state, in which dominion was exercised from Mohammed through his successors by charismatic leaders, whose charisma was institutionalized and subject to hereditary transmission. All the tremendous early successes of this imperialism were due to the uncomplicated identification of military and political objectives with the will of Allah. The complicated readjustments which had to be undertaken by a pastoral community, which had not yet achieved integral nationality, to the wider expanses of an imperial community, were regulated by laws drawn from its sacred scriptures. Religious fanaticism was curiously mingled with military prowess in carrying the followers of the prophet from success to success. Islamic imperialism, according to Schumpeter, was driven by a self-perpetuating fanatic energy:

> War was the normal function of this military theocracy [he declares]. The leaders might discuss methods, but the basic issue was never in question. The point emerges with particular clarity, since the Arabs, for the most part, never troubled to look for even flimsy pretexts for war, nor did they even declare war. Their social organization needed war; without successful wars it would have collapsed. War, moreover, was the normal occupation of the members of the society. When there was no war, they would rebel or fall upon each other over theological controversies.[8]

Schumpeter admits that this picture is not quite accurate for the later eras of Islamic imperialism, when its dominion was consolidated and the cultural centers of Cordoba, Cairo, and Baghdad were developed. But in both the early and late periods of Islam

---

[7] Ignaz Goldziher, *Mohammed and Islam*, New Haven, Yale University Press, 1917, pp. 27–28.
[8] J. A. Schumpeter, *Imperialism and Social Classes*, The Noonday Press, 1955, p. 37.

the remarkable combination of religious passion and military prowess continued. The unifying force of the imperial community, which first cemented the Bedouin tribes into a cohesive force and later gave unity to such diverse conquered regions as Egypt, Persia and Iraq, and Spain, was undoubtedly the religious belief. The commandments of Allah and the doctrines of the prophet, declares Schumpeter,

> ... pervaded and dominated Arab life with an intensity that has few parallels in history. They determined daily conduct, shaped the whole world outlook. They permeated the mentality of the believer, made him someone who was characteristically different from all other men, opened up an unbridgeable gulf between him and the infidel, turning the latter into the arch enemy with whom there could be no true peace.[9]

It must become obvious, even before the analogy be studied more closely, that the absolute distinction between the believer and the unbeliever with the resulting fanaticism and the relation between political and religious dynamism, suggests the similarity between Islamic and modern communist imperialism. Communism is a religion within the framework of a modern secular culture in which the "logic of history" takes the place of Allah as the absolute source of meaning, and the writings of Marx and Lenin become the sacred texts, analogous to the Koran.

At one point Islamic fanaticism is differentiated from both ancient and modern religious fanaticism. The unbeliever or infidel is not exterminated; and his subjugation is qualified by a tolerant attitude towards his beliefs and institutions, so long as he pays the tax to the conqueror. It was this policy which extended the life of the Islamic imperialism for centuries. The analogy between Islamic and communist determinism is most significant particularly because in both cases this determinism, this confidence of an ultimate plan to which human wills must conform, was, contrary to modern voluntaristic opinions, the source of an almost demonic historical dynamism.[10] At only one point does the difference be-

[9] *Ibid.*, p. 38. [10] See Goldziher, *op. cit.*, p. 94.

tween Islam and Communism betray the gulf between a classical religion and a modern secularized one. Islamic faith produced a movement of mystic world-flight which, analogous to medieval asceticism, represented the expression of the uneasy conscience of sensitive individuals to the power realities of the Islamic empire; and which had its historic warrant from the early portions of the Koran, when the military successes of the prophet were not yet secured. The change from world-flight to world conquest was very rapid.

> Even before his death and notably immediately after, the watchword had changed [writes Goldziher]. In place of the denial of the world came the idea of the conquest of the world. Confession of Islam was to result for the faithful in 'the attainment of material prosperity, in supremacy over the Arabs and subjection of the non-Arabs, and besides all this a kingly estate in paradise.' [11]

The final otherworldly promise and hope has, of course, no analogy in Marxist utopianism, in which prosperity and the supremacy of the proletarian messianic class is promised for this life only.

SIMILARITIES AND DIFFERENCES BETWEEN THE EASTERN CHRISTIAN AND THE ISLAMIC EMPIRES

In addition to the similarities in the structure of prestige drawn from a universal religion, in all three empires, it is necessary to note the marked ideological distinctions between the two religions. Islam had an uncomplicated idea of the relation between the will of Allah and the achievements of the prophet-warriors who had conquered and ruled in his name. In the Christian faith the figure of Christ in the Biblical revelation was at once the symbol of the ultimate virtues, which transcended historic possibilities, and of the reconciling divine mercy, which accepted the fragmentary and contradictory moral realities of history. In terms of theological principle and logic it should have been impossible for any person, and particularly for any complex of power and authority, to claim identity with Christ or the authority to speak in his name. Actually

---

[11] *Ibid.*, p. 149.

the emperors of the East claimed religious authority equal to any Islamic claims; and although they were subject to reproof by the Patriarch of Constantinople, the power realities made the idea of separate but equal authorities, the one spiritual and the other temporal, irrelevant to actual politics. The treatises on the authority of the emperor invariably assert that he rules by divine right and exhort him to imitate the divine justice. The blandness of the moral exhortations, and the absence of any consideration for the power realities of the imperial rule, reveal a remarkable similarity not only with the moralism of Islamic ideology but with the consistent moralism of the Chinese Confucian reformers, who from age to age sought to overcome the despotism of the Chinese empire by counselling the emperor to rule in the spirit of the idealized sage-emperors of the Chou dynasty. Thus in an Introduction (Epanagōgē) to "a revision of the ancient laws" instructing the emperor at the beginning of the Macedonian dynasty, presumably written by the Patriarch and scholar Photius (circa 880), we read these sentiments:

1. 'The Emperor (*Basileus*) is a legal authority, a blessing common to all his subjects, who neither punishes in antipathy nor rewards in partiality, but behaves like an umpire making awards in a game.

2. 'The aim of the Emperor is to guard and secure by his ability the powers which he already possesses; to recover by sleepless care those that are lost; and to acquire by wisdom and by just ways and habits those that are not [as yet] in his hands...

5. 'The Emperor ought to be most notable in orthodoxy and to be famous for holy zeal,... in the matter of the doctrines laid down about the Trinity,...

6. 'The Emperor must interpret laws laid down by the men of old; and ... decide the issues on which there is no law.' [12]

This conception, which makes the piety and orthodoxy of the emperor the source of his authority, is frequently varied with a

[12] Quoted from Ernest Barker, *Social and Political Thought in Byzantium*, Oxford, Clarendon Press, 1957, pp. 89–90.

moralistic approach which combines piety with universal goodwill; and this goodwill is identified with universal dominion. Thus Theophylact, the Archbishop of Bulgaria and the tutor of Constantine, the son of the Emperor Michael VII (1071–8), gives his conception of religion and the imperial authority:

> A true king, knowing that his throne should have a firm foundation...makes religion his cornerstone...he acts and speaks, at all times, as one who surely knows that God sees and hears all things. Loving God, he is known as a man who is loved of God; for a man who loves God will be loved by Him. Wherefore God will be all in all to him—father and brother; soldier and fellow fighter, giving him victory in war and raising trophies by his side. ...Who then has greater prosperity than the man who loves God? Who is more invincible in battle?...Indeed a man of his stamp—but only such a man—may well be king of the whole world. For if the world is God's; if the man of whom I speak is agreed by all to be the friend of God; and if the goods of friends are their common property—it follows that the man who is dearest to God will be king [along with God who is his friend] of the whole world.[13]

The conception of piety as the basis of universal dominion is not always as simply conceived, even in Byzantine culture; and it may be discounted as a pious clerical interpretation. It is nevertheless true that the Byzantine conceptions of dominion had little relevance to the power realities of empire, to the dynastic struggles in which dynasty after dynasty perished or gave way to another; and to the imperial wars with both the western and the Islamic empires.

The relation of piety and moralism to power in the theocratic Islamic empire was even more obvious, and the frictions between the religious and the political aspects of empire were more frequent, despite the fact that the dynasts were both religious and political rulers. The friction accounts for the supplanting of the Omayyad dynasty with the Abbaside house, the latter accusing the former of secularism; and to legitimatize their claim, they "over-

---

[13] *Ibid.*, p. 147.

flow[ed] with unctuous piety in the endeavor to restore the sanctity of prophetical recollections. ...They wish in this way to
emphasize the contrast between themselves and their predecessors
[the Omayyads]." [14] The political realities were illumined as little
by these interpretations of religious dominion as they were in the
Byzantine empire. This is not to say that there were not a few who
interpreted the social realities in moral terms, as there were, for
instance, also in the Chinese Confucian empire.

Thus in the heyday of the North African Islamic empire in the
fourteenth century, the famed scholar Ibn-Khaldun interpreted the
cohesive power of a religious faith in both ideological and moral
terms:

> To conquer, one must rely on the allegiance of a group animated
> with one corporate spirit and end. Such a union of hearts and
> wills can operate only through divine power and religious support.
> ...When men give their hearts and passions to a desire for
> worldly goods, they become jealous and fall into discord. If, how-
> ever, they reject the world and its vanities for love of God...
> jealousies disappear, discords are stilled, men help one another de-
> votedly; their union makes them stronger; the good cause makes
> rapid progress, and culminates in the formation of a great and
> powerful empire.[15]

The identification of an empire with God, and of rivalries and
jealousies with the quest after the "vanities" of the world, gives a
vivid picture of the powerful religious force of cohesion is this
quasi-universal empire, without, of course, doing justice to the
rivalries and jealousies which were constantly apparent in the formation of the empire. Nothing could express so vividly the amalgam of religious devotion and political will to power which characterized all these medieval empires. It was so potent that one
must raise the question whether any secular analogy can be found
for this ideological frame of empire. One must answer that question tentatively in calling attention to the quasi-religious creed of

[14] Goldziher, op. cit., p. 52.
[15] H. Graetz, History of the Jews, IV. Quoted from Will Durant, The Reformation, New York, Simon & Schuster, 1957, p. 693.

Communism as the only force in modern culture which faintly approximates the religious dynamism of the medieval empires. Among the many similarities it is significant that Communism, so realistic in analyzing the power realities of the capitalist world, is equally oblivious of the power factors in its own empire. At least its prophets and priests are equally bland in treating these realities.

This analysis of the similarities of the medieval empires suggests the following conclusions: first, that the most rigorous monotheism cannot prevent, and may support, the pretensions of a great imperial community to be the universal community and the claims of the rulers to have their sovereignty by divine decree. Secondly, that the difference between the Islamic faith—with its primitive historical dynamism—and Christianity—with its understanding of the difference between the historical and the divine—is obscured by the similarities in the religious justification of empire when Christ becomes simply an anchor of power. The Christian community, in its indictment of Communism as "atheistic materialism," does not seem to realize the significance of these striking similarities. These similarities prove it almost inevitable that the community, particularly the large imperial community and its rulers, should overcome all religious scruples, however integral to their professed religion, and should engage in the idolatrous claim of absolute validity for a community and a dominion which is so obviously historically contingent. The secular protest against religious politics, which identifies the historical with the divine, must be regarded as an inevitable reaction against this danger. It is compounded in Christian culture of an essentially religious antireligion and of a more purely secular protest against all ultimates, which contain the danger of false ultimates. Immediate goals, proximate ends, and the web of tolerably decent values are found more sufferable than the falsely ultimate values. From this perspective, the defect of Communism is not that it is atheistic but that it has a false god. It indulges in the perennial religious mistake of identifying its political idealism and will to power (not a unique but a typical combination) with its god, or source of ultimate meaning—the historical dialectic.

The power of the impulse of dominion to make use of any and all religions, historical and non-historical, worldly and other-worldly, can be illumined not only by calling attention to the similarities between christian, islamic, and communist forms of religious devotion, but in analyzing the service which such an otherworldly mystical religion as Buddhism (perhaps the purest of all religions because the least given to historical responsibility) can offer imperial rulers. An interesting use of Buddhism as an instrument of dominion is found in Chinese history, when the Sui dynasty came to power in 581 B.C. and unified China after three centuries of disunity. The founder of the dynasty was a Buddhist, the Emperor Wen-ti, who artfully combined confucian with buddhist traditions to create a more potent imperial ideology. The Sinologist Arthur F. Wright analyzes his religious and political motives in terms which establish a real analogy with the Christian Emperor Constantine.

> Wen'ti [declares Wright] was a devout Buddhist, but he was also a shrewd and calculating man in pursuit of great power and universal dominion. ... From beginning to end Buddhism was under firm state control, and support of Buddhism, as well as the ideological use of Buddhism, were calculated in terms of the problems facing the dynasty.[16]

Tibet is not a community of imperial proportions, but it is worth noting in passing that the Lamaism of Tibet, regnant to this day, represents an interesting form of dominion in which a religion of world-denial is made an instrument of domination, and the agents of domination are the very monks who are most adept in the techniques of life-denial.[17]

In short, the impulse to dominion on every level, but particularly on the imperial level, is able to use the most varied and contradictory religious impulses and philosophies as instruments of its purposes. The similarities which we have noted in the three occi-

---

[16] Arthur F. Wright, "The Formation of Sui Ideology, 581–604" in Fairbank, *Chinese Thought and Institutions*, pp. 93–94.
[17] Cf. Charles Alfred Bell, *The Religion of Tibet*, Oxford, Clarendon Press, 1931.

dental empires point to a pattern of community which is more universal than western history. It is possible to derive an axiom from this pattern. It is that quasi-universal community and dominion is bound to use religious quests for ultimacy and universality as instruments of its purposes. No pattern of history could give a more vivid evidence of a perennial fruit of one aspect of human existence. That aspect is that man has the freedom over nature to create communities in ever larger proportions. He also has the freedom to transcend these political constructions and to envision a meaning and system of ends which transcends these historically contingent and precarious political configurations. But the rulers also can make use of this final flight to the absolute and harness it to political ends. The question is whether they could be so successful if men did not give themselves willingly as tools for this enterprise, perhaps because they seek collective compensation for their individual insignificance.

But this analysis of similarities threatens to obscure a consideration of the significant differences in the empires of the Middle Ages. These differences are many, but we must center our attention on the difference between the western empire and the other two, because so much of what we know as the characteristics of western culture and political life are to be found in embryo in these differences.

CHAPTER VIII

The Uniqueness
of Western Christendom

WE have previously considered the three medieval empires, and analyzed the similarities in their development of dominion and community. If we now single out the western empire for special consideration, and if we define the subject as "Western Christendom" rather than the western Christian empire, it is because its history manifests very significant differences from the other two empires. Some of the differences are so great that it is not accurate to speak of the "Western Empire" as a definitive term. There was indeed a western empire, beginning with Charlemagne, continuing its insecure life throughout the Middle Ages, during which the Hohenstaufens and the Hapsburg emperors tried vainly to maintain themselves against the more potent church on the one hand and the rising nations on the other hand. It was not the empire but the universal church, with its claims of spiritual and temporal dominion, which was the most powerful historical agent in the life of the West. The position of the church, as we have previously recognized, was due to historically contingent factors. The dominance of the Pope in the political life of the Middle Ages was initiated in the period between the fall of the Roman empire and the rise of the western Frankish empire; and the Pope's policy in transmuting the Frankish king into the western emperor contributed considerably to the dominance which was never lost, though it could be argued that the papal power was destroyed through its effort to humiliate its junior, but necessary, partner: the empire.

In terms of purely political organization the character of western Christendom seems not to be too different from the other empires. The most marked distinction is that the priest rather than the soldier-king had the dominant prestige, thus exhibiting an interesting version of the age-old partnership between priest and soldier in the building of imperial communities. But it would be an error to regard this distinction as insignificant merely because the dominance of the priest gave the western empire a different structure of force and prestige. For this dominance involved two characteristics which had consequences for the whole of western culture and not merely for its political life. The two characteristics may be defined briefly as: first, the sharper separation between the religious and the secular sphere than in the other empires; and secondly, the unity of the ecclesiastical institution achieved by the prestige of the Pope, particularly since Gregory VII. This gave the church a monolithic structure, which tried to subordinate all the national and intellectual vitalities of the culture. Modern western culture has in fact acquired most of its distinguishing marks in political and cultural rebellion against papal dominion, so that the overarching unity of the church would seem to be no more than negatively significant. But whether negative or positive both the dominance and the unity of the church created the background for the rise of modern culture in all the richness and variety of its political and cultural life.

The sharper distinction between the religious and the secular in western Christendom is easily obscured by the attempt of the church to exploit its religious prestige for the sake of temporal dominion. This development, which we have previously analyzed, and which reached its triumph in the power of Innocent III and in the claims of Innocent IV and Boniface VIII, did indeed partly annul the distinction. Thus Innocent IV could claim:

> [God] has established in the apostolic throne, not only a pontifical but a regal monarchy, committing to the blessed Peter and his successors the government of both an earthly and a celestial empire, which is duly signified by the plurality of the keys; in order to make known by the one key which we have received applicable over the earth in things temporal and by the other over the heavens

in things spiritual, that the vicar of Christ has received the power of judgment.[1]

In one of his glosses on the decretals, Innocent IV becomes even more explicit in the claim of dominion. "We believe," he writes, "that the Pope, who is the vicar of Jesus Christ, has power not only over Christians, but also over all infidels." [2] It would be irrelevant to our interest to trace the long history of the papal claims of dominion, of the contest with the empire, and the varying forms in which the claims were expressed, sometimes emphasizing both temporal and spiritual dominion and at other times merely affirming the supremacy of the Pope in the ecclesiastical institution. Even Boniface VIII declared in his famous Bull *unam sanctam* (1302):

> ...We declare, we affirm, we define, and pronounce that for every human creature it is absolutely necessary for salvation to be subject to the Roman Pontiff.[3]

It will be noted that the claim of dominion is universal, but in this case not political but soteriological.

It must be admitted that the superior prestige of the church and papacy, and the consequent exploitation of that superiority over both religious and political life, obscures the distinction between the religious and the secular which is so marked in the life of the western world compared to both the Byzantine and Islamic empires. Yet while the distinction is blurred, it is not effaced. The proof that it is not is given by the historical consequences which flowed from the distinction and gave western culture its peculiar color. The distinction may have been one of the most creative in the history of culture even though the maintenance of ecclesiastical dominion, by means of the authority derived from a scheme of salvation, aroused so much resentment, even before the Reformation and Renaissance.

On the political side the distinction became the basis for a

---

[1] Quoted from Charles Howard McIlwain, *The Growth of Political Thought in the West*, New York, Macmillan Co., 1932, p. 234.
[2] *Loc. cit.*   [3] *Ibid.*, p. 245.

secularized political order, which was elaborated in various forms through the subsequent centuries. But it is significant that only a century after the theory of papal supremacy was fully developed, Marsilius of Padua, in his *Defensor Pacis* (1324), elaborated an anti-papal conception of the political order in which Aristotle furnished the stuff for the political structure and Augustine gave the justification for the radical distinction between the two realms of the political and the ecclesiastical—of nature and grace—of reason and faith. Marsilius' theory, which has been widely regarded as the beginning of modern political thought, presented a rather more viable definition of the two realms than Luther presented two centuries later. Luther, as Marsilius, was indebted to Augustine; but his "earthly realm" was conceived as a realm of coercive order in a world of sin. It lacked the concern for discriminate justice which was the fruit of Aristotelian thought in the Middle Ages.

Even more significant than Marsilius' secularization of the political order is Dante's conception in his *De Monarchia*. For here the great Christian poet, without challenging the Catholic faith, opposes papal absolutism and seeks to rescue Christian universalism from the odium into which it fell because of the papal use of religious authority for the sake of gaining universal dominion. Dante believes in the necessity of a universal monarchy, in the first instance to save Italy from the anarchy into which its various principalities and states had fallen; and, secondly, to assure universal peace, an ambitious purpose which the author believed to be within reach if the community of mankind had but a single ruler. His conception of peace through an omnipotent ruler who, having all he desired, could have only disinterested motives, is naturally utopian. It was projected in history, when all historical factors revealed that the community of mankind was larger and more subject to competitive tension than Dante's theory assumed. But the theory was significant for two reasons:

(1) It provided a secular and rational support for the political order and eliminated the religious justification for the empire, a justification which our study has shown to be a source of confusion. Dante provided the political community with its own justi-

fication through an analysis of the necessity of community for human self-fulfillment. In this enterprise he disassociated the basic Aristotelianism, which Aquinas had used in his synthesis of classical and Christian doctrine, from its religious component and made the self-justifying political community independent of the Church. It had its justification immediately; it was not mediated through the Church.

(2) Dante, despite his anti-clericalism, insisted on the validity of the realm which the Church controlled and which corresponded to the dimension of the human, as private rather than public, existence. He did not challenge the Church in this realm as the Reformation did subsequently.

> Just as the Church has its foundation [declared Dante], so has the Empire. For the Church's foundation is Christ. Hence the Apostle's word to the Corinthians: 'Other foundation can no man lay than that is laid, which is Christ Jesus.' He is himself the rock on which the Church is built. But the Empire's foundation is human justice.[4]

It may seem hazardous to venture the opinion that Dante's radicalism restored the distinction not only between the religious and the secular, but between the public and the private dimension of life. It was the original genius of the Christian faith to establish this distinction, but it had been obscured by ecclesiastical authority over the political empire, an authority which claimed control of the "keys of heaven."

Dante's radicalism did not prompt him to deny the value of this ultimate form of fulfillment. He was sufficiently orthodox not only to affirm this promise of eternal felicity but also to give the church precedence as an agent of grace in this ultimate dimension of life. D'Entrèves observes that in the closing paragraphs of his treatise Dante warns, lest he be misunderstood, that his theory does not suggest the equality of the two powers. "Let Caesar observe that due reverence for Peter, which a first-born son should

---

[4] Dante, *De Monarchia*, introd. by Donald Nicholl, Library of Ideas, New York, Noonday Press, 1954, Bk. III, Ch. 10.

observe to his father," warned Dante, and proved how far the medieval system of politics and salvation could be challenged without being destroyed.[5]

The modern mind will appreciate Dante's achievement in the secularization of politics more than his rigorous distinction between the public and the private dimension of existence, which also involved the further distinction between the proximate and the ultimate ends of man's quest for fulfillment. Before passing judgment upon the relative merits of these achievements it is necessary to analyze each more fully.

Dante's secularization of politics, we have suggested, clarifies the distinction between the political and the religious sphere which was implied in the original synthesis between classical and Christian culture but obscured by the papal political supremacy. This distinction was defined in Augustine's *De Civitate Dei*, but the distinction was obscured when the papalists identified Augustine's *civitas dei* with the church without reservation and, moreover, with the politically potent church. Significantly, not only Marsilius of Padua and Dante used Augustine, together with Aristotle, to restore the radical dualism, but Luther based his doctrine of the two realms upon Augustinian ideas. He made the political realm more coercive and less productive of discriminate judgment than either Marsilius or Dante. In this, as in other cases, the pre-Reformation Renaissance was both more modern and more Catholic than the Reformation.

Naturally the Aristotelianism in Dante's thought prompts him to an interpretation of political reality, quite contrary to Augustine's realistic account of the power realities of the *civitas terrena*. Dante thinks the universality of the monarch's dominion would guarantee his disinterestedness. For

> when there is nothing to be desired there can be no cupidity, because the passions cannot remain when their objects have been eliminated. But the Monarch has nothing to desire, since the

---

[5] A. P. D'Entrèves, *Dante as a Political Thinker*, Oxford, Clarendon Press, 1952, p. 58.

ocean alone is the limit of his jurisdiction,—unlike other princes, such as the Kings of Castile and Aragon, whose jurisdictions are limited by one another's frontiers. It follows that of all mortals the Monarch can be the purest incarnation of justice.[6]

This lack of realism is significant for it reveals that the rebellion against ecclesiastical pretension prompted Dante to idealize the temporal, or earthly, empire. This sacrifice of the Augustinian realism, partly evident in Aquinas, was to be characteristic of political thought throughout the Renaissance, except for rebellious realists such as Machiavelli.

The purity and disinterestedness of the universal monarch was rationally adduced; and so was the conception of the necessity of a universal empire derived from the universality of the divine governance of the world. Dante writes:

> A son's condition is most perfect if the son, as far as his nature allows, reproduces the perfection of the father. Mankind is the son of the heavens, which is perfect in all its works; but man is begotten by man and the sun (according to the second book of the 'Physics'). Therefore mankind's condition is most perfect when it reproduces the perfection of heaven, so far as human nature allows. And just as the heavens are governed by a single mover, which is God ... so, if our argument be correct, mankind is at its best when all its movements and intentions are governed by one Prince as its sole mover and with one law for its direction.[7]

To this argument, deriving the perfection of a universal monarchy from the perfection of God, Dante adds another argument in which he seeks to prove that universal monarchy is necessary for the fulfillment of human freedom.

> The human race is at its best when it is most free. ...If the judgment completely directs the appetite and is in no way deflected by it, then it is free; ...This is why brute beasts cannot enjoy free judgment; because their judgments follow their appetites. ... Once this is realized, it becomes clear that this liberty, or this principle of all our liberty, is God's most precious gift to human nature. ...But this plenitude of freedom it enjoys only under a Monarchy.[8]

---

[6] Dante, *op. cit.*, I, xi.   [7] *Ibid.*, I, ix.   [8] *Ibid.*, I, xii.

It is obvious that one of the defects of Dante's rigorous distinction between the public and the private realm, or more exactly between the realm of the public and temporal welfare and the private and eternal blessedness, is the definition of the public reality in terms of classical rationalism which derives evil from the influence of the passions and is oblivious to the mystery of the contradiction in human freedom, namely that man's freedom becomes the source of evil when it is used to aggrandize the self and not to serve the community. Evil, as Augustine observed, is rooted in the self and not in the passions of the body.

Dante's universalism was projected at a moment in history in which all universal and quasi-universal communities were doomed, both because the community of mankind was revealed to be more extensive than it had been supposed (a realization for which Columbus' discovery of America was symbolic) and because the parochial and particular communities were stirring to challenge the dominion of the empire. Dante's rational perfectionism, as indeed his universalism, remained as a permanent characteristic of one element in the secularized politics of culture. This development suggests that it is scarcely possible to carry through a too radical distinction between the public and the private, between the proximate and the ultimate good, and certainly not if secular politics, valuable in itself, is based upon one theory of human nature and the theory of personal fulfillment is based on another. A secular politics is necessary because it deals with proximate goals and ends; and the religious intrusion of ultimates is a source of confusion. But if the ultimates are introduced in secularized forms utopia is substituted for the "eternal felicity" of the Catholic scheme of salvation. Dante's *De Monarchia* is thus a very important document. For it introduces both the virtue and the weakness of optimistic political thought: the virtue of seeking the proximate happiness which is attained by the harmony of the historical community and the weakness of setting goals for this community in terms of both perfection and universality which are beyond the capacity of mortal man to attain, since he is both finite in his perspectives and suffering from an inner contradiction in the use of his freedom. Perhaps it is not too hazardous to claim that there is an inner connection, though no obvious historical chain, between the logic of *De Monarchia* and the communist vision of a universal empire. The utopianism of Dante, however, was not a universal characteristic of the post-medieval age. It was challanged both by the secular realism of Machiavelli and of Hobbes and by the Pauline realism of the Reformers. All of these realists, incidentally, were excessive in their estimate of the egocentricity of man and oblivious to the fact that human rational faculties always display both creative and destructive tendencies, building just communities on the one hand, and on the other disturbing the peace of the communities by the rationalization of particular interests.

We have suggested that the creative influence in Western Christendom was partly derived from the dualism which separated the "temporal" from the "eternal" end of man, identifying the one with his political life and the other with private hopes and fulfillments which transcend any communal attainments and realizations. Dante does not clarify the private nature of the "eternal" end, for he leaves the church in complete control of the guarantee of the eternal end. Yet his orthodoxy is significant because it leaves the ultimate dimension standing, if only as a façade. Both the Reformation and the Renaissance were to explore the private possibilities of the self in its transcendence over the communal situation. The Reformation emphasized the individual character of the relation of the self to the divine; and the impossibility of any human fulfillment bridging the chasm between the fragmentary character of the historical and the divine. The Renaissance was to explore all the individual intellectual and cultural possibilities of the self once it was freed of ecclesiastical authority. But both explorations depended upon that radical distinction between the political or communal and the "eternal" or private end of man, which Dante had maintained.[9]

---

[9] It is one of the many virtues of Boris Pasternak's Nobel Prize-winning novel, *Doctor Zhivago*, that it emphasized the distinction between individual and collective destiny. The novel was erroneously interpreted as purely anti-communist. It is critical of all purely collectivist interpretations of life.

To understand the importance of this ancient and reemphasized distinction it is necessary to explore the relation of the human self to the community. It is a paradoxical relation, for the community is at once the fulfillment and the frustration of the self. It is the fulfillment because the self cannot fulfill itself within itself but only because a true self as its interests and creativities are engaged in the community. Aristotle rightly declares that only a beast or a god is able to live without the *polis*. The meaning of human life and the fulfillments of those meanings is provided by the community.

But the individual has the capacity to transcend the community, to conceive of ends which are only indirectly relevant to the community, and to survey the human condition radically so that no social or political fulfillment can answer the problem which arises. This problem can be defined in two ways: first, that the self is able to conceive ends which transcend the possibilities of history as bound to nature. The proof that this transcendence is real is given by every heroic death or martyr's achievement in which the warning is heeded: "Fear not them which are able to kill the body." The fulfillment of man's physical life and historical success must be sacrificed for the attainment of this integrity of spirit. This is the "eternal"—as distinguished from the temporal—end of human existence. In a secular age this dimension is regarded with scepticism or even contempt, because there is no scientific or metaphysical proof of a "supernatural" world in which the frustrations of history are overcome, the injustices abolished, and the highest hopes fulfilled. Nevertheless, it was the contribution of the Christian faith to emphasize this transcendent dimension; and its emphasis left a deposit in modern life even in the secularized culture of the French Enlightenment, which never tired of emphasizing the "dignity" of man, though it was not fully conscious of the final communal irrelevance of this dignity. Modern bourgeois culture has always been the product of a compound of the religious appreciation of the incongruous individual, rising above all social meanings and communal fulfillments and frustrations, and the social individualism of the commercial classes whose social mobility, flexible forms of property, and emancipation from traditional vocations, established their dignity.

The second way in which the dimension of individual selfhood must be defined is the situation of self-contradiction, mythically suggested in the Biblical legend of the fall of Adam, which has informed all Christian ideas of the human situation, and which is vaguely suggested even in the Stoic idea of a difference between the Golden Age and actual history, in which, for some undefined reasons, the final possibilities of social virtue cannot be realized. This self-contradiction, usually termed "original sin," is as offensive to modern culture as it was irrelevant to classical culture. Yet it points to a fact of human existence, more proved by human experience than any other affirmation of the Christian faith. That fact is that the capacity of human freedom to transcend a finite situation does not lead inevitably to a more valid or universal norm of conduct; but it can lead, and often does, to the sanctification of the finite and contingent situation as the ultimate one. This is the *hybris* in which all human spirituality is involved, and which makes all efforts to remove general evil by a progressive elimination of particular causes of particular evils so abortive. In every new historical or social situation, some individual, class, nation, or social force, will claim more than its share of the goods of life and pretend to more dignity than is its by right because it looks at the common situation, not from a transcendent and disinterested perspective but from its own perspective which it falsely identifies with the ultimate perspective. This human situation is partly subject to remedy and partly not. It is subject to remedy insofar as it is recognized. For every recognition of this determining factor in man's behavior leads to a measure of emancipation from this determination. Hence, "grace" is defined by the Christian faith as the accretion of a new power of righteousness, consequent upon true repentance. In an ultimate sense, there is of course no remedy. Every achievement of moral virtue and every technological progress in human culture and every triumph of the human mind remains subject to the ambiguity of human existence. Man is both creature and creator of history, and inevitably he forgets the limits of his creaturely finiteness and pretends to a transcendent and universally valid perspective upon common problems which is beyond the capacity of mortal man. Intellectual sophistication and the accumulation of knowledge can reduce this tendency and an adequate sociology of knowledge can mitigate it. But no force in culture or history can eliminate it.

The whole of Christian culture distinguishes itself from both classical and modern culture by making the figure of Christ the central symbol of the frame of meaning for life. Christ is the expression of both dimensions of human existence, which we have analyzed. His goodness (that is, his death upon the cross) is the symbol of the fulfillment of selfhood in a trans-historical dimension; it is a failure in history but a perpetual reminder that historical man must not take historical success too seriously. But the Christian gospel entered the world not merely by insisting on the trans-historical possibility of the fulfillment of life but also as an assurance of the divine mercy, which closes the chasm between all fragmentary human virtues and the ultimate goodness. The message that "God was in Christ, reconciling the world unto Himself" gives authentic Christianity that paradoxical combination of pessimism and optimism which is a perpetual source of creativity so long as it does not become the historical symbol of the very nullification, either optimistic or pessimistic, of the original message. The pessimism prevents every eminence in history, cultural or political, from claiming absolute validity. The optimism prevents the drama of history, with all its patches of meaninglessness, from being conceived as a "tale, full of sound and fury, signifying nothing." The modern mind is sceptical of any metaphysical foundation of the realm of meaning in which perfect virtue finds fulfillment; but all but the most consistently naturalistic philosophies must concede a dimension of meaning for human existence, which hovers precariously over the communal realities and destinies of collective man and comprehends the individual in the grandeur and incongruity of his freedom and finiteness—in his dignity and in his misery.

It is this dimension which Dante seeks to recognize in his retention of the Catholic dogma of eternal blessedness as the final end of man. "In order to grasp this," declares Dante, "it must be realized that man is unique amongst all beings in linking corruptible things with those that are incorruptible." He proceeds to explicate the incongruity of human existence in purely Aristotelian terms. He goes on:

> ... If man is considered according to his essential constituents, that is, his soul and his body, he is corruptible in regard to the one, the body, but incorruptible according to the other, the soul. Thus, in the second book of *De Anima*, the Philosopher rightly says of the incorruptible constituent of man: 'and this alone, being eternal, is capable of separating itself from the corruptible world.' Therefore man is, so to say, a middle term between corruptible and incorruptible things, and since every middle term participates in the two extremes which it unites, man must participate in the two natures.[10]

This view of the double dimension of human existence hardly did justice to facets of human nature which the Renaissance developed on the one hand and the Reformation on the other. Aristotle's conception of the incorruptible part of man was hardly adequate to the private and individual character of man's freedom, for the incorruptible part of man was the impersonal *Nous*. The whole of modern culture, beginning with the Renaissance, was to elaborate this sense of biographical individuality which has become one of the hallmarks of modern culture. Nor did Dante's conception of man's incongruity illumine the inner experience of that incongruity, which it has been the service of various forms of existentialism to explicate.

Nor does Dante anticipate the emphasis of the Reformation that it is impossible for man, by virtuous conduct, to overcome the contradictory and fragmentary character of all human virtues. "Eternal blessedness" for the Reformers is the fruit not of the realization of perfection but of a sense of forgiveness, that is, of acceptance, despite the inability of man to reach the impossible goal of perfect virtue. The Reformation, as we shall see, was not

[10] *Ibid.*, III, xvi.

very successful in relating these religious visions to the collective life of man, but it gave a valid account of that part of the human situation which deals with both its incongruity and with the abortive efforts to overcome or to obscure that incongruity. Thus Dante is not the herald of the Reformation and only partly of the Renaissance. His achievement at the very end of the medieval period was that he sharply distinguished the two realms of collective and individual destiny, of historical and trans-historical possibilities, which clerical absolutism had obscured, thus clarifying one of the elements in the structure of Western Christendom, which distinguished it from the Islamic and Byzantine empires.

If the truth of the Christian faith should rest, as I think it does, upon the validity of its interpretation of the human situation, and if the Reformation interpretation of that faith correctly states this situation and accurately defines what is remedial and what irremediable in man's destructive use of his freedom, it follows that both Dante's and the Reformation's stricture against Catholicism reveal that it is possible to use an ultimate truth as an instrument of power and prestige, and that a truth can be appropriated for forms of pretension which it is designed to refute. The fact that papal absolutism should dominate the political life of a religious age, and that it should be unmindful of all those Biblical reminders of the gulf between the historical and contingent and the divine, reveals how readily human creativity should defy the religious warnings designed to set limits for its inordinacy. It may prove also that the ultimate truths of the Christian faith are acceptable only to the individual, and are almost bound to be misused by collective man and his majesties. Only the individual has the self-transcendence to measure the distance between his finiteness and the ultimate source of meaning. And only the individual can know of the impossible possibility of life transcending nature-history in some act of heroism and sacrifice which defies all rational calculations and points to an ultimate, if not eternal, end.

Even among individuals there is no certainty that piety will have the fruit of a broken spirit and a contrite heart. Historically piety may be the source of both humility and fanaticism; and the Christian faith has been productive of both, as everyone knows. But in the collective life of man piety is usually more productive of fanaticism for the simple reason that the collective achievements are sufficiently impressive to lend themselves to identification with the ultimate. It was this fanaticism against which the modern age revolted, beginning with Dante's *De Monarchia*, running through the Reformation's indictment of the papacy as the "Whore of Babylon," and continuing in the resentment of the French Enlightenment against "priests and their hypocritical tools." Some of these indictments made the almost universal mistake of attributing a general inclination of the human heart to a particular historical force or institution in which it is momentarily embodied.

Nevertheless, the refutation of papal absolutism was a significant challenge to religious imperialism. The significance could be explained more fully if it is remembered that the West had no religio-political force to hold the larger community together such as the Islamic and Byzantine empires had. The force of universal cohesion was not the empire but the church; and it used an authority drawn not from the meaning of a community but from a dimension of human existence transcending the community. When the legitimacy of this form of authority was challenged, and when it did indeed prompt the most potent resentments, the doom of the unity of the western community was a foregone conclusion, which the Renaissance and the Reformation elaborated—the one protesting against papal pretension in the name of the dignity of rational man, and the other in the name of the majesty of God.

Meanwhile the partly secularized West developed many cultural and political vitalities, among them chiefly the economic force of the new commerce and the political force of integral nations long held in subjection to an ecclesiastical authority. The forces in the realm of politics and the cultural force of the awakened reason of man all made for a creative chaos which it was impossible for an inflexible system of order either to contain, to deflect, or to reformulate. Thus the modern age began in every realm of human vitality with a force which we recognize, with

the wisdom of hindsight, as an inevitably triumphant one. The
unity of civilization and culture had been shattered. Henceforth
mankind was never again to have this unity, culturally or politically. Those who look back to the Golden Age with regret are apt
to predict the inevitable doom of our own precarious order so close
to the edge of chaos. Modern culture did not indeed anticipate, in
its early stages, how difficult it would be to establish a viable community on either the national or international level. The eighteenth and nineteenth centuries did not anticipate the tragic predicaments of an age of nuclear warfare. Man's conquest of nature
was assumed to contribute directly and inevitably to human welfare. The idea of progress gave meaning to life, and utopia sup-
planted the "eternal blessedness" of Dante's vision.

This optimism prompts the final question in our consideration
of the uniqueness of Western Christendom. The question con-
cerns the fate of the realism which Augustine first introduced to
western culture and which he laid in the foundation of that culture
in his doctrine of the "two cities." From the ideal vantage point
of the "City of God" he was able to survey and analyze the political realities of the "earthly city" with penetrating realism, dis-
covering all the conflicts of interest and power in any historic community. This was a new note of realism, quite distinct from the
bland analyses of political realities in all the empires of history,
which had in fact the common characteristics of a religious source
of authority and a moralistic estimate of the power realities. This
common characteristic covers, as we have seen, such diverse cultures as China and Islam, Byzantine, and Stoic Rome.

The answer to the question is that this note of realism had a
curious and ironic fate in Western Christendom. It was appropriated by the church, which presumed to be the "City of God," to
discredit the moral pretensions of the emperors and princes.
"Kings have their dominion," said Pope Gregory the Great, "by
perfidy and plunder." The first great Pope's realism was matched
by the founder or restorer of the mediaeval papacy, Gregory VII,
who was even more rigorous in his condemnation of the secular
rulers:

> Who does not know [he asked] that kings and rulers had their
> beginning in men inspired by the Devil, the prince of this world,
> to turn away from God and presume in the blindness of their
> lust and their intolerable arrogance to bear rule over men, their
> equals, through pride, violence, fraud, bloodshed and almost every
> known crime? [11]

The Augustinian motifs in the indictment are revealing; and
they give the clue to the papal realism. The Popes, assuming to
speak from the standpoint of the "City of God," which they had
transmuted into an instrument of dominion, criticized the "earthly
city" exactly as Augustine did. Papal realism was naturally limited
to an analysis of the political rulers and was therefore discredited
among those who resented the papal dominion, either because
they were in conflict with the Popes, as were the Hohenstaufen
emperors, or because they objected to papal dominion as a matter
of principle, as did Dante.

Thus the anti-papalists were Augustinian in their conception of
the church as a community of grace rather than an instrument of
dominion; but they inclined to the blandness of classical estimates
of the community when dealing with the temporal order, leaving
no trace of the Augustinian realism in their political thought. This
realism had therefore no secure place in the post-medieval culture. Machiavelli shocked the world and became a whipping boy
for the medievalists by blurting out the real facts about the political order without subjecting them to criticism because they
did not correspond to the moral norm. He declares in his advice to
the prince that

> ... it appears to me more appropriate to follow up the real truth
> of a matter than the imagination of it, for many have pictured
> republics and principalities which in fact have never been known
> or seen. ...[12]

It may be significant that three realists of the post-medieval
period, Machiavelli in the fifteenth and sixteenth centuries, Luther

---

[11] Quoted from McIlwain, *op. cit.*, p. 207.
[12] Machiavelli, Nicolo, *The Prince*, Ch. XV, trans. by W. K. Marriott, Everyman's Library, London, J. M. Dent & Sons Ltd., 1908, p. 121.

in the sixteenth century, and Hobbes in the seventeenth century, while informed by various and contradictory philosophies, were all influenced by resentment against the claims of papal dominion. Machiavelli nonchalantly advises the prince of his city-state how to achieve power in his dominion, and suggests it is sufficient to observe the outward forms of morality if his policy be in the service of the state.

Hobbes is concerned chiefly with establishing the order and dignity of the national community; and with elaborate sceptical arguments, proceeds to banish the Pope from temporal dominions on the ground that he is dealing with another world:

> ... If a man consider the original of this great ecclesiastical dominion, he will easily perceive that the Papacy is no other than the ghost of the deceased Roman Empire, sitting crowned upon the grave thereof. For so did the Papacy start up on a sudden out of the ruins of that heathen power.
>
> The language also, which they use, both in the churches, and in their public acts, being Latin, which is not commonly used by any nation now in the world, what is it but the ghost of the old Roman language?
>
> The fairies in what nation soever they converse, have but one universal king, which some poets of ours call King Oberon; but the scripture calls Beelzebub, prince of demons. The ecclesiastics, likewise, in whose dominions soever they be found, acknowledge but one universal king, the Pope.[13]

Obviously Hobbes has a more virulent resentment against papal universal dominion than Dante, and the structure of faith has been completely destroyed. If there is still an Augustinian motif in his description of political reality it is not obviously indebted to Augustine.

Of all the post-medieval realists, Luther was most obviously indebted to Augustine, understandably enough, because of his early training as an Augustinian monk. His doctrine of the two realms is an adaptation of the Augustinian concept of the "two

---

[13] Thomas Hobbes, *The Leviathan*, ed. by Michael Oakshott, Part IV ("Of the Kingdom of Darkness"), Ch. 47. Oxford, Basil Blackwell, 1955, p. 457.

cities." But in his thought the idea of the two cities is perceptibly changed. The "heavenly realm" is not, like the "heavenly city" of Augustine, formed by the love of God but by the divine forgiveness, and the *agape* which flows from the security of being forgiven. The earthly city of Luther's conception is more clearly Augustinian. Its order is maintained by "chains, laws, courts and the sword." But it lacks the expansive dimensions of Augustine's *civitas terrena*. It is, in fact, simply defined as *obrigkeit*, or authority. The imperial authority is vaguely in the background, but the relevant authority is the princely elector, who became Luther's protector. Luther does not concern himself with the problem of a universal order, but only with the order in the parochial community of his experience. In that community order is maintained by coercive authority; and Augustine's conception of a relative justice, derived from the balance of social forces, disappears. So strong is Augustine's influence on Luther, however, that, despite the Reformation conviction that the redeemed are still sinners (*"justus et pecator simul"*), Luther divides the two realms as if one were for the believing and the other for the unbelieving.

> God has established magistracy for the sake of the unbelieving, insomuch that even Christian men might exercise the power of the sword, and come under obligation thereby to serve their neighbor and restrain the bad, so that the good might remain in peace among them. And still the command of Christ remains in force, that we are not to resist evil. So that a Christian, although he bears the sword, does not use it for himself nor to revenge himself, but only for others; moreover, this is the mark of Christian love, that with the sword we support and defend the whole Church. ...[14]

Practically, the doctrine of the two realms established an ethical dualism between public and private, between inner and social, morality. In the one sphere the perfectionism of the *agape* ethic of the Sermon on the Mount prevailed. In the other order, rather than justice, was the norm. Luther's policy in regard to the peasant

---

[14] Commentary on Peter and Jude in J. M. Lenker, ed. of *Works of Martin Luther*, Vol. XIV, pp. 127f., Minneapolis, The Luther Press, 1903–1910.

revolts, which he wanted to suppress with rigorous severity, was evidence that something of the spirit of discriminate justice, which was supplied in medieval Christianity by the Aristotelian-Thomistic concern for a rational examination of conflicting rights, had disappeared.

It is, in short, significant that post-medieval political realism, whether expressed in the cynical terms of Machiavelli or the materialistic terms of Thomas Hobbes or the pious terms of Martin Luther, was betrayed by the rigor of its anti-papalism and the virulence of its reaction to previous political sentimentality, into an irresponsible attitude toward problems of discriminate justice. The realists were all proponents of the parochial community; and the problem of the larger order between parochial communities disappears from the moral horizon. The realities of power and interest are recognized but only for the sake of justifying a coercive power which will bring order into the conflict of interests. Western society was to suffer for a long time by the fact that the spiritual descendants of Dante had an unrealistic approach both to the problems of the world community and toward justice in the local community. The realists, on the other hand, became the fountain source of an uncritical political absolutism and particularism. In a sense, the bridging of this chasm by putting political realism into the service of justice, however defined, remains one of the paramount problems of an adequate political ethic.

The devotees of the "medieval synthesis" may well regard this contradiction between idealistic and realistic approaches to the problem of community as an indictment against the modern approach and a vindication of the idea of a universal culture. If, however, our analysis be valid that the resentment caused by ecclesiastical universalism and expressed in varied forms was inevitable, then only nostalgia could prompt a return to this comparatively uncomplicated past. The historical evidence is that the day of the quasi-universal empire is over. The parochial and particular forces which must be managed are too vital and autonomous, and the overarching ideological framework is not sufficiently strong to furnish one of the forces of cohesion. This is particularly true in a day when the whole non-western world has been discovered as part of the community of mankind, which of course it has always been, and since a secularized western culture would not think of accepting ecclesiastical dominion. We live in the world of autonomous nations which must achieve such precarious order and peace as is possible for them in our kind of world. But before we dismiss empires altogether as an outmoded form of community, we must again be reminded that Russian Communism has challenged the West with a new, and yet old, form of quasi-universalism—in the form of a secularized and utopian version of the Christian culture. Its appeal is still very powerful. Some of that appeal is derived from contemporary conditions; but we will not understand the whole force of the appeal until we set it in comparison with the ideological systems of the empires of the past.

CHAPTER IX

The Historical Basis
for National Autonomy

A SURVEY of the history of the empires which partially integrated the communities of mankind suggests the inevitability of their decay—though in the strict sense nothing in history is inevitable and though the decay proceeded by various processes, which would make it inadvisable to discern any "logic" in this decay. Nevertheless, it is possible to hazard certain conclusions:

(1) The medieval empires ceased to be effective instruments of order, leaving only an ideological system which gave prestige to the wielder of power. Thus the western empire had only the political force of the very attenuated Hohenstaufen dynastic power; and suffered further disintegration when the Hapsburgs tried desperately to preserve their dominion by marital alliances which were insufficient in themselves to furnish a solid core of political authority. The decay of the empire and its increasing weakness under the challenge of the two first autonomous nations, England and France, began not in the modern period but at the height of the Middle Ages. Thus in the thirteenth century, according to Pirenne, the empire was:

> ... anarchy in monarchial form; that perhaps is the best description of an extraordinary political entity, which had neither common laws, common finances nor a common body of functionaries. ... Compared with France and England, it seemed amorphous, illogical, almost monstrous. ... The necessity of an Emperor, who no longer corresponded to any existing reality, was imposed by tradition. Since the King of Germany was Emperor-designate, to suppress him would have been to abolish the Empire. He therefore continued to exist, and by the most paradoxical of destinies,

he retained his illusory monarchial power only to secure an Imperial power which had become even more illusory.[1]

Pirenne's estimate of the impotence of the imperial power refers
to the period of the election of Rudolf of Hapsburg to the imperial
throne in 1273. Since the Hapsburg dynasty presided over some
kind of empire until the Austro-Hungarian empire disintegrated
in the First World War, we may draw the conclusion that its fate
is symbolic of the slowness of historical processes, however seemingly inevitable.

(2) In the case of Western Christendom, as we have noted, it
was not the core of political power but the religious authority
incarnated in the papacy which was the potent instrument of
order. The claim of incarnating an ultimate principle of order and
of representing a universal community was bound to be subject to
a law of diminishing returns. It was subject to such a law even
before the modern nations arose to challenge any form of imperial-
universal dominion. It may be observed that the conflict between
the three medieval empires was bound to reveal the implausibility
of the claim of universality, just as the comparative vitality of the
so-called "free world," in competition with Communism, is bound
to challenge the communist pretension of universality.

The other empires of the Middle Ages, the Byzantine and the
Islamic, had one similarity with the western empire despite the
differences we have analyzed. The religious authority which over-
arched the empire proved more lasting than the political power
held by the emperors, sultans, or dynasts. The Islamic empire was
under the political and military power of various dynasties, Arabian
and Persian, and finally was reconstituted by the Ottoman Turks.
In the case of the Byzantine empire, when Constantinople was
conquered by the forces of Islam, the Russian nation, having been
converted to Byzantine Christianity, took over the political power
in the remnant of empire and became the "third Rome." The important development in both of these imperial transfigurations is

---

[1] Henri Pirenne, *The History of Europe*, New York, University Books, 1955,
pp. 448–49.

that political force and religious prestige were intimately united in the political rule and made for a system of absolute power. This absolute power in each case became so vexatious that it was obvious that it is possible to pay too high a price for the boon of large-scale order. The order of both the Russian and Ottoman empire became increasingly uncreative. It was unable to give play to the ethnic and cultural vitalities in the realm of their dominion and imposed a more and more restrictive autocracy. Thus the Ottoman empire was in obvious decay before the First World War, and the Russian empire collapsed under the exertions of that war with the curious consequences, of course, of generating out of this decay the new and revolutionary version of despotism.

The conclusion is obvious that both the degree of political power and the height of the ideological pretension which is necessary to give unity to a larger community of mankind is incompatible with freedom and cannot do justice to all the cultural and ethnic vitalities of an imperial community.

The modern period, judged in terms of the internal organization of the community, begins in the seventeenth and eighteenth centuries. The modern age, measured in terms of the autonomy of the parochial and integral community, begins in the Renaissance and Reformation when the nations defied the universal authority of the church. Judged from the perspective of a faith which regards the medieval order as ideal, this is the beginning of the political anarchy whose final fruit is the contest of power in which we are now involved. Judged from another later perspective, the anarchy of modern autonomous nation-states was the inevitable consequence of a culture in which every technical advance, including the invention of printing and gunpowder and the development of modern industry, favored the smaller integral community in competition with both the still smaller feudal and the larger imperial community; in short, everything favored the emancipation and consolidation of the nation-state. But since the conditions for the emergence of the nation out of the old empires were so various, and sometimes contradictory, it is safe to draw the conclusion that the negative pre-conditions for nationalism were probably as important as the positive conditions which made for national autonomy.

If the negative condition of autonomous nationalism is the loss of power, that is, the loss of both prestige and force of the super-sovereignty, or its degeneration into oppressive forms of authority and coercion, the positive condition is the capacity of the integral community to establish a single organ of dominion, a governing state, over the sometimes heterogeneous and sometimes homogeneous political elements in the parochial community, and to triumph over the lower sovereignties—feudal, tribal, or sectional —which threaten the integrity of the community. A single organ of will and order is an absolute prerequisite of any community, as our founding fathers argued eloquently in the Federalist papers. If there is such a single government, source of a single system of law and of taxation, it may be possible to unify nations, even though some of the forces of cohesion and unity are absent. But pure dominion, or the authority of government, cannot create a community if there are not some horizontal forces of community at work.

The forces of cohesion for the integral community which are most potent are: common language and a sense of ethnic kinship, geographic unity and contiguity, a common historical experience, and frame of political thought, a common area of economic mutuality, and, sometimes, the fear of a common foe. Any of these forces may be defective, but they cannot all be defective if the unity of the nation is to be preserved. A common religion was usually regarded as an equally important prerequisite until modern religiously pluralistic nations, particularly our own, refuted the theory. It is worth noting, however, that only solid communities, bound by other ties of mutuality, can afford the luxury of religious pluralism.

A religiously divided India could not preserve unity after independence removed the imperial unifying force. It fell into division and two nations emerged, the one essentially informed by the

Hindu faith, though fortunately a secularized state rather than a sacerdotal one. The other nation, Pakistan, has nothing but a common Islamic faith to give it cohesion.

Pluralism of language, race, and religion represents a particular peril to the unity of the national community if the differences are localized and people of one language or religion live in the same region. Yet the unifying elements in the Canadian nation were strong enough to overcome the peril of separatism in the French-speaking and Catholic Quebec. It is worth noting, however, that this unity only grew slowly, so that in the two world wars of this century the Federal Dominion government found it necessary to be very circumspect in its conscription laws in order not to offend the sensibilities of Quebec. Significantly, the expansion of the nation into the virgin territories of the west had a unifying effect, much as the earlier occupation of the west and northwest had helped to unify the American nation.

The classical refutation of the necessity of a common linguistic or ethnic bond is the little nation of Switzerland, carved out of the Hapsburg empire in the late Middle Ages, and having as the only source of cohesion a common devotion to liberty, a common experience in resisting authority, upon the basis of which grew the unifying forces of common laws, common taxation, and the mutualities of trade. Switzerland still speaks three languages, and the language and ethnic areas are very localized. These facts must discourage any bold generalizations about the basis of unity of a national community.

Any survey of the many forms of integration which have taken place in the history of nationhood must include the emergence of the first two autonomous nations, England and France, as well as the new and small nations which have established their autonomy through the disintegration of the two residual empires of the Middle Ages, the Ottoman and the Hapsburg empires, or through the tutelage in independence given them by the British Empire and (in the case of the Philippines and Cuba) by the U.S. and the new nations, such as Indonesia and Vietnam, Laos and Cambodia, which have declared their independence from the

Dutch and the French empires in Southeast Asia. Such a survey must prove that generalizations about the forces of unity and integration in nationhood are very hazardous.

If we consider the rise of the first two western European nations to political unity and autonomy the significant similarities and differences in integral nationhood will be both disclosed. Their paths were very different, but the forces of integration were very similar, though not chronologically identical. In both cases, the royal power was the initial organ of unity and autonomy, and democratic forms were the subsequent organs of the national will. In the case of England and Great Britain, the dynastic institution was important not only in unifying England but in giving unity to the United Kingdom of England and Scotland. Dynastic marriages and legitimacy were very potent forces of unity. When James VI of Scotland succeeded Queen Elizabeth the first chapter in the unification of the ancient foes of Scotland and England was written, just as the marriage of Isabella and Ferdinand, in the sixteenth century, united Castile and Aragon and laid the foundation for Spanish unity. Dynastic prestige is thus certainly an instrument for the unity of two communities, otherwise separated, though other forces of cohesion must enter to strengthen the bond. Dynastic authority is also the first instrument of the integrity of the national community in its contest with the super-sovereignties of church and empire and the subordinate sovereignties of the feudal aristocracy. But it is not the sole or the final source of authority. This fact is vividly illustrated in the rise to autonomy of the first two independent western nations. In both cases the causes of their autonomy lie deeply imbedded in the medieval period, but bore fruit in the late Middle Ages and in the beginning of the modern period, that is, in the sixteenth to eighteenth centuries.

The first chapter in the integral unity of England may well have been written in the Norman conquest, which gave the conquering king superior authority over the feudal nobles. The next chapter may have been the granting of the Magna Carta by King John. This document not only was the foundation of British liberties, but it established in parliament another organ and symbol of unity for the nation. England, therefore, did not have to gain its unity by the absolute triumph of the king over the nobles; and both monarch and parliament became symbols of the national unity and organs of the national will. Thus dynastic and democratic institutions of national unity were intertwined in English history, while in France they followed each other chronologically. This partnership in England was, of course, subject to historic growth. The Tudor monarchy under Henry VIII was still the most effective instrument of English independence in the sixteenth century; and the causes of this quest for autonomy were deeper and more various than the king's desire to divorce his Spanish queen.

In France it was the king alone, and not king and parliament, who was the agent of the growing national autonomy. The earliest chapters of this story were written at the height of the Middle Ages, when at the end of the thirteenth century, Phillip the Fair challenged the authority of Pope Boniface VIII in temporal dominion over the nation. Thus the long history of Gallicanism began, in which a Catholic country with a Catholic monarch, using an increasingly autocratic royalism, asserted the autonomy of the nation against the Pope and bound the nobles to the throne by making them purely courtiers to the royal house, without the local quasi-sovereignty which the British nobility enjoyed. Thus there is a clear line of history from Phillip the Fair to Louis XIV, in which French nationalism comes into its own.

Their histories are so different, yet on close analysis some similar factors appear, though in different chronological order. These similar factors are the relation of the throne, the middle class, and democracy to nationalism. In the words of a well-known study of nationalism:

> A struggle for power was bound to ensue between the old order and the new, between the barons and the Church on the one side and the new merchant class on the other. But the king, who had his own reasons for fearing the turbulent feudal lord and the equally insubordinate abbot or bishop, had already taken up the struggle against him on his own account. It was natural that the

merchant class should give its support to the only power which
was likely to establish the settled conditions on which its liveli-
hood depended, and it was natural that the king should readily
accept an alliance which gave him the money and mercenaries
essential to the assertion of his authority. The king and the merchant had a common interest in the growth of a centralized State
and an organized bureaucracy subordinate to the royal authority.
Thus, in Western Europe that transformation of the economic and
social order which is marked by the emergence of a middle class
was first the result and then in part the cause of the establishment
in each State of a supreme and sovereign government. As Acton
observes, 'The development of absolute monarchy by the help
of democracy is the one constant characteristic of French history.'
In its origin the centralized State was in no sense the product of
national feeling. But once the process of consolidation had begun,
a group feeling began to be generated, and no doubt became before long a contributory factor to the continuation of the process.[2]

Perhaps this judgment, relevant to France, does not cover the
growth of national feeling in the whole of western history. Even
in the case of France it is necessary to add that the same middle
classes which supported royal power for economic motives became,
in the next centuries, the generators of democratic revolt against
the royal power; and that the democracy which they established
gave the national feeling a new impetus. Thus it was Rousseau
who was, in a sense, the father of French nationalism. His chapter
on "Civic Religion" insisted on the moral, as well as legal, autonomy of the national state or community. It is significant that
the sixteenth century protagonist of royal power, Jean Bodin, who
championed the king in the interest of order in an era of religiously
inspired civil wars, was also the first to make the protection of
property the criterion of the justice which would distinguish true
kingship from tyranny.

> A true king [declares Bodin] is one who observes the laws of
> nature as punctiliously as he wishes his subjects to obey his own
> laws, thereby securing to them their liberty and the enjoyment

[2] *Nationalism*, Royal Institute of International Affairs, New York, Oxford
University Press, 1939, pp. 13–14.

of their property. I have added these last qualifications in order
to distinguish kingship from despotism.[3]

The bourgeois bias in the emphasis on the rights of property is
as obvious as the same emphasis in the democratic theories of
John Locke, whom Bodin anticipated by more than a century.
Royalism, democracy, and the middle classes represent the same
triangle of forces in both England and France. But in England the
democratic revolt came a century earlier under Cromwell. Monarchy and parliament, in effect, developed together as the twin
organs of the nation made the break less violent and permitted a
restoration of a constitutional monarchy.

In both of these nations the democratic organs of community
were more potent in expressing the sentiment of national patriotism than monarchy, not only because they corresponded to the
interests of the middle class bearers of the national sentiment,
but also because they gave the national community a stronger
sense of cohesion than the monarchial dominion. Voltaire expressed the combination of patriotic sentiment with the passion
for liberty which characterized the democratic movement, in his
Dictionnaire Philosophique:

> When those who, like myself, possess fields and houses, gather
> for their common interests, then I have my voice in that gather-
> ing; I form a part of the whole, a part of the community, a part
> of the sovereignty; *voilà ma patrie.*[4]

If the sentiment of nationalism expressed itself in France in
terms of enthusiasm for the newly established democratic community, the democratic ferment in the Cromwellian revolution of
England, having a religious inspiration borne by the Puritan sects,
expressed itself in a religious sense of the peculiar destiny of England under divine providence. Thus John Milton exults in his
Areopagitica:

---

[3] Jean Bodin, "Concerning Royal Monarchy," *Six Books of the Commonwealth*, abridged and translated by M. J. Tooley, Oxford, Basil Blackwell,
Bk. 2, Ch. 3, p. 59.
[4] Quoted from Hans Kohn, *The Idea of Nationalism*, New York, Macmillan
Co., 1944, p. 219.

> God is decreeing to begin some new and great period in his church, even to the reforming of the reformation itself; what does he then but reveal himself to his servants, and as His manner is, first to his Englishmen; I say as His manner is, first to us, though we mark not the method of his counsels and are unworthy.[5]

The national spirit of the new American nation was fed by many sources: pride in the establishment of a free society was analogous to the French sentiment, and the idea of being the beneficiaries of a providential destiny drawn from the same Puritan sources from which Milton drew his idea. These two were usually mingled. Thus President Ezra Stiles of Yale, in a sermon on "The United States Elevated to Glory and Honor" (1783), spoke of the covenant of Israel with Moses "as introductory to a discourse on the political welfare of God's American Israel." [6] The idea of the nation as a "chosen people" in analogy to the covenant with Israel was a favorite Puritan nationalistic theme. The anology, incidentally, was not confined to America. Jefferson expressed the idea of a unique national destiny in more secular terms:

> We exist [he wrote in 1820] and are quoted as standing proofs, that a government so modelled as to rest continually on the will of the whole society, is a practical government. ... As members therefore of the universal society of mankind, and as standing in a high and responsible relation to them, it is our sacred duty ... not to blast the confidence we have inspired of proof that a government of reason is better than one of force.[7]

National sentiment and pride, nurtured by the thought that the nation is making an ultimate contribution to the welfare of mankind, is an unvarying characteristic of democratic nationalism. The three western democratic nations of the late eighteenth century— England, France, and America—were informed by a new sense of community, by pride in the novelty of a free community, and by

---

[5] *Works of John Milton*, New York, Columbia University Press, 1931–38, Vol. IV, p. 340.
[6] Kohn, *op. cit.*, p. 279.
[7] *The Writings of Thomas Jefferson*, edited by Andrew Lipscomb and Albert Ellery Bergh, Thomas Jefferson Memorial Assoc., Washington, D. C., 1903–04, Vol. XV, p. 284.

a sense of being providential instruments for the attainment of free governments throughout the world.

But it would be wrong to place too much emphasis upon the relation of democracy to the national spirit merely by singling out these three nations, two of which first used and discarded the monarchial instrument of national unity and identity, while the third founded the national life *de novo* on a virgin continent on democratic principles. For this approach obscures the fact that all these nations, including our own ethnically pluralistic nation, could take ethnic and linguistic homogeneity for granted. The nation is, in terms of communal factors, primarily a community of people who feel themselves unified by a common language and by ethnic kinship. Even in America the preponderantly Anglo-Saxon ethnic strain in the population of the colonies was an unconscious source of community, the importance of which can be measured if our community be compared to South Africa, for instance, where even the most generous settlement of the strife between English and Dutch settlers after the Boer War did not result in an integral national community. The tragic conflict with the African natives in the Union of South Africa is the more insoluble because of the subordinate ethnic tension between the English-speaking and Dutch-speaking citizens of the Union.

Properly to gauge the force of the language and ethnic factors in the rise of the nation one needs only to compare the frustrated cultural nationalism of the two European nations, Germany and Italy, who arrived belatedly in the nineteenth century at the goal of integral nationhood, despite the fact that they were conscious for centuries of their ethnic and linguistic sense of kind. A contributing factor to the growth of German nationalism was Luther's translation of the Bible into German which gave the Saxon dialect supremacy over all the other dialects.[8] Both nations were frustrated in achieving a state which could be the organ of the will and of the integrity of the national community. Both were the seats of

---

[8] In the same way, the translation of the Bible into a Low German dialect in the Netherlands established the Dutch language as an independent language and contributed to the national feeling of the Dutch people.

the two forms of medieval internationalism, the empire and the papacy. Both were riven by conflicts between sub-national sovereignties and by foreign usurpations over their national community. Both went through a tortuous history in achieving the goal of nationhood. In the case of Germany the liberal democratic nationalism having failed in the revolution of 1848, the nation had to wait for its unification until the Prussian monarchy, which achieved hegemony in the German nation through the military power founded by Frederick the Great, finally unified the nation after the war with France in 1871. In the case of Italy the liberal nationalism of Mazzini, the idealism of Garibaldi, and the statesmanship of Cavour, were all required to rescue the Roman capital from the papal state and to unify the nation under the dynasty of the Piedmont state. In each case a community lacked an organ of dominion to act as an instrument of its communal will until dynastic triumphs finally achieved this unification. In both cases the lack of a strong middle class, or at least of an independent middle class, retarded both democracy and the growth of nationality as a political force.

The flowering of cultural nationalism in Germany under the impact of the Napoleonic victories over Germany, the romantic glorying of national particularism in the thought of Herder, the patriotic appeals to the German nation by Fichte, and the metaphysical justification of the nation-state by Hegel were all of no avail in creating a German nation-state. The sense of community lacked an organ of integration in a state which would speak for the single national community. The flowering of German culture in a situation of political fragmentation, which was not healed until Bismarck healed it by blood and iron, is an instructive piece of evidence about the difficulties confronted by a national "soul" unable to be incarnated in a national body. It is evidence which might well warn the apostles of world government who think it easy to create both an international community and an international government by an act of will.

The experience of the frustrated nations, who had a sense of ethnic and linguistic community long before they could express that sense in political terms, is a reminder of the reciprocal relation between dominion and community. The sense of an international community is certainly less potent than the sense of a German community in the eighteenth century. Even if it were more potent, it could not furnish an organ of will and a center of authority by purely rational and volitional means, because the authority of government rests upon the twin pillars of prestige and force. The prestige, which induces habits of loyalty and implicit consent, grows by organic and historical process. The possession of force does not guarantee the right to use it. That right or authority is derived from a clear mandate to speak in behalf of the community. Force alone may initiate the authority, but it is subject to the law of diminishing returns if the community does not grant implicit consent to the authority which uses it. There is, thus, a reciprocal relation between the community and its organ of government, which explicit covenants may influence or change but which they cannot create out of whole cloth.

The American experience of having been created a nation by a constitution has prompted excessively voluntaristic estimates of the possibility of creating and enlarging both national communities and corresponding governments. But these forms of voluntarism obscure the fact that there was a community of common culture and language and the more potent sense of community, derived from common experience in the war of independence, before the constitution; that all these forces of community, supported by the fortunate common experience in occupying a virgin continent and by the equally fortunate means of communication which developed at the precise moment of our westward march, did not prevent some of the states from challenging the authority of the federal government, and could not persuade a high-minded Southerner, such as Robert E. Lee, though he disliked slavery, to give his loyalty to the government of the United States rather than to the state of Virginia.

The Latin American states, established in the nineteenth century by independence movements and rebellions against the Spanish and Portuguese Empires present us with another facet of the anatomy of the parochial community. Even if the political skill of the imperial nations had been more resourceful, the independence of these nations would have been a foregone conclusion because of geographic factors. These factors made life under a single sovereignty centered in Europe intolerable for parochial communities on another continent. Their desire for independence was prompted by some of the same factors as our desire for independence from the British crown, though they remained essentially feudal in social organization, and lacked the strong middle class which would make for the capacity of self-government as well as the technical means which would extend the national community over a continent. Geographic factors also contributed to this lack of unity among the Latin American states, for the Andes were forbidding barriers to continental communications. Yet the Latin American nations all spoke either Spanish or Portuguese, and they were all ethnically a mixture of Latin and Indian blood, with some slight admixture of Negro blood. This mixture, incidentally, contributed to the class structure, much in the same way that the caste system of India is partially determined by the mixture of blood of the Aryan conquerors of India and the indigenous population. The Latin American republics have, for the most part, not been able to establish a stable democratic authority, and are therefore subject to various forms of dictatorship, chiefly military; and they have not been able to achieve federation on any large scale. Their nationhood does not represent ethnic particularity, as in the case of the European nations. Ethnic and linguistic similarities transcend nationhood, as they do in the Arab states. Their life is therefore a reminder of the importance of the geographic factors in the life of the nations, and of the need of technical advances in education and communication in achieving integral community on the national level on a wider scale than the small parochial community. Their limited achievements also remind us that while democracy is the only source of stable community in a technical age, it is beyond the present capacity of many nations, not only the nations of Asia and Africa.

The establishment of the independence of two small nations,

Ireland and Israel, after the First World War and the Second World War, respectively, must serve to remind us of two facets of nationhood which add to the complicated picture of the nation. Ireland represents one of the failures of the otherwise successful achievement of Britain, both in establishing nationhood transcending the ethnic community and in establishing an empire in which subject peoples are nurtured in the arts of self-government and finally given their freedom. The "United Kingdom" originally embraced England, Scotland, Wales and Ireland. But Irish objection to the larger community was persistent and stubborn; and the same England which had made so many mistakes in regard to Ireland, finally after bloody struggles allowed the nation its freedom.

It would be pretentious to offer a brief explanation, exceeding the competence of any but the specialist in Irish affairs, of the failure of Britain in Ireland. Part of the cause for the failure was geographic, the island separation from the larger island; but that certainly was not the chief cause. Part of the failure to cohere was due to the religious differences, Ireland remaining Catholic when Britain made the quasi-Catholicism of the Anglican establishment the fixed instrument and concomitant of its nationhood. But the difference between Presbyterian Scotland and Anglican England did not prevent the union between the two nations; there is always the possibility that the stubborn Catholicism of Ireland was partly the consequence and the instrument of its purpose to maintain its own identity. Certainly the economic policy of the Anglo-Irish landowners in their Irish estates and the exploitation of Ireland may have been more productive of Irish recalcitrance than any of the factors previously mentioned. The recalcitrance proved resistant to every kind of blandishment and concession, including the granting of representation in Parliament and the establishment of Home Rule. An additional word must be said about the ethnic factor. It is significant that northern Ireland, composed of Protestant Irish of Scottish ancestry, has proved as stubborn in resisting inclusion into the Irish nation as the Irish nation has been in resisting inclusion in the British nation.

The case of Israel is so unique that it warns us against almost every type of generalization about nations. In a sense, Israel is the oldest of all the nations. The Greek culture flourished in the Hellenic city-states and the culture of the Middle East grew in the great empires of the ancient world; but Israel was a nation. Its nationhood was grounded in a religious covenant experience. It had been "called out" by God, through Abraham and through Moses, to be a separated nation, seeking not its own survival but the realization of the will of the transcendent creator God. Yaweh was not the exclusive possession of Israel, according to the prophets, who interpreted and enlarged the conception of the covenant even while they thought only on the basis of the covenant presupposition. Yaweh was a God of all the nations who had brought "the Philistines from Caphtor, and the Syrians from Kir." [9] This was not the "great God" of Cyrus, who was an instrument of the national will. This God represented the mysterious source of creation and of historical destiny, transcending the vicissitudes of any particular nation. The history of the nation was a tortuous and tragic one, as it lived its precarious life at the crossroads of the great empires, was destroyed and restored by them, and finally lost its homeland and maintained its identity in the Diaspora in Islamic and European nations. Its will to survive was stubborn and it used some of the same religious instruments for its survival which it may have been too rigorous to use in establishing its security in history.

It is certainly a question whether the Jews lost their homeland merely because they were small, or because their monotheism was too rigorous to permit them to identify their own destiny with the ultimate mystery and meaning of the cosmic order.

This precarious life of a people without a homeland lasted throughout the Middle Ages and well into the modern period, in which the Jews—debarred from the land and from the professions till recent liberal emancipation—conducted the trade and banking of the Middle Ages and earned the resentments of both the

[9] Amos 9:7.

nobility and the peasants and exposed the Jewish minority to economically inspired prejudices, as well as the prejudices arising from its non-conformity in the ethnic and in the religious spheres. Both the Crusades and the Spanish inquisition heightened these prejudices.

But these prejudices did not threaten the Jews with extinction. It required the religio-political fury of Nazism and the gas chambers of the Nazi tyranny to awaken the sense of racial and religious cohesion, which an age of liberalism and assimilation had partly dampened, and to give added political impetus to the age-old desire of the Jews for a homeland. The first step towards this came through the partial concession of the Balfour Declaration in the First World War, which gave returning Jews a foothold in their ancient territory, long since occupied by the Islamic conquerors of the Middle East. The next step came with the Second World War, with the pressure of immigrants from every continent fleeing the new insecurity of what was once a "liberal" world. The uneasy conscience of the Christian world about the Nazi atrocities provided the climate of opinion for the granting of independent nationhood by the United Nations; and the generosity of the Jews of the Diaspora furnished the new state with the economic resources to organize a productive agricultural and industrial economy, partly capable of supporting the phenomenally increased population. No nation has ever been "so conceived and so dedicated" by such a variety of social, moral and religious forces and factors, some in the Jewish and others in the non-Jewish world. This new Jewish state maintains a precarious existence in a hostile Islamic world, and preserves its unity despite the sharp rift between the secular Jews, intent upon founding a secular state, and the religious parties, who represent an archaic orthodoxy.

Despite its basic ethnic homogeneity the new nation is not altogether secure in its internal unity, since a very generous immigration policy has inundated it with a population of diverse cultural and economic backgrounds, as varied as those of the European nations on the one hand and of Yemen on the other. But the unifying factors, in addition to the Jewish patriotism, are also very strong. Among these are the highly competent army—recruited by a policy of universal military service, and ever alert—a high standard of technical competence in both agriculture and industry, and a rigorous and comprehensive educational program. All of these factors give promise of unifying the nation and of mitigating the cultural differences.

Thus far we have considered only three types of nation-states, the first consisting of the British, French, and American democratic states, of which two came into existence or achieved their autonomy by the use of both royal and democratic instruments of dominion, while America established its independence and its democratic forms in the same historical act. The second type may be defined as the frustrated nations, Italy and Germany, which waited long before the organ of dominion became a tolerable instrument for the expression of nationality. The third category consists of two unique nations, Ireland and Israel. The first achieved independence by a stubborn resistance to the unity of the British nation. The second became a nation only after a homeland was supplied for a people who once were a nation, but who had lived long ages without a homeland. The diversity of causes entering into the formation of these nations would discourage any hasty generalization; but before we come to any generalizations at all it will be necessary to consider other very radically different types of nations.

CHAPTER X

The World
of Autonomous Nations

Our cursory study of the various types of autonomous nations and of the varied paths by which they achieved independence has not yet dealt with three categories which we must now proceed to analyze. They are: (a) those independent nations which were not under imperial domination; (b) the nations of imperial dimensions, particularly China and Russia, who unified great territories in imperial terms but whose populations were relatively homogeneous; and (c) the great number of ex-colonial nations who extricated themselves or were graduated from some imperial system, either from one of the empires of the Middle Ages or from modern national empires such as those of Britain, France, Holland, America, and Japan. The emancipation of some of these nations, as, for instance, the Netherlands and Belgium, took place in the early modern period. But most of the emancipated nations achieved their independence after the first or the second world wars. These nations represent a tremendous disparity in size, strength, cultural achievement, and integral unity of their community.

The Scandinavian nations clearly belong in our first category. They were always independent of the western empire because they were geographically remote. The Scandinavian region was under the independent rule of the Danish kings since the late Middle Ages. Norway's and Sweden's independence was not established for centuries, though there was a sense of separate nationality which could not be implemented because the northern region was not strong enough. The Protestant Reformation and the establishment of three national churches contributed greatly to the heightened sense of nationality. The religious wars after the Reformation gave Sweden, under Gustaphus Adolphus, the opportunity both of independence and of imperial expansion. His empire around the Baltic was short-lived, however, not outlasting its founder by many decades. Sweden and Norway were regarded as separate nations under a single crown. They did not achieve separate governments or dynasties until 1905. The history of the Scandinavian nations reveals the importance of geographic and linguistic factors in their affinities and their differences. Their languages, being dialects of the same tongue, prove both the force of affinity and of separateness in the building of nations. Geographic factors have also contributed to their collective, as well as separate independence. Their collective independence was due to their remoteness from the main currents of imperial politics, and their separate independence was due to the water barrier between Denmark and the two northern countries and to the mountain barrier between Sweden and Norway and, of course, also the increasing economic strength of Sweden in the nineteenth century.

Among the nations which were never under the necessity of establishing their independence, we must count Japan and Thailand. The one is an island kingdom, boasting a single dynasty of god-kings from the dawn of its history to the Second World War when Japan's defeat prompted the transmutation of an absolute monarchy into a constitutional one. Japan, as the first industrialized oriental nation, used its power conventionally for building an empire at the expense of less powerful neighbors. It dominated Korea and Formosa, and would have established the more inclusive "co-prosperity sphere" if it had not suffered defeat with Germany in the Second World War. Thailand, much weaker than Japan, was geographically too isolated and remote to come within the grasp of the European imperial powers and has a long history of independence and of a fairly cohesive national life under a traditional monarchy.

In terms of traditional history the Korean Nation would also belong to the category of nations which did not have to win their independence. In terms of modern history, Korea fell under the dominion of Japan in the nineteenth century, and northern Korea is now unfortunately under Russian dominion.

The beginnings of the Korean nation, situated on a peninsula adjacent to the Chinese mainland, lie in the legendary past. The population represents both Chinese and Japanese migrations. The unity of the nation was achieved in the ancient past; and the fact that it did not fall under the dominion of stronger nations until the nineteenth century is a curious exception to the general destiny of small nations.

Both China and Russia are nations of imperial dimensions in the sense that the integral territory under a single sovereignty is vast but they are nations rather than empires because a degree of ethnic and linguistic homogeneity is part of their cohesive force.

We have previously considered China under the category of "empires," and have observed that the religious claims of the emperor as "son of heaven" was the source of the prestige of the sovereignty, which controlled a large bureaucracy, through which the great nation was held in a kind of order subject to periodic decay and feudal disintegration. For our present purposes, however, it is important to consider the other imperial nation, Russia, which integrated a partially homogeneous community in the sense that the Russian people were mostly Slavic. But the Russian domain was vast and all the imperial sources of prestige were required to give cohesion to a multinational nation.

The first center of unity and dominion in Russia was the Kievan state. The Tartar invasion subjected this unity to external domination. The Princes of Muscovy finally defeated the Tartars. To this military basis of dominion the ideological prestige was added that Muscovy claimed to be and was acknowledged as the "Third Rome," the bearer of Orthodox Christianity. This made Russia the legatee of the Byzantine Empire. This ideological claim was succinctly stated by Philotheous, a monk in the monastery of Pskov, who, writing to the Grand Prince Basil III in the sixteenth century, declared:

> The first Rome collapsed owing to its heresies, the second Rome fell a victim to the Turks, but a new and third Rome has sprung up in the North, illuminating the whole universe like a sun. The first and second Rome have fallen, but the third Rome will stand till the end of history, for it is the last Rome...; a fourth Rome is inconceivable.[1]

The good monk could hardly have anticipated that the fourth Rome would rise on the site of the third Rome in Moscow; for Russia has the unique distinction of being twice the beneficiary of the integrating effect of a trans-national creed. The Russian nation was and is, under either dispensation, a league of Slavic nationalities, in which a common ethnic core and a religious impetus furnish the two sources of national cohesion. The idea of "Holy Russia" has been potent both in the integration and in the ossification of the Russian monarchy; and nationalistic messianism has been so powerful that a Russian theologian, who had suffered at the hands of both tsar and communist, could seriously speculate on the plausibility of the communist realization of the Russian dream of world salvation.[2]

The communist unification of Russia through a non-national idea has been even more successful than the orthodox idea. Lenin conceived the state as a loose federation of nationalities in which each nationality had the right of self-determination, including the right of secession. That this idea was compounded of both Marxist internationalism and a more traditional idea of ethnic homogeneity can be seen from the fact that Lenin did not expect either Poland or Finland to secede, and assumed that the other nationalities would adhere though given freedom to depart. Fin-

[1] Quoted from Chapter V, "The Rise of Russian Nationalism" in *Nationalism, op. cit.*, p. 62.
[2] Cf. Nikolai Berdyaev, *The Russian Idea*, New York: The Macmillan Co., 1948.

land and Poland indeed did establish their own national life, partly because they had a strong sense of national identity, partly because they had the force of arms to resist the Red Army, and partly because the economic and social factors were not propitious for the spread of the communist creed. Finland, as we know, has kept its independence until the present day, while Poland, after a brief hour of independence between the two wars, now enjoys a precarious semi-autonomy within the Russian satellite system. But this brings us to the dimension of communist imperialism rather than the imperial dimension of the Russian state. Only the states within the Russian Soviet orbit which could muster the force to preserve their independence exercised the "right of self-determination." The Baltic states maintained themselves between the two World Wars, but were reabsorbed after the Second World War, military power and communist infiltration being the forces of unification.

The international principle of Communism removed some of the resentment of subject peoples against Russification of subject peoples. At the same time, the class creed and the political organs based upon this creed served as forces of unification. Stalin, speaking at the Twelfth Party Congress in 1923 revealed the limits of the idea of self-determination in the communist creed: "There are instances," he said,

> when the nations' right of self-determination conflicts with another, higher principle, namely the right of the working class to consolidate its rule once it has seized power.[3]

Stalin was prompted to this reservation by the situation in Poland and Finland, but the principle proved ultimately effective in the Ukraine, where, despite separatist tendencies, the communist forces ultimately prevailed; and the Ukraine is now a part of the Soviet Union. One might speculate whether only strategic considerations in the civil war determined the result or whether the ethnic kinship, the common language, and the traditions of

---

[3] Quoted from Georg von Rauch, A *History of Soviet Russia* (tr. by Peter and Annette Jacobsohn), New York: Frederick A. Praeger, 1957, p. 84.

eastern Orthodoxy may not have contributed to the Ukrainian absorption into Russia, when even the small Baltic nations, Poland and Finland, maintained, for a while, their independence.

The communist universalist creed thus unified Russia more effectively than had the creed of eastern Orthodoxy. Nevertheless, it required a defensive war to complete the unification of the nation. The communist government subordinated its revolutionary dogma to national patriotism in the war to which the communist oligarchy consistently refers as "the Great Patriotic War." It was only after, and not before, that war that Stalin could finally overcome Marxist internationalism in the field of linguistics. Refuting the Russian specialist in linguistics, Professor N. Y. Marr, who died in 1934, and who had taught that the victory of Communism would make a new "supra-national" language, the language of socialism, necessary, Stalin participated in the debate on language in 1950 and in his "Letters on Linguistics" ordained the following principles:

1) language belongs neither to the super-structure of society nor to the basis; it is independent; 2) language is not the concern of individual classes but of the people as a whole; 3) language is not limited in time but eternal and lives through many historical periods; 4) when several languages clash they do not merge to form a new language but one of them prevails over the rest. The Russian language has always been victorious.[4]

One may question Stalin's expertness in linguistics but one can hardly deny his touch with the historical realities, because the Russian language actually became victorious in the monolithic state created by the communist creed; and a multilingual nation became practically monolingual. Many of the resentments against Russification in traditional tsarist Russia were removed by the principle of self-determination, which had the effect of presenting Russia as a federation of many nations. The Second World War both solidified the nation and gave the Russian component in the multi-national state complete dominance. The communist oli-

[4] *Ibid.*, p. 405.

garchs subordinated the revolutionary creed to the pride of nation and its history.

Thus Zhdanov, speaking in 1946 to the Russian writers, declared

> Where will you find such a people and such a country as ours? Where will you find the magnificent qualities which our people displayed in the Great Patriotic War...? ...we are not the same Russians we were before 1917, our Russia is different, our character is not the same. We have changed and grown along with the great reforms which have profoundly changed the face of our country.[5]

The rewriting of history in favor of the patriotic—rather than the revolutionary—theme included the rehabilitation of Tsar Ivan the Terrible as one of the creative forces of Russian history. But the revolutionary creed is also artfully interwoven with the patriotic one. Thus the official organ of the teaching profession made a statement in which the patriotic and the revolutionary creed are clearly combined:

> Love of one's socialist motherland is linked inseparably with hatred of her enemies. It breeds in the hearts of Soviet youth apphorrence and contempt for slavery and oppression, for the dark forces of reaction, for all enemies of progress, civilization, and democracy...[6]

But the amalgam of revolutionary ardor and patriotism after the war never subordinated the patriotic theme. Thus *Pravda* repeated a toast of Stalin in 1950:

> Sublime is the history of Russia. From time immemorial the Russian plains were inhabited by our ancestors, of remarkable endurance, of great vitality, of inquiring mind, of active disposition, of rare tenacity. During the entire course of their history the Russians never submitted to foreign usurpers. They never bowed their head before the enemy.

---

[5] Quoted in George S. Counts, *The Challenge of Soviet Education*, New York: McGraw-Hill Book Co., 1957, p. 115.
[6] *Ibid.*, p. 123.

> Sublime is the history of the Russian people. They have enriched mankind with immortal creations of mind and talent.

The revolutionary creed was naturally added, though in a subordinate form:

> The Russian proletariat, the most revolutionary in the world and led by the great Party of Bolsheviks, by the Party of Lenin and Stalin, brought the peoples of our country to the victorious socialist revolution and opened a new era in the history of all mankind.[7]

The communist supernational creed was more inclusive than the Orthodox Christian one. It was able to win many of the Asian Moslem peoples into the Soviet Union. The Soviet success with Islam has been so great that an Islamic institute under communist auspices could actually be organized in Tashkent.[8]

This hasty survey of Russia as an imperial nation under two dispensations is not meant to include the imperial dimensions of the communist creed in extending Russian dominion over other nations. Russian and communist imperialism must be analyzed subsequently. Now we are concerned only with the unity of a great nation, partly homogeneous ethnically and partly heterogeneous and finding non-national ideological systems to be potent instruments of its national unity.

We must consider first two ex-colonial nations, which have had such a long history of independence that they are usually not counted among the ex-colonial nations: Holland and Belgium. Both of them subsequently achieved empires of their own. The "low countries" gained their independence at the beginning of the modern period in the sixteenth century. They were culturally and economically among the most advanced peoples of the continent, but were under the sovereignty of the Hapsburg dynasty because a dynastic marriage had given the Hapsburgs dominion

[7] *Ibid.*, p. 125.   [8] Rauch, *op. cit.*, p. 413.

over the Burgundian dukedom. The architect of the independence of the Netherlands was William the Silent, of the House of Orange. Religious and socio-economic factors similar to those which expressed themselves in England a century later, operated to make subjection to a feudal empire intolerable.

Belgium, the "Austrian Netherlands," was not liberated until the Napoleonic period and was forced into a union with the Netherlands by the treaty of Vienna. It was separated from the Netherlands in the nineteenth century. Catholic Belgium, partly French (Walloon) and partly Flemish, declared its independence from the predominantly Protestant Netherlands. The two nations possess a high degree of integral unity and economic health.

We have already considered in another context the Latin-American nations who established their independence from Spain and Portugal in the nineteenth century. We can, therefore, proceed to a survey of the colonial nations whose independence is recent. Such a survey of the many small and large nations who became autonomous, particularly in the period of the two world wars, naturally includes nations of every type of unity, stability and power. It includes the predominantly Anglo-Saxon dominions of Great Britain who have gradually achieved their essential autonomy as members of the British Commonwealth of Nations. Their progress in this respect corresponds to the gradual evolution of the empire into a commonwealth. Of these commonwealths, Australia and New Zealand offer no particular variant to the pattern of community and dominion among the nations. Both of them are ethnically homogeneous, though New Zealand has performed the remarkable feat of gradually drawing the indigenous Maori people into the national community. The solidity of both communities is furthered by geographic factors of island isolation. Canada is a more complex example of integral nationhood. It has a strongly localized French minority in the Province of Quebec, which had preserved a strong local patriotism and was dangerous to the unity of the nation throughout the nineteenth century. But the unity of the nation has become very solid in this century. The gradual exploitation of western lands and the mineral resources of the north have been among the unifying factors, as a century earlier the western expansion helped to unify the thirteen original states of the United States.

The state of South Africa is radically different, for there the original ethnic and cultural struggle between the English and the Dutch settlers has never been resolved; and the generous peace offered the Boers after the war between the two groups has not mitigated the tension nor prevented the Dutch farmers from gaining political control of a nation in which English and cosmopolitan interests dominate the industrial life, particularly diamond, gold, and uranium mining. The tension between the groups aggravates the problem of giving justice to the native Negroes, so necessary for the industrial life of the nation and seemingly so threatening to what the Dutch feel rather passionately to be the racial integrity of the "white" nation. The future of South Africa both as a nation and as a member of the British Commonwealth of Nations is therefore insecure. The resources for a tolerable justice between the white minority and the native majority are lacking. And flagrant injustice will destroy any parochial community even though it may be impossible to define the standards of a tolerable justice.

It may be significant that the non-white nations in the British Commonwealth waited until the close of the Second World War for their independence. They had to fight for their autonomy, and only a weakened Britain yielded it to them. The ambiguity of imperialistic ventures, to be examined presently, is such that it is impossible to reach an "objective" conclusion on the question whether the grant was delayed because of incapacity of the Asian dominions for self-government or because the sense of ethnic kinship was lacking. The subsequent history of the newly freed nations, exhibiting the precarious stability of many of them, would seem to favor the first alternative. It is significant, however, that the missionary passion of Great Britain for founding democratic communities did not obviate the necessity of bringing pressure upon the imperial nation to grant the subject nations freedom. The reluctance may well have been compounded of honest apprehensions about the capacities for self-government of the former dominions and the love of dominance in the rulers. The motive of economic exploitation, so emphasized by the Marxists, was certainly not a dominant motive in the twentieth century; for the British rule of subject nations created financial burdens equal to, or exceeding, the profits of imperialism.

The unifying results of imperial dominion is proved in the case of the inability of the two communities of India, Hindu and Moslem, to preserve their unity in one nation, the Moslems separating themselves from India and founding the state of Pakistan.

India is undoubtedly the most promising large democracy among the new nations, though the democratic institutions can make their way but slowly against the feudal-agrarian background and the small percentage of literacy in the population. Significantly its only common language is one borrowed from the former masters. It is also indebted to the former imperial connections for its common laws and its system of communications. Pakistan, separated in two halves by a thousand miles, has a more precarious existence.

Two small nations of the Orient, Ceylon and Burma, previously connected with India, have also achieved autonomy and a fairly stable nationhood. In both an interesting combination of traditional Buddhism and modern socialism informs the cultural life of the nation. Even more recently the Federated Malay States —after conquering, with the help of their imperial tutors and masters, the communist guerrillas who sought to destroy the rubber forests of the new nation—have achieved unity and independence. But forces of national integration are not as powerful as in Burma and Ceylon. Geographic and historic factors are hazards to the unity of the new state.

The British concern for tutelage in democracy has been more vividly displayed than in any other instance in the grant of independence to Ghana, the former Gold Coast colony. The prospects are hopeful even though the national sentiment, based in the commercial life of the coast, must contend with the powerful residual tribal loyalties, particularly of the strong Ashanti tribe.

The contrast between the new nationalism and the old tribalism is characteristic of many of the budding nations and may be regarded as the consequence of the impingement of a pattern drawn from a more advanced culture upon a more primitive one. Both nationhood and democracy can be exported from advanced cultures to those which would have been unable to develop political plants, which may or may not be transplanted to this alien soil. In Africa Britain has promised national independence in the proximate future both to Nigeria and the central African federation; and in each case the question is whether there are sufficient forces of integral community to support the independence. Obviously there are limits to the success of transplanting the political fruits of one culture to gardens of a more primitive culture. But the impingement of techniques upon the primitive culture is changing the economic basis of politics so rapidly that the hazards of political change seem justified.

The most recent venture by Great Britain in launching a new nation has been undertaken in the West Indies where the Federation of the West Indies has been formed under British tutelage. The geographic and other factors are not too propitious for this new nation's success. The venture has certainly revealed the consistency of the British "missionary" motive in empire-building and the comparative success in transplanting a western pattern of integral community upon cultures which could not have developed the pattern out of their own resources.

Not only the British but the Dutch empire suffered a loss of strength. Among the new nations achieving independence is the former Dutch colony—now the nation—of Indonesia. This nation, too, uses forms of cohesion and communication which would not have been possible without the help of a technically competent imperial power. The Dutch had made their first contact with the Indonesian people through trade interests, as did the British in India, and gradually had consolidated their political dominion to insure their commercial interests. The unity and, therefore, the future of the new nation is beset by many hazards. The scattered islands of the archipelago represent a geographic danger.

The island, which is the seat of the Indonesian government, Java, is poor but populous, while Sumatra, politically less powerful, is rich in many resources, more particularly oil deposits. This disparity between the two large islands makes for political tension. Ethnically the islands are heterogeneous and culturally the people are divided between the dominant Islamic faith and the Christian minority, composed of both Protestants and Catholics. Indonesia gained its independence partly because the Dutch could not reoccupy the islands after the Japanese conquerors were dislodged. According to some Dutch opinion, America's rather dogmatic anti-imperialism may have unduly hastened them in the grant of independence. But this raises the question whether the desire for independence and the idea of national self-determination has not become such a universal impulse and pattern that political policy must reckon with it even if the factors for integral nationhood are not too propitious. This is the more true since the desire for independence is constantly fanned by communist "anti-imperialism" to which the West must respond for political reasons, even if it has lingering, and not dishonest, apprehensions about the capacity of the new nation to achieve stability and unity.[9]

Three nations, or more correctly four, emerged as the result of the sanguinary struggle between Indochina and the French imperial power: Laos, Cambodia, and North and South Vietnam. Their culture, their lack of preparation for self-government, and their geographic circumstances make their freedom precarious. They are certainly endangered by the Chinese Communist power. Only South Vietnam reveals some of the resources of integral and independent nationhood. Some of the resources were acquired with the help of western nations, anxious to prevent the absorption of the new nation in the communist bloc.

Two more categories of the newer nations which achieved autonomy through the disintegration of either ancient or modern empires in the two World Wars must be briefly described to complete the picture of diversity lurking under universality of

[9] For a brief survey of the Indonesian situation, see *South-East Asia* by Brian Harrison, New York: St. Martin's Press, 1954.

the general pattern of nationhood—the nations which achieved their independence through the decay of the Turkish empire and those who became independent through the decay of the Hapsburg empire after the World Wars. Most of the nations in both categories represented very old political entities, with ethnic and political roots in the ancient or the medieval world and possessed integral nationhood in varying degrees before becoming incorporated into the empires.

The nations of the Islamic Empire must be divided between the European nations, who extricated themselves from the Islamic yoke before the First World War, and the Middle Eastern nations, who became independent before, during, and after the first and second world wars, some of them falling briefly under British or French dominion in the period between the two wars. Among the Islamic nations a distinction must be made between the Turks, former bearers of the imperial power, who established an integral, ethnically homogeneous nation under Kemal Attaturk in the period after the First World War and now have achieved the most stable condition of national independence, and the Arab nations. Some of the latter live on the ground of ancient civilizations, Iran on the ground of the old Persian empire, Iraq on the ground of the Mesopotamian civilization, and of course, Egypt, the most ancient of all but subject to various imperial conquerors throughout the millennia of human history. It now conceives the ambition to revive the glories of the Islamic empire with the dictator Nasser imagining himself as a second Saladin. But included among the Arab nations there is another category of desert kingdom created by British policy after the First World War. It comprises the three kingdoms of Syria, Jordan, and Saudi Arabia. The absorption of Syria into the United Arab Republic, under Egypt's Nasser, is one of many indications of the lack of force in Arabic integral nationalism in tension with Islamic supra-nationalism.

The desert kingdom, Saudi Arabia, is a most curious national configuration. Its unity was achieved by absolute monarchy, but the absolute monarch maintains his authority partly by appeasing the desert tribal chiefs and partly by being the recipient of fabulous oil riches, poured into his coffers by the petroleum interests of the West. No one can prophesy how the growth of a class of technicians and middlemen, by-products of the oil interest, will affect the social and political structure of this autocracy, qualified by tribal anarchy. The wealth of Saudi Arabia is certainly no guarantee of its stability.

Arab nationalism or nationality is embarrassed not only by the social and economic facts arising from the impingement of technical civilization and oil wealth upon Bedouin-tribal political forms qualified by an artificially induced autocracy, but by the fact that ethnic and linguistic factors, which are marks of distinguishing identity in other nations, are too universal to be the basis of national integrity. Nuseibeh writes about the problem of language and nationality as follows:

> In the literature on Arab nationalism considerable space is devoted to a definition of an Arab nation and analysis of the components of such a nation. This is essential because of the multifarious connotations which the term Arab has acquired over many generations. In modern use, the term Arab stands for a political concept and has no ethnic or social significance;* its definition follows closely the Western concepts of nationhood. ...
>
> In formulating the postulates of Arab nationalism, Arab writers have drawn upon two principal sources. The first one is the legacy of the past. The community of language, of tradition, and of historical experiences have all been stressed as common denominators of an Arab nation. ... Nearly every theorist of Arab nationalism in the past two decades has been at pains to stress that the term Arab does not possess ethnic signification and they have done so with an eye principally on Egypt, which, though the most important Arab country, would not be happy if exclusive racial prerequisites were established.

---

* After the late Abbassid period, when the Arab kingdom had been transformed into a cosmopolitan Islamic empire, the term Arab reverted to its earlier meaning of bedouin or nomad, becoming in effect a social rather than an ethnic or political term. ... It is only since the beginning of this century, when the European idea of a nation began to make headway, that the term Arab has again acquired political connotations. ...[10]

[10] Hazem Zaki Nuseibeh, *The Ideas of Arab Nationalism*, Ithaca: Cornell University Press, 1956, pp. 65–66.

The fact that a common language but not a common race is stressed with an eye to Egypt does not obscure that in Arab nationalism neither language nor race are distinguishing marks of an integral national community. It also explains why federations of Arab states are comparatively easy. Arab nationalism may be so frantic because it represents the adaptation of western patterns for social reality which do not quite conform to the requirements of integral community. By contrast the stability of the ethnically-based Turkish state points to the defect in Arab nationalism.

The two North African nations, Morocco and Tunisia, which had come under a French protectorate after the disintegration of the Islamic empire, have recently achieved their qualified independence and possess geographic and economic forces of cohesion superior to the Middle Eastern Arab states. Tunisia aspires to become a secular state, eliminating the sacerdotal character of an orthodox Islamic state. The case of Algeria is very different and very tragic. Its incorporation into Metropolitan France represents a curious compound of the old imperialism and the new liberalism. The liberal concepts of the "rights of man" were expected to eliminate national and ethnic distinctions; and in justice to the French it must be noted that they are more free of ethnic prejudices than any other European peoples. Nevertheless the liberal concepts obscured, but did not efface, the fact that Algeria was a budding nation, ethnically and religiously distinct and culturally on a different level. The consequent single community of France and Algeria does not correspond to the cultural and ethnic facts; but meanwhile a single economic unity has been created which, if severed, will create serious economic problems for both France and Algeria. This tragic conflict between the two nations might well be a reminder of the limits of constitutional forms and structures in overcoming basic ideological ethnic and cultural disparities.

If the new nations formed out of the Islamic empire, particularly the Arab nations, are usually wanting in marks of ethnic identity, the nations which have declared their independence from the Hapsburg empire, or were released from it by its disintegration in the First World War, have been troubled by the ethnic confusion. The empire had held German, Slav, and Magyar nations in one political unity, but not without scattering the nationalities so much that only a few nations could emerge with a clear ethnic distinction.

The nations which have become independent after the First World War all have an ethnic core and a political history reaching into the early Middle Ages; but most of them have no clear ethnic integrity. Czechoslovakia represents the ancient kingdom of Bohemia and another tribe of Slavs in Slovakia. A German minority long resident in Bohemia and included in the new nation by the peace-makers, partly for strategic reasons, proved the undoing of the nation when Hitler's fierce German nationalism prompted the German minority in the Sudetenland to espouse the cause of Pan-Germanism and provided Hitler with a force of disruption. Serbia and Croatia, united in the new state of Yugoslavia, have a common Slav kinship, but are culturally at variance since the nation was divided between the Eastern and Western empires in the Middle Ages and consequently became informed by two different versions of Catholicism, Orthodox and Roman. The religious factor sometimes operates divisively in ethnically homogeneous nations. Sometimes, as in the case of Roman Catholicism in Poland, it becomes the servant of the national community when the imperial community (Russia) professes a different faith. The relation of Roman Catholicism to Polish nationalism under the pressure of communist imperialism is an interesting bit of evidence on the continued potency of the religious factor in even a secularized communist state.

Hungary, which fled to the Hapsburgs to be saved from the Moslems and became one of the two sovereign powers in the "dual monarchy," became independent only on the disintegration of this anachronistic dynastic construction. It has since lost its independence under the communist imperialism, to which so many eastern European nations have become subject. Its abortive and heroic struggle for freedom belongs to modern history, and its failure is one index of the importance of strategic and power factors in the life of nations. Russia evidently could not afford the independence of Hungary ideologically or strategically and was willing to taint the communist legend of anti-imperialism to hold Hungary in subjection.

Two small nations, Rumania and Bulgaria, having become free with the disintegration of the Islamic empire at the end of the nineteenth century, are now incorporated into the communist empire, together with Czechoslovakia.

This rapid survey of the life of great and small nations in a world of autonomous nations (except as they have fallen victims to the communist empire) leads to these conclusions: The conditions and prerequisites of integral nationhood obviously vary very greatly. Ethnic, linguistic, geographic, and historical factors are all present in the formation of the integral nation; but it would be hazardous to draw conclusions about the relative importance of each of these factors. The necessity of a single organ of political authority and power is the most obvious fact. It is also apparent that the state alone cannot guarantee the unity of the nation if the factors of integral community are too deficient. One or another of the linguistic, ethnic, and geographic factors may be deficient but they cannot all be deficient. In an industrial age the factor of economic mutuality as a basis of integral national community has become particularly important. Modern means of communication have also achieved increasing importance in achieving a solid integral community. This is one reason why some of the new nations, with low literacy standards and with few journals, cannot possibly meet the requirements of healthy nationhood as quickly as is expected of them by those who have made the autonomous nation into the final form of community.

The disparity in the power of the nations, from the two great "super-nations" to the smallest of the new nations, presents a problem, not of nationhood but of the organization of the community of nations, to which we have previously referred and which we must study more specifically in a later chapter.

CHAPTER XI

The Vague Universalism
of Liberal Democracy

OUR own nation, as we have had previous occasion to observe, is confronted by all the responsibilities of a great power. Indeed, it is now one of the "super-powers." For the performance of these responsibilities it is equipped by only a few decades of experience and a tradition: the liberal-democratic tradition.

We must enquire closely into the origins and the character of the foreign policy tradition of liberal democracy which has so strongly influenced our attitudes. We can distinguish four sources of the liberal democratic view of foreign policy. One is derived from the French Revolution, and its most vivid spokesman is Rousseau. In this tradition a sharp rent with the past is assumed, and a boundless hope for the future obscures all the permanent and recurring forces of national behavior with which foreign policy must deal. The second source is to be found in the liberal nationalistic idealism of the frustrated nations, Germany and Italy, particularly in the romantic idealism of Herder and the moralistic idealism of Mazzini.

The third source was the liberal-democratic tradition of England, or more precisely of Britain, in which there was constant tension between the new democratic forces and the facts of empire. The prejudices of liberal democracy against empire made for a combination of idealistic and realistic appraisals of problems of foreign policy, which we find lacking in the other sources of the liberal-democratic creed. The fourth source of the tradition is in our own nation, which developed a democracy on virgin soil and was so free of the problems and turmoils of European international relations as to seem able to afford all the illusions about

182

the realities of international behavior which characterize the purest forms of irresponsible idealism. But recently we were suddenly vaulted into a position of world leadership where we must exercise power and responsibility in terms and categories which make the sharp distinction between authority "by the consent of the governed" and authority by the right of conquest rather irrelevant. For the authority and prestige by which we function in today's harassed world is not subject to explicit "democratic consent" (except within our boundaries), and we certainly do not "conquer" any nation—even if we do force Guatemala, for instance, to get rid of a pro-communist government.

The chief characteristic of the liberal democratic tradition in foreign policy, which is preserved with a remarkable degree of consistency in all the versions of the tradition (except in Britain), from the seventeenth to the nineteenth centuries, is indifference to any form of dominion or community above the level of the nation and below the level of the "community of mankind." This "community of mankind" is naturally vaguely conceived and its organization was not contemplated until the projection of the League of Nations in the First World War and the United Nations in the Second World War. This consistent characteristic is evident whether the inspirer of the tradition is John Locke, the father of pure liberalism, or Rousseau, the father of both liberalism and totalitarianism.

Perhaps the reason for this consistency lies, first, in the fact that liberal democracy grew up against the background of an established nation, as in the case of Britain; or democracy and the national spirit had a simultaneous birth, as in the case of the United States; or the two seemed coterminous, though they were not, as in the case of the French Revolution. The spirit of nationalism originally had a royal rather than democratic instrument, but the revolutionary impetus and the thought of Rousseau were so potent in reviving and strengthening that spirit that the revolution seemed to be a new beginning. In any case, democracy developed within the confines of the nation-state and assumed the integral community as the ultimate community, except for its vague consciousness of the community of mankind.

The community of mankind, the idea of a universal community, was both an inheritance of Stoic and Christian universalism and the consequence of the sense of a more all-embracing community which the voyages of discovery from Columbus through the whole sixteenth century gave the concept. But this community was not considered in specific terms as subject to organization as Dante, for example, had conceived it. The old principle of organization was discredited; and in any case the newly-discovered continents made it impossible to conceive of Europe as the center of its organization. Hence the universalism was bound to be vague.

John Locke expressed this vagueness by asserting the simple principle that conquest gave the victor no permanent rights. "The conqueror," he declares, "even in a just war, hath by his conquest no right of dominion; they are free from any subjection to him, and, if their former government be dissolved, they are at liberty to begin and erect another to themselves." [1] One assumes he means "morally free" for the concept has no relevance to any power realities.

What we have defined as the vague universalism of John Locke's theories, expressed in concern for the community of mankind, which will presumably benefit from the annulment of tyranny on every level, is not confined to Locke or to the seventeenth century. It becomes the consistent characteristic of liberal nationalism from the seventeenth to the nineteenth centuries whether the ideological foundation of the liberalism be romantic or rationalistic.

Rousseau, whose thought was the potent source of both nationalism and "democratic" idealism in France as well as throughout Europe, assumed the nation to be the final form of community. In his chapter on "civil religion" he specifically excluded a Christian or any other form of universalism which might qualify

---

[1] John Locke, *op. cit.*, Ch. XVI, par. 185, p. 93.

devotion to "La Patrie." He dismisses the problem of the relation of the nation to other communities in a final chapter of his "Social Contract" with these words:

> Conclusion: Now that I have laid down the true principles of political right, and tried to give the state a basis of its own to rest on, I ought next to strengthen it by its external relations, which would include the law of nations, commerce, the right of war and conquest, public right, leagues, negotiations, treaties, etc. But all this forms a new subject that is far too vast for my narrow scope. I ought throughout to have kept to a more limited sphere.[2]

His attempt to limit social discipline and the consequent moderation of selfish interest to the nation is specifically stated in his "civil religion." He objects to Christianity for two reasons: (1) Its otherworldliness prevents it "... from binding the hearts of the citizens to the State, it has the effect of taking men away from all earthly things. I know of nothing more contrary to the social spirit." [3] And (2), as he declares in his "Letter from the Mountain," it is too universal: "Although far from taxing the pure Gospel with being pernicious to society, I do find it in some way too sociable, embracing too much of the human race, for a system of law which ought to be exclusive; inspiring humanity rather than patriotism, and tending to form men rather than citizens." [4]

Rousseau's sentiments admirably define the relation of nationalism to vague universalism in liberal thought, far beyond the bounds of romanticism. It rightly sees the difficulty of embodying the larger community into a "system of law" and, therefore, wrongly dismisses all problems of community which

---

[2] Jean-Jacques Rousseau, *Social Contract*, translated with intro. by G. D. H. Cole, Everyman's Library, London: J. M. Dent, 1913, Book IV, chapter IX., p. 116.
[3] *Ibid.*, Book IV, part VIII, p. 111.
[4] Jean-Jacques Rousseau, "First Letter from the Mountain," in *Political Writings of Rousseau*, ed. C. E. Vaughan, London, Cambridge University Press, 1915, Vol. II, p. 172.

cannot be embodied into a system of law. Rousseau does, of course, hope for a system of unorganized peace after tyranny had been removed from the local community and imperialism abolished. The larger community will be not exactly unorganized, but will achieve peace through minimal organization. Rousseau was convinced that a free people would never attack another people. He was tremendously impressed with the utopian vision of the Abbé de Saint-Pierre, embodied in his "Project for Perpetual Peace." This work was published in 1713 and Rousseau sought to popularize it by publishing a condensation of the prolix treatise. He simultaneously published his "Judgement in regard to Perpetual Peace," which provided for arbitration between the nations and a minimal system of "collective security." Rousseau's thought influenced Kant in his treatise "Zum Ewigen Frieden," thus showing that romanticism and rationalism in the eighteenth century had a vague universalism in common. The old Christian and Roman universalism qualified the national particularism of all eighteenth and nineteenth century idealists. But no one asked the question how the power impulses above the level of the nation would be channeled and organized. It was simply assumed that the aggressiveness and self-seeking of the nations was due to the specific cause of monarchy or "tyranny."

The German romantic philosopher, Herder, had an even simpler version of the relation of the particular community, not necessarily the nation, to the community of mankind. He gloried in the diversity of cultures and languages and felt that Christian missions had violated the genius of primitive peoples by displacing, rather than purifying, their primitive faiths. His appreciation of the genius of every people did not prevent him, of course, from having a special appreciation of the genius of the German people, so that he was at the same time a nationalist, or at least an inspirer of German nationalism, and also a cosmopolitan and humanitarian, who would have been shocked by the use made of his thought by German nationalism in the subsequent centuries. If Rousseau was certain that a free people would not violate another people, Herder was certain that if each "folk"

would be left alone to express its peculiar genius, "all father-
lands would live peacefully with each other." The conception
hardly does justice to the dynamic cultural and linguistic competition in history above and below the level of conscious political
imperialism.

The idealist philosopher, Fichte, could hardly be termed a liberal democrat, but he was an idealistic nationalist whose thought
exhibited the same ambivalence between particularism and universalism. Influenced by the Napoleonic defeat of Germany, and
feeling called upon to fan the patriotism of the Germans to a
new heat, he tried to combine respect for Frederick the Great
with a vaguely conceived loyalty to the community of mankind.
He accomplished this double purpose by declaring that only
the Germans, with their bent for philosophy, could combine
love of the fatherland with love of humanity.

These forms of idealistic nationalism joined with a vague universalism were particularly popular in the two frustrated nations,
Germany and Italy, which had a strong sense of national community based upon a common language, but had been prevented
from having a common state because both were seats of the two
medieval imperialistic systems, the empire and the church. In the
nineteenth century Mazzini professed the same combination of
nationalism and universalism which had flowered in Germany in
the eighteenth century. Giuseppe Mazzini (1805–1872) was one
of the most childlike and naïve nationalists, who wanted both to
unify Italy and to place the nation in the service of humanity.
Italy, he declared, had once ruled the world by force through
the Roman Empire. Then she had ruled the world by authority
through the Papacy. The third Italy would "lead the world by the
common consent of the people"; thus, Italy of the people "radiant
and purified by suffering will move as an angel of light among
the nations which thought her dead." It would substitute for
the "rights of man" announced in the French Revolution the
"duties of man," and would usher in a new era of "collective energies." Nations have an important moral function to perform. They
must educate and train their citizens in the "moral law" and

direct their energies in behalf of humanity at large. According to Mazzini "nationalism is what God has ordained for each people in the work of humanity."

This form of idealism was certainly not lacking in influence in arousing the people of Italy to a sense of unity and mission; but it was scarcely as relevant as the activities of Garibaldi and Cavour, who dealt with the vexing problem of finding a sovereignty which would give dominion for the shattered nation of Italy and thereby give it unity. The nationalism of Mussolini in the twentieth century offers a pathetic contrast between the ideals and the realities of history. The universalism remained a kind of faint aftermath of the Christian universalism of the Medieval Papacy, which neither Italy nor any other nation found it easy to embody in a practice. The universal community of mankind does not have a body until this day, despite the hopes of the various idealistic nationalists that their particular nation would give it a body or perhaps a soul without a body.

These versions of Italian and German idealism did not come into sufficient contact with realities and responsibilities to be interesting. If we return, therefore, to the two great Anglo-Saxon nations, the one involved in imperialism and the other by history and conviction "anti-imperialistic," we shall find additional causes for the vagueness of the policies beyond the integral nation. One is that the democratic form of government has relevance only for the integral community where "consent" can be established and measured in free elections. Proposals for world government are efforts to extend these democratic instruments to the universal community. But most of the proposals ignore the fact that a full-blown system of communication, which overcomes parochial loyalties and permits judgments in the total community transcending these loyalties, is a prerequisite of the "democratic" method.

John Stuart Mill tried to envisage a federal organization of states which would most closely approximate to the justice of democratic societies. But the conditions he set for federation made the concept practically irrelevant to any historical problems. He wrote in his *Representative Government*, that "Portions of mankind who are not fitted or disposed to live under the same internal government, may often with advantage be federally united as to their relations with foreigners both to prevent wars among themselves, and for the sake of more effectual protection against the aggression of powerful States." [5] For the federation he prescribes these conditions: "mutual sympathy among the populations" resting on common language, religion, and identity of interests. The second condition is that "the separate states be not so powerful as to be able to rely, for protection against foreign encroachment, on their individual strength. ...A third condition, no less important than the two others, is that there be not a very marked inequality of strength among the several contracting States." [6] In short, his conception of a federation corresponds as closely as possible to the conditions of a democratic integral community. The reservations specifically exclude the very conditions under which the two great alliances of nations now function, each with a hegemonous nation with dominant power. Mill, however, accurately states the ideal in its purity which has governed the foreign policy of the democratic world. Woodrow Wilson's "League of Nations" tried to substitute the principle of "collective security" for the precarious, and in his opinion wicked, "balance of power" principle which had created some kind of order in the European anarchy. Collective security was dependent upon the principle of "equal sovereignty" of the nations. This principle is ambiguous. In one sense, if big and little nations are autonomous they are equal; but in another sense if sovereignty includes the power to determine one's own destiny, nations are not equal; and their inequality is more marked than the inequality of individuals in integral communities. Even the United Nations, despite the provision of a Security Council composed of the more powerful nations, has not come to terms with the dilemma of equal sovereignty. This was particularly obvious when frustration in the Security Council persuaded the West to give more

[5] John Stuart Mill, *On Liberty and Considerations on Representative Government*, ed. with intro. R. B. McCallum, Oxford, Basil Blackwell, 1948, p. 298.
[6] *Ibid.*, pp. 298–99.

power to the Assembly in which each nation, despite a great disparity of power, has a single vote. Woodrow Wilson stood squarely in this tradition when he announced at Versailles, "Without straining a point we are representatives, not of governments but of peoples."

Democratic liberalism is vague in its universalism, not only because the international structures of dominion and community, as they exist, do not correspond exactly to the norms of the democratic nation, but also because the liberal democrats had the conviction that democracy had, or would, radically alter the nature and the motives of states. This idea, born in the French Enlightenment, exerted a considerable influence in both Britain and America, but particularly in America. There were, of course, both realist and idealist schools of thought in foreign policy in Britain and America. In both nations the two traditions are vigorous. In our own nation Jefferson stands for the one tradition among our founding fathers, and Madison, Hamilton, and Adams for the other. In Britain the imperial experience of the nation naturally gives greater strength to the realist tradition, according to which democracy neither invalidates nor makes impossible the "balance of power" among the nations nor absolutely condemns the imperial structure of international organization.

Among our founding fathers who accepted the idea that democracy had materially altered the behavior of states Thomas Jefferson is a good example. Thus he animadverted on the war between France and Britain in terms which obscured the distinction between individual and collective morality. "My own hope," he wrote, "is that by giving time for reflection and retraction of injury, the sound calculation of their own interests will induce the aggressing nations to return to the practice of right. But the lot of our nation happens to be cast in an age when two nations, whose circumstances have given superiority over others temporarily, the one by land and the other by sea, throwing all restraints of morality, all pride of national character, forgetting the mutability of fortune and the inevitability of doom, which the laws of nature pronounce against all departure from justice, individual or national, have dared to treat her acclamation with derision, to set up force, rather than reason as the umpire of nations. Degrading themselves thus from the character of lawful societies into lawless bands of robbers and pirates, and abusing their brief ascendancy by desolating the world by blood and rapine." [7] Jefferson's version of the Augustinian description of the morality of states as that of "robber bands" is a modern and more optimistic appraisal of the morality of nations, which rests upon the assumption that nations, if they reflect on their true interests and on the nemesis which overtakes them if they defy the law of nature, will cease to be robber bands and return to the obedience of the law of nature.

In fairness to Jefferson one must remember that his insights and actions as a responsible statesman do not quite conform to his theories as a radical political thinker. As the third president of the new republic he was responsible for the purchase of the Louisiana territory from Napoleon. He also initiated the expedition of Lewis and Clarke. These policies reveal a realistic awareness of the future continental potentialities of the new nation. He also had the foresight to see the strategic significance of the Caribbean, though he would have been shocked by our method of wresting Cuba from Spain. Of Jefferson's policy Gerald Stourzh declares:

> The apt name of 'protective imperialism' which has been coined for Jefferson's foreign policy may be applied with equal justication to Benjamin Franklin. This kind of imperialism, motivated by security considerations rather than by other political or economic motives, presents an interesting precedent, if we accept recent interpretations of American foreign policy, which lays particular stress on the persistent and paramount importance of extensive security concepts of American foreign policy. [8]

[7] *The Writings of Thomas Jefferson*, ed. by Andrew A. Lipscomb and Albert Ellery Bergh, 20 Vols., Thomas Jefferson Memorial Assoc., 1903, Vol. 13, pp. 355–56.
[8] Gerald Stourzh, *Benjamin Franklin and American Foreign Policy*, Chicago University Press, 1954, pp. 251–52.

Responsible statesmen, whatever their theories, may not always be as astute as Jefferson, but they are usually more astute than the pure theorists.

The French Enlightenment which influenced Jefferson was more influential in the political thought of our nation than in Britain. It had more influence in a virginal nation than in one in which revolutionary ideals encountered historical experience as in Britain. But ideas are influenced partly by collective experience and partly by individual experience, or lack of it. A typical British idealist, William Godwin (1756–1836), lacked Jefferson's political experience and responsibility. He, therefore, revealed the vague universalism of the liberal tradition in a purer form. He believed that democracy would radically alter the behavior of nations, for

> ... For wars do not originate in the unbiassed propensities of nations, but in the cabals of government and the propensities that governments inspire into the people at large. ... Where nations are not brought into avowed hostility all jealousy between them is an unintelligible chimera.[9]

Godwin's conviction that the aggressive behavior of nations was always due to governments, and never to the innocent people, was thoroughly refuted by subsequent history, but his theory echoes in the thought of modern democracy well into the twentieth century.

Naturally illusions in regard to the behavior of nations generated corresponding illusions in regard to the structure of the community above the level of the nation. For centuries the anarchy of European nationalism was slightly mitigated, particularly between the Napoleonic Wars and the First World War, by strategies which generally come under the category of the "balance of power." Godwin thought this strategy a wicked device. "The pretence of the balance of power," he wrote, "has, in a multitude of instances, served as a veil to the intrigue of courts; but it would be easy to show, that the present independence of the different states of

[9] William Godwin, "Enquiry Concerning Political Justice and Its Influence on Morals and Happiness," ed. F. E. L. Priestly [facsimile of 3rd edition corrected] Toronto, U. of Toronto Press, 1926, Vol. II, pp. 192–93.

Europe, has in no instance, been materially assisted, by the wars undertaken for that purpose." [10]

There was a realist tradition in American thought, exemplified particularly by Madison, Hamilton, and Adams. But, since the problems of the international community were beyond the interests of the new nation, isolated on a virgin continent, we must turn to the moderate British liberals for a realistic account of the structures of dominion and community above the level of the nation. The two structures which concern us particularly are the balance of power and the empire. If we consult the thought of the more circumspect liberals of Britain, particularly David Hume, Adam Smith, and Edmund Burke, we will find both a realistic account of the behavior of nations and an understanding of the structures of power which stand between the nation and the community of mankind.

David Hume makes the necessary distinction between the morality of individuals and of nations. Hume declares that

> There is a maxim very current in the world, which few politicians are willing to avow, but which has been authoriz'd by the practice of all ages, *that there is a system of morals calculated for princes, much more free than that which ought to govern private persons...*
> ...Shou'd it be ask'd *what proportion the two species of morality bear to each other*...one may safely affirm, that this proportion finds itself, without any art or study of men. ...The practice of the world goes farther in teaching us the degrees of our duty, than the most subtile philosophy, which was ever invented.[11]

This is an admirable statement of the real situation in world history, in which the commonsense of mankind acknowledges both collective standards and the difference between collective and individual standards, which philosophies infrequently acknowledge. If the "realists" acknowledge the difference they make the disparity too great, as in the tradition of Machiavelli. Hume was

---

[10] *Ibid.*, p. 156.
[11] David Hume, *A Treatise of Human Nature*, ed. L. A. Selby-Bigge, Oxford, Clarendon Press, 1951, pp. 568–69.

no Machiavellian. He recognized a moral standard for the nation. Its principal commandment was the keeping of covenants. "For no one, of ever so corrupt morals," he declared, "would approve of a prince, who voluntarily, and of his own accord, breaks his word, or violates any treaty."

Hume's realism naturally prompted him to view the structures of community and power in the international field in a different light than did Godwin. This applied particularly to the "balance of power" principle of which Hume gave a classical description. "But whether we ascribe the shifting of sides...to jealous emulations or cautious politics, the effects were alike and every prevailing power was sure to meet with a confederacy against it, and that often composed of its friends and allies." [12] This is not the only possible description of the balance of power, and it certainly does not give a picture of the balance which preserves a precarious peace between two blocs of nations today. But it has the merit of realizing the necessity of some kind of principle of intermediate order within the chaos of international relations, which cannot be overcome by any system of "collective security."

Edmund Burke, informed by the same realistic estimate of the possibilities and the limits of international morality, speaks of the duty of nations to enforce common standards of justice (against Napoleonic imperialism, for instance) and declares, "If England shows herself indifferent or unconcerned when these powers are combined against the enterprises of France she is to look with certainty to the same indifference of these powers when she may be at war with that nation." [13]

Burke's principles of international federation and co-operation not only accurately describe the motives which prompted the alliance against Napoleon, but the alliance which now is loosely formed against Russia. Both Hume and Burke envisaged the real-

[12] David Hume, "Of the Balance of Power" in *Essays Moral, Political, and Literary*, Vol. I, Pt. II, Essay VII, p. 349.
[13] Edmund Burke, "Heads for Consideration of the Present State of Affairs," *Works of the Right Honorable Edmund Burke*, IV, p. 398; quoted from Arnold Wolfers and Lawrence W. Martin, *Anglo-American Tradition in Foreign Affairs*, New Haven, Yale University Press, 1956, p. 112.

ities which seem to recur in the field of international relations, particularly the reality of defensive alliances, far more clearly than did the purer liberal theorists.

The imperial community above the level of the nation must be specially analyzed in a subsequent chapter. The moral ambiguity inherent in the structures of power and community is obviously raised to a high level in the structure of empire. Imperial ventures have given the West an uneasy conscience. Our own nation, with only a brief excursion in imperial dominion after the Spanish American War, has been particularly self-righteous about the alleged sins of its allies. Yet whatever the moral judgment upon empire may be, we must recognize the fact of empire as one of the recurring patterns of large-scale community which will persist as long as strength impinges on weakness, either exploiting that weakness or supplementing it.

It may seem strange to call Adam Smith to witness as a realistic liberal on the question of empire, for he was a critic of the imperialism of his day. But he criticized it for different reasons than did the other liberal critics; and his criticism assumed empire as a possible and valid structure of community. His criticisms dealt not with the injustices which the colonies suffered from empire but with the injustice to the "mother" country, caused by her bearing the sole burden of defense for the colonies; and also with the general injustice of mercantilist imperialism which established a monopoly of trade with the colonies. "The European colonies of America have never yet furnished any military force for the defence of the mother country," he declared.

> Their military force has never yet been sufficient for their own defence; and in the different wars in which the mother countries have been engaged, the defence of their colonies has generally occasioned a very considerable distraction of the military force of those countries. In this respect, therefore, all the European colonies have, without exception, been a cause rather of weakness than of strength to their respective mother countries.[14]

[14] Adam Smith, *An Inquiry into the Nature and Causes of the Wealth of Nations*, ed., Edwin Cannan, London, Methuen & Co., 1904, Vol. II, p. 94.

Adam Smith was a liberal imperialist, who objected both to trade monopoly between the colonies and the mother country—arguing that this was not ultimately beneficial to the imperial country—and to the burden which the mother country bore for defense. He believed in a fair scheme of taxation but also recognized that the colonies could not be taxed without representation. Every one of his policies, in short, if applied, might have prevented the American Revolutionary War. They were not applied because the imperial impulse is not motivated by purely economic motives. The indifference to political and other motives in community building was, as every one now knows, the defect of classical economics. In this context it is important only to recognize that Adam Smith could envisage a just imperial structure. He even could envisage a structure in which the central authority of the empire could move across the Atlantic because of the superior economic power which he thought was in prospect in the American colonies. This eventuality came to pass, but not within the limits of an imperial structure.

Adam Smith was, of course, dealing with the realities of the empire which Britain lost—because it did not observe the wisdom of Smith and the other critics. He did not anticipate the realities of the new empire which Britain gained after the loss of the first one. It consisted of two portions—the Anglo-Saxon colonies, in which democratic self-government gradually loosened the ties of empire and permitted the dominions to emerge as self-governing nations—and the Asiatic part of the empire which had a much more tortuous history on the road to the freedom of the dominions of India, Pakistan, Burma, and Ceylon.

In short, if the more naïve liberals could not envisage the structures of power and community which would form above the level of the nation, even a sagacious liberal, such as Adam Smith, could not anticipate all the communal formations which would be constructed below the level of the "community of mankind" and also above the level of the nation. The naïve liberals were right in assuming that the integral nation was, and would increasingly become, the community of significant loyalty for modern men. They were right also in affirming that the democratic principle of "consent of the governed" would be both a force of justice and a means of communal integration, though the increasing means of communication tended to favor the nation in contrast to the imperial community, even if democracy had been unavailable. For the written word and the multiplication of pamphlets and newspapers were mighty instruments of increasing the intensity of social cohesion. But they did not increase the breadth of cohesion.

The more naïve liberalism was wrong however in assuming that democracy would seriously alter the self-regarding motives of nations, or that the aggression of nations was due chiefly to the machinations of kings and diplomats. Democracies are indeed slow to make war, but once embarked upon a martial venture are equally slow to make peace and reluctant to make a tolerable, rather than a vindictive, peace. Both types of liberals, the more naïve and the more sagacious, were right in assuming that community without the instruments of democratic checks would not achieve a consistent justice; but they were wrong in affirming that such supra-national formations, which lacked the democratic instruments, should not be formed. They will inevitably be formed, though the justice they achieve will be more deficient than that in the nation.

Those we have defined as the more "judicious" liberals, particularly David Hume and Adam Smith, were right in their interpretation of the behavior of even democratic nations and in their interpretation of the political structures which transcend the nations—alliances, balances of power, and empires. But they could not have anticipated the various methods of community which have actually taken place, or those forms of the impingement of strength upon weakness in which both traditional nationalism and traditional imperialism are transcended. If one tries to distinguish between the perennial and the emergent factors and forces in history in regard to the patterns of nation and community above the level of the nation there are perhaps at least two patterns which remain fixed which both the naïve and the more sagacious nationalists observed, though the naïve thought the second would become outmoded.

The first pattern or form is the integral and autonomous nation. The idea of the autonomous nation has achieved universal acceptance, even though the disparities in the culture and the economy of the various peoples raise the question whether some of the less developed cultures provide the nascent nation with sufficient forces of cohesion to make autonomy feasible. Many of the nations, emancipated since the First World War, and even many of the Latin-American nations, which have achieved their autonomy from Spain and Portugal in the nineteenth century, have certainly lacked the resources of a democratically controlled autonomy. They are subject to various types of military dictatorship which create neither justice nor stability; but it is a question whether an imperial structure of community would be productive of more justice. The case of Mexico comes to mind, suffering for ages under dictatorships as grievous as the previous imperial power. But the revolution at the beginning of this century under Madero, Carranza, and Obregon finally made real progress both in justice and stability.

The pattern of autonomous nationality is so universal that it will finally prove a great hazard to the communist imperialism, even though this latter hides its violations of autonomy by ruling subject nations through subservient communist parties. In Africa and Asia communist imperialism runs less immediate danger because it can always pose as the emancipator of subject nations; but in the long run it must run into the same intractable problem.

The pattern of autonomous nationhood is so generally accepted that imperial power can only express itself in relation to smaller nations by accepting the sovereignty of the nation as a fixed norm of international morality. Our nation finally came to the conclusion that if Mexico desired to nationalize her sub-soil wealth it was unwise to challenge the right; under the administration of Calvin Coolidge, Ambassador Dwight Morrow liquidated the tension between the two nations by the simple expedient of substituting contracts between owners and producers for the previous right of foreign ownership. Britain, within recent memory, resolved the long tension with Iran by the same expedient.

The second permanent pattern of international community is one which was discerned by the more sagacious liberals. It is the pattern of alliance and co-operation between the nations below the level of the collective security of the community of mankind. But there are more variations in this pattern than either David Hume or Adam Smith anticipated. Among the variations are regional defensive alliances, such as the North Atlantic Treaty Organization, which offers mutual security to the western nations of the Atlantic community; and the politically more dubious alliances of the Baghdad Pact and of SEATO in the Pacific.

In addition there are such economic alliances as projected originally in the Marshall Plan, which are certainly not in the category of "imperialism," though condemned as such by the communists. In these alliances the power of a strong nation is brought into terms of mutuality with the weaker nations, not for the sake of exploitation, but also not in terms of pure generosity of the strong nation. The category of "imperialism" has become irrelevant to these formations. The communists have recently followed similar patterns, which do not fit into the category of "imperial" control of the subject satellites. They are intended to woo and to bind the hitherto neutral nations. Though these arrangements are condemned in each case by the opposite bloc as imperialistic, they are not essentially different from each other except as the power impulses of the communist nations are informed by a more restrictive dogma than the power impulses of the democratic nations.

It is necessary to include in the variety of these patterns of international life the increasing economic penetration of weak nations by strong ones (the "economic imperialism," so-called, over the "banana republics" of South America is a case in point). One must also include the industrial enterprises which transcend the national sovereignties of both weak and strong nations as, for instance, the oil companies, which exploit the oil resources of the Middle East, which are partnerships of American, British, and

Dutch oil interests. In a technical and industrial age it is even more difficult to contain the economic vitalities of peoples within political limits than it has been in previous ages. The economic interrelatedness of a technical age and the necessity of economic mutuality, particularly in specific geographic areas, is an invitation to modern statecraft to seek forms for these nascent economic communities which will extend economic mutuality with a minimum of injustice. The European "Coal and Steel community," conceived and organized by the imaginative Frenchman, Jean Monnet, is an example of the necessary inventiveness. Perhaps the European "common market" is another such example.

The variations in the pattern of international community vary endlessly. But the fixed pattern in all these variations is a combination of dominion and community above the level of the nation and below the level of the community of mankind. It is safe to predict that no future history will annul this pattern though it may produce hitherto unknown variations in the pattern.

CHAPTER XII

The Character
of National Imperialism

THE western world is embarrassed by the communist charge that
it is "imperialistic." All the western nations in fact have engaged
in imperial ventures, and their rivalries and conflicts have been
aggravated by their imperial interests. The wars of the nineteenth
century and the First World War were occasioned in no small
degree by the conflicts of national empires. The communist charge
of imperialism against the West is particularly plausible in the
continents of former colonial nations, animated by real and residual resentments against the present or former masters. It is also a
source of confusion between the two great Anglo-Saxon nations,
who must be the bulwark of the "free world." For one of them is
by tradition and liberal democratic conviction "anti-imperialistic"
while the other was involved in imperial ventures in every part of
the world.

In the triangular struggle between the three imperial nations,
Spain, France, and Britain, the latter was the most successful in
imperial ventures, dominating the politics of the nineteenth century, as Spanish power and adventure dominated the seventeenth
century and France the early eighteenth. The German bid for
imperial power was eliminated in the First World War as the
Japanese bid was eliminated in the Second World War.

It is usually assumed that the imperial dominance of the European nations was the result of the superiority of European military
power. Guns were no doubt used in all imperial ventures, but the
superior strength was frequently furnished not by guns but by
the superiority of social and political cohesion. The impingement
of power upon weakness was often the impingement of a system

of order upon either anarchy or an inchoate political and social situation.

The occasion for this national imperialism was furnished primarily by the discovery of the virgin continent of America and the contact between Europe and Asia and Africa. This contact was originally furnished by the adventurous voyages of the sailors of Latin countries, Italy, Spain, and Portugal; and was encouraged by the increasingly effective means of navigation and communications. These contacts inevitably placed the highly integrated nations of Europe in juxtaposition to the politically less integrated nations of Asia and Africa. The people were either on the primitive level of tribal life; or, as in the case of India and China, they represented ancient cultures deficient in the technical means of communication which are important sources of cohesion in an integral community.

There are almost invariably three motives of the extension of dominion by vital nations. The one motive is missionary, the desire to extend the fruits of a culture, whether conceived in religious, political or technical terms. In the case of modern communist imperialism the missionary zeal of the secular religion of communism is combined with the zeal for making the non-technical nations technically competent. This combination was of course not unknown in the history of European imperialism. The "missionary motive" of nations must not be confused with genuine Christian missions, which, if they are uncritical, become inadvertent instruments of political prestige, but which are, at best, transcendent to political and interested motives.

The second motive is economic. We have previously dealt with the absurdity of the communist charge that imperialism is purely the product of capitalism. While communist propaganda interprets imperialism as purely exploitative and while the motive of either economic exploitation of the resources of subject peoples or the extension of trade often plays a large part in imperial ventures, it is never the sole motive of imperial expansion. The third motive is more difficult to define. It consists of the expression of a national vitality and of the desire for power and glory, for the enhancement of the prestige of the imperial power. This desire for power and glory is usually expressed in European imperialism in the racial arrogance of the white Europeans in relation to the colored races of Asia and Africa. Such arrogance was certainly a more powerful source of resentment of the subject peoples than economic exploitation. These are the resentments which modern Communism exploits, though its theory gives purely economic interpretations of imperialism.

The missionary motive is invariably related to the conviction that the imperial power either represents a universal community or that it is able to bestow a value of universal validity. The fact that particular nations, rather than the classical universal-imperial communities, dispense this boon is one of the greatest moral hazards of modern imperialism. It is at this point that the seemingly more plausible communist claims put the West at a disadvantage, though if catastrophe does not overtake the world one may predict that the claim of universality of Russian imperialism will become as implausible as the claims of the original Spanish imperialism seem to us now. And the combination of the missionary and the exploitative motives will also be equally apparent.

The original impetus for the Spanish imperial venture undoubtedly was given by the triumph over the Moors, after centuries of struggle. The battle with the Moors hardened the martial vigor of the conquistadors and gave them a sense of incorporating the ultimate values of a Christian civilization, whether fighting the Moors or exporting Christianity to the heathen of America. Thus Columbus addressed Ferdinand and Isabella: "Your Highnesses, as good Christian and Catholic princes, devout and propagators of the Christian faith, as well as enemies of the sect of Mahomet and of all idolatries and heresies, conceive the plan of sending me, Christopher Columbus, to this country of the Indies, there to see the princes, the peoples ... and their disposition and the way one might convert these regions to the Holy Faith." [1]

Inevitably Columbus' motives were not so unmixed as his ad-

---

[1] La Casas version of Columbus diary, quoted in Louis Marie Émile Bertrand and Sir Charles Petrie, *History of Spain*, translated by W. B. Wells, p. 164, London, Eyre and Spottiswoode, 1952.

dress to Isabella and Ferdinand suggested. Imperial motives are
never unmixed. Describing Columbus' missionary and economic
motives, Bertrand and Petrie declare: "Without the least hypocrisy
these two motives could coexist in one and the same person. Columbus had two things together, a converter and exploiter of the
natives. He wanted gold not only to satisfy his real avarice, but
also to maintain those who followed him, to justify the promises
of paradise, which he had lavished on the Spanish sovereigns, and
finally to plant the cross and build chapels on foreign soil." [2] Thus
the first great explorer gives us a vivid example of the mixed motives of what developed into imperialism. One need question only
one phrase in the description of the mixture of motives by the
eminent authors. It is rather naïve to observe that the mixture oc-
curred "without hypocrisy," when the very nature of hypocrisy
in both the political and individual life is to cover and veil the
less noble motive by the more noble one.

The mixture of motives was more vividly displayed by the Spanish conquerors than in any subsequent imperialism. Perhaps it
would be better to say it was more naïvely displayed. But what was
displayed was a permanent characteristic of the imperial urge
which was revealed, for instance, in the policies of the two great
founders of the British Empire in India, Lord Clive and Warren
Hastings.

Cortez was a fit successor of Columbus in more ways than
one. A self-made lay catechist, Cortez addressed the emperor of
Mexico, declaring that we are all children of one father and that
it grieved his great sovereign that so many souls are led to perdi-
tion by the worship of idols. He had been sent to redeem the
Mexicans of idolatry. Montezuma replied with dignity: "We have
our gods whom we have long worshipped, holding them to be
good. Yours may be good too. For the moment do not concern
yourselves to speak to us of them." [3]

The missionary impulse was directly related to the impulse of
dominion in a curious way, for in the words of Bertrand, "the
Spaniards came to America to convert the Indians. The best way

---

[2] *History of Spain,* Bertrand and Petrie, p. 177.
[3] Bertrand and Petrie, *op. cit.,* p. 181.

of doing so was to reduce them to slavery. So there was established the notorious regime of 'commanderies of Indians.' " This is not the whole story about the relation of the two impulses. In nineteenth century England the evangelical reformers, the "Clapham sect" particularly, used imperial dominion to abolish slavery in the whole British Empire.

The fact is that beside the phenomenon of mixed motives of empire there is a more significant phenomenon of the conflict of motives. In the second British Empire the motive seems to have been primarily economic. But when Adam Smith refuted the economic reasons for empire the other two motives became more popular. In the nineteenth century, when the great triumphs of British imperialism were recorded under the stress of a constant debate between imperialists and anti-imperialists, Disraeli championed the motive of prestige for imperialism (as did Winston Churchill years later). In his Crystal Palace speech in 1872 he declared that the Empire was proof of "the commanding spirit of these islands." Langer writes: "His policy was essentially concerned with questions of power and security, all pointed at the security of the routes to India, and the safeguarding of the Indian empire itself. ...the emergence of the principle of nationality and the growth of the German empire called forth a corresponding feeling of national pride among the English, which resulted in a new appreciation of the Empire, which was not in keeping with the Manchester doctrine." [4]

If pride of power and prestige became a later motive of British imperialism the new combination of motives took place in the latter part of the nineteenth century when the missionary motive was combined with the impulse to dominion. Thus Joseph Chamberlain, whose efforts failed to establish imperial tariffs in the teeth of the British free trade tradition, was one of the apostles of the missionary motive of imperialism, the peculiar British mission being, in his esteem, to be "trustees of civilisation." "I believe," said Chamberlain, "that the British race is the greatest of

[4] William Langer, *Diplomacy of Imperialism*, New York, Knopf, 1935, Vol. I, p. 70.

governing races which the world has ever seen. ...We alone among the nations of the world have been able to establish colonies under different conditions in every part of the world. We have maintained them to our advantage and to theirs, and we have secured not only the local attachment of British subjects, but the general good will of the races, whether they be European or native, that have come under the British flag." [5]

Lord Rosebery expressed the same pride in the success of the British political mission in the words: "The empire is sacred to me for this reason: I believe it to be the noblest example known to mankind of a free adaptable just government. ...When a community is in distress or under oppression, it always looks first to Britain." [6]

These claims will appear extravagant and to be in fact good examples of hypocrisy and pretension of empires in general. They will be discounted by the national patriots of British colonies who defied Britain in the twentieth century to win the independence of India, Ceylon, and Burma. But the claims are closer to reality than many similar claims of other nations.

The conflict and mixture of motives was frequently evident in the same person and the one could not be distinguished from the other. At the beginning of the nineteenth century when the doctrines of free trade began to undermine the economic reasons for empire and when humanitarianism was fostered both by evangelical religion and the Enlightenment, Sir Thomas Stamford Raffles, one of the eloquent proponents of the imperial idea, combined the two motives succinctly. After arguing that Britain would profit economically from the organization of India he continued, "This comprises no presumptuous view of our character. It is Britain which now gives the standard of all that is excellent. It is to British manners and customs that all nations now conform themselves —Britain leads the fashion and gives the law, not only in the tinsel of dress but in the whole frame of social acquirements. It appears that there is something in our national character and condition which fits us for this exalted station. I think too that there is a kind of destination of this character and condition to these services. It was the privilege of Britain to receive first the purest beams of reformed religion." [7] The derivation of British moral excellence in imperial rule from the first reception of "the purest rays of reformed religion" links Raffles' ideas to those of John Milton's conception of "God's Englishman." Thus moral religious pride is related to the pride of dominion and all these virtues are united with the hope of economic profit.

Naturally there were cynical reactions to the mixture and confusion of motives, not only in Britain but in the foreign world. In Britain Sydney Smith criticized the mixture with devastating irony, "To introduce European population, and consequently the arts and civilization of Europe into such untrodden countries as New Holland," he wrote, "is to confer a lasting and important blessing on the world. The savage no sooner becomes ashamed of his nakedness, than the loom is ready to clothe him." [8]

The conflict of motives and the mixture of them in the heart of single individuals and in the national soul has prompted the charge of hypocrisy against British politics, particularly by continental statesmen, who in the late nineteenth century saw in Gladstone the perfect exemplar of this "cant."

But one must raise the question whether we are not dealing with a general characteristic of both individuals and nations. It is universal human inclination to veil egoistic motives behind nobler ones. In the case of British imperialism the interesting fact is that the achievements of British empire were such that they always partly validated the moral claims. The triumph of British imperialism, first over Spanish and then over French imperialism, was of course not a purely moral one; but if military power was the decisive factor, moral and political achievements also entered into the British ascendancy.

An examination of the causes of the British triumph discloses

---

[7] Klaus E. Knorr, *British Colonial Theories 1570 to 1850*, Toronto University Press, 1944, p. 247.
[8] Knorr, *op. cit.*, p. 247.

the same mixture of forces and motives as the fact of empire itself. No doubt the triumph over French imperialism was hastened by the defeat of Napoleon, though there were many encounters between the two systems after that defeat and many reasons why Britain gained the ascendancy both in India and in North America despite the loss of the American colonies. Part of the superiority must be ascribed to the power of the British navy and part to the skill and resourcefulness of British navigators and tradesmen. But the Dutch navigators and tradesmen were equally resourceful. They simply lacked the supporting power of a strong navy.

The British ascendancy may be partly ascribed to the political genius and cunning of Britain, particularly its ability to insinuate its power by indirect rule, that is, by supporting, guiding, and finally dominating ruling princes, whether in Egypt or in India. But this cunning would not have availed if the political genius had not contained another component than cunning. British rule in India gradually insinuated the standards of political justice into the patchwork rule. The British established an independent system of courts, gradually modified the role of the princelings, and gave India a system of communications which contributed to the final achievement of integral nationhood. Critics may observe that it required a very long time to get rid of the anomaly that India was ruled by a trading company. But the friendly observer will note that the elimination of the company proceeded by gradual but inexorable stages.

The British ascendancy in empire undoubtedly rests partly on the early achievements of British industrialism. These provided the goods for trade, hastened the quest for markets, and developed the means of communication. The first steamboats were not capable of crossing the oceans, fuel consumption for long journeys being too high, and not until 1825 did the first ship round the Cape of Good Hope mostly under steam.[9] The introduction of

[9] Cf. C. E. Carrington, *The British Overseas*, New York, Cambridge University Press, 1950; particularly chapter IX on "Markets, Money and Men in the Age of Free Trade."

the deep sea cable further improved the communications of the empire and enhanced the imperial authority.

The moral superiority of British imperialism, certainly over Spanish imperialism and to some extent over French imperialism, is partly derived from, and would not have been possible without, the development of the free parliamentary institutions of Britain. All imperial reforms were achieved by a combination of external and internal pressures. The achievements of democracy in the character of imperialism are of course not confined to Britain. The Belgian imperialism in the African Congo began in the horrors established by the private monopoly of the King of the Belgians, Leopold. The African colony was gradually brought under the control of the democratic institutions of the constitutional monarchy; and the pressure of world opinion and of Belgian democracy prompted many reforms until the Belgian Congo became one of the better African dependencies. It has not given the natives political rights but it has tried to prevent white settlers from exploiting the natives and in theory it is preparing the natives for self-government by a generous educational program.

In Britain parliamentary authority gave three forces of reform the scope they needed. One of these forces consisted of the critics of empire. Some of these criticized the economics of empire, as did Adam Smith and Ricardo. Their criticisms resulted in the abolition of mercantilist monopolies and the establishment of free trade. Without this achievement the empire could not have survived. Others criticized the very fact of empire, holding it to be the source of injustice or the cause of war. Bentham in fact regarded the abolition of empire as the chief hope of universal peace. Richard Cobden, an ardent disciple of Adam Smith, put his confidence in free trade as the principle of mutuality which would eliminate war. Some of the critics, such as Edmund Burke, were critical of the actual operations of empire, whether in America or India; and their criticisms did much to raise the tone of imperial relations.

The second force making for higher imperial standards was furnished by the reformers, who did not so much criticize the empire as use it for the spread of their reforms. The agitation for the abolition of slavery began in the early nineteenth century, the chief proponent being the evangelical "Clapham sect," influential in high places. The last slaves in the colonies were emancipated in 1839.[10] Thus under the difficult colonial conditions, with the variety of cultures, the empire accomplished without war what America accomplished decades later in a bloody war. Other moral reforms such as the abolition of "suttee," the immolation of widows on the death of the husband, were carried through in India. This reforming zeal overcame the customary British tendency to interfere with native custom as little as possible. The British reformers, who used the imperial community for the wider effectiveness of their reform program, gave the imperial community a moral meaning which surpassed that of any other empire. Their effectiveness was, of course, due to the freedom of agitation which they had in the democratic culture of Britain.

The third force of the political superiority of the British empire must be identified as the large group of British proconsuls who combined the impulse of dominion with a strong impulse of responsibility toward subject peoples, and a passion for raising the general cultural level of the colonies. These proconsuls are almost too numerous to mention and the inclusion of some of the names in this category might be disputed. One is not quite certain whether Clive and Hastings, who laid the foundations of the Indian empire, would deserve inclusion in the list. Yet both of them had a creative impact upon India.

Most of the creative proconsuls functioned in the latter nineteenth century when British imperial achievements reached their height. They included Lord Cromer in Egypt. The original purpose of occupying Egypt was the strategic one of protecting the route to India. But once the relation of dominance was established, men like Cromer used it to bring order and economic improvement to the Egyptian nation, boons that have been forgotten in this day when Egypt is the fomenter not only of nationalism but

---

[10] Carrington, *op. cit.*, p. 294.

of a new Pan-Islamic imperialism which threatens the vital flow of Middle Eastern oil to Europe. British rule in Egypt established an honest, efficient, and solvent administration; and one of Lord Cromer's final achievements was the founding of an educational system, including a new university. The essential problem of the poverty of the Egyptian peasants and the venality of the Egyptian landlords was not, of course, solved and has not been solved to this day. The involvement of Britain in the Sudan was not at all to the discredit of the imperial power. British arms under Kitchener put down the rebellion of the Islamic dervishes after General Gordon lost his life in the siege of Khartoum. The problems of the Sudan have not been solved by the Egyptians after the Anglo-Egyptian condominium was destroyed by the rising nationalism. Egypt has little inclination to give credit to these British achievements.

New nations are usually integrated partly by the force of resentment against their masters and partly by the means of community supplied by the imperial power. This double source of nationalism is not fully appreciated by either the imperial masters or their subjects. It is one of the hazards of imperial rule that it so obsesses the colonial peoples with the evils arising from imperialism that some time is required for the emancipated nations to come to terms with the economic and political problems, which are not derived from imperial dominion. Some of these arise from lack of experience in self-government.

Among the creative proconsuls of the British Empire in the late nineteenth century one might mention at least two more good examples: Lord Lugard, whose field of creativity was Africa, more particularly Nigeria, and Sir George Golden, who laid the foundations for Lugard's achievements by acting as adviser and guide to the tribal chieftains of the region. Lord Lugard brought about the union of the territories of the lower and middle Niger under a centralized administration by partly beguiling and partly forcing the Moslem aristocracy of the north into the union. The cultures of this vast region—comprising everything from barbarism to advanced civilization, and Moslem and Christian as well as primitive religion—are too diverse to make the outlook for an integral national community very bright, though the venture of dominion status is soon to be made. Naturally the present nationalistic patriots criticize many of Lugard's achievements; but these criticisms cannot obscure his passion for justice and for education of a great population in the arts of government. It is safe to say that without such men as Golden and Lugard there would have been no possibility of an independent Nigeria. Lugard and Golden, with Lord Cromer, are exemplars of the innumerable British proconsuls in every part of the world who have followed the principle elaborated by Lugard in his "Dual Mandate in Africa" (1922). "Europe is in Africa," he wrote, "for the mutual benefit of her own industrial classes and the native races, in their progress to a higher plane. That the benefit can be made reciprocal, is the aim and desire of civilised administration in the dual mandate." [11] This principle is also a very succinct statement of what is valid in the mixture of motives in all imperial enterprise, and for that matter is a definition of a valid political ethic in every sphere and relation. For the essence of political morality is the attainment of a responsible relation of strength to weakness on the one hand and the achievement of reciprocity on the other hand. There can be no complete self-sacrifice or even "generosity" in political or collective relations.

This record of the political achievements of British imperialism must finally include the transformation of the Anglo-Saxon parts of the empire into a commonwealth of nations, comprised of self-governing dominions who throughout the nineteenth century developed into integral and self-conscious nations and by the First World War, or through their voluntary exertions in that war, became virtually independent, with only loyalty to the common crown as the symbol of the larger connection. The achievement of the British Commonwealth of Nations is one of the great political triumphs of the modern era. While many statesmen were involved in these achievements it is perhaps enough to say that the commonwealth was the product, on the one hand, of the lessons which

---

[11] Carrington, *op. cit.*, p. 829.

Britain learned in the American War of Independence and, on the other hand, of the philosophy of the Whigs, which throughout British history tried to extend political freedom in Britain and with a fair degree of consistency, refused to deny to the new nations which Britain spawned the rights which the Britons claimed for themselves. It is necessary to distinguish between the Anglo-Saxon portions of the empire which attained their independence without a political struggle in the nineteenth century and those Asian and African portions of the empire which were emancipated after the Second World War, and rather more reluctantly than the English-speaking dominions. The greater reluctance of the imperial power may have been due to the fact that the inhabitants of these dominions could not claim the historic rights of Englishmen, or perhaps they were not deemed ripe for self-government. In any case the achievement of the transformation of the empire into a commonwealth of nations is an impressive witness to the British political genius.

A comparison favoring British over Latin imperialism would be neither fair nor complete without presenting a characteristic of Anglo-Saxon imperialism which presents us with a moral perplexity and illumines the curious relation between individual and collective standards and between the moral and the political order. Anglo-Saxons exhibit more race pride than the Latins, whether French, Spanish, or Italian; and all the achievements of British rule cannot obscure the fact that British dominion insisted on a separation of the dominant and the subject peoples, while Latin rule allowed intermarriage more consistently and made little of the distinction between white and colored peoples. The Latins were not more just to the subject peoples but they were more tolerant of intermarriage. Thus Spanish imperialism both enslaved the indigenous Indian population and mingled with them. The consequence was a half-Indian, half-Spanish culture, politically reproducing the ancient feudalism of Europe with the difference that the class or caste system was ethnically colored and determined. Our Puritans, on the other hand, while engaging in sporadic missions to the Indians, assumed that they were building a "new

England" on American territory. Not all the Indians were liquidated, but it is significant that remnants of the Indian tribes now
exist as wards of the Federal Government in their reservations.
Some of the difference may be found in the higher degree of culture among the Indians of Mexico and Peru than among our
North American Indians. But this does not explain the whole difference in strategy. Some of the difference may be due to different
emphases in Catholic and Protestant cultures; and other differences
may be explained in terms of the weight given to ethnic feeling
in Latin and Anglo-Saxon cultures. It is sobering to observe that
race prejudice is so intimately related to Anglo-Saxon achievements in empire that, indeed, it may even be basic to its success.
Of all the Nordic peoples the Anglo-Saxons stand below only the
German Nazis and the Dutch in Africa in the consistency of their
preference for an ethnically integral community. They have of
course not developed ethnic prejudice and solidarity to the last
degree of consistency and inhumanity as the Dutch in South Africa
have, where British humaneness offers a valuable counterpoise to
Dutch intransigence in the the treatment of the Negroes. It is
also true that in New Zealand, after bloody wars with the indigenous Maoris, the dominion has succeeded in incorporating them
into the national community. It is also true that of late the
British have prepared multi-racial communities in Africa for autonomy, notably Kenya and the Union of Central Africa; but the
constitutional position of the Negroes is not secure in them. The
most hopeful experiment in nationhood under British auspices is
the former Gold Coast colony now known as Ghana. This new
nation is almost completely Negro and the tension between the
races does not complicate its youth as in the other colonies.

In America our treatment of the Negroes is based upon the
national presupposition that they will be fully incorporated into
the national community. The insistence on the Bill of Rights, with
its demand of equality before the law, dramatized by the Supreme
Court decision abolishing segregation in the schools, represents
the national will at its best in conformity with the humanitarian
and moral principles of both Christianity and the Enlightenment.

But the increasing resistence of the Southern states, where the Negro minority is large, is a witness of the real hazards of racial integration between races who are ethnically and culturally disparate; and to the fact that on the whole integral communities require ethnic homogeneity, or at least a racial situation which makes the amalgam of races fairly easy. Among the emerging nations we have yet to see how successfully the Malay States and the West Indian Federation will be able to achieve national unity and integrity despite ethnic heterogeneity. Yet Hawaii has been accepted for statehood within the American nation, despite the ethnic heterogeneity of its population.

Whatever be the achievements of Anglo-Saxon culture in race relations, they cannot obscure the difference between the Anglo-Saxon and Latin ethnic attitudes. Britain has in most instances planted purely white colonies, and if it exercised dominion over other races it gave them a just administration but offended them by racial arrogance. The French, on the other hand, ruled in Indochina and North Africa with much less ethnic feeling; but they did not invest Vietnam with sufficient capital of autonomy to make the struggle against Communism morally viable. Perhaps the weakness of the French attitude toward races and diverse cultures is most clearly revealed in Algeria, where the long-standing insistence that Algeria is a part of Metropolitan France has frustrated the national ambitions of a budding nation. The future will reveal with what success the new policies of the Fifth Republic will come to terms with this stubborn problem.

Thus a survey of the permanent and variable characteristics of national forms of imperialism, developed from the sixteenth to the nineteenth centuries reveals that the presence of the three motives, missionary, economic, and political—that is, the desire for power and glory—is a constant factor in imperialism. But the proportion between the motives and their respective success vary among the nations and in different epochs. The invariable mixture of the motives gives a certain moral ambiguity to the imperial enterprise, which may be regarded as an accentuated form of the moral ambiguity of the whole political order.

This heightened ambiguity may be obscured for a brief season by the utopian illusions which inform the communist imperialism. But in the long run the illusions will aggravate what they provisionally obscure. We must proceed to study this interesting historical phenomenon more carefully in the subsequent chapters.

CHAPTER XIII

The Utopian Basis
of Soviet Power

THE world is confronted with what seems to be an entirely unique emergence in history; a despotic and imperialist political system based upon rather implausible utopian illusions. This system of power on the foundation of utopia may, however, not be as new or unique as it seems to our generation. Our horror of the despotism and our surprise at the comparative success of this political system inclines us to merely polemical reactions, which may deter us from an impartial study of the structure of dominion in order to determine what is new and what old in the system.

To understand the nature of the Soviet achievement fully we must inquire into: the relationship of utopia to revolution, not only in modern Communism, but as we know it in modern history; the relationship of utopia to a totalitarian political organization; and the possible reasons for the technical success and the imperial dimensions of a political project with so impossible a foundation.

UTOPIANISM AND REVOLUTION

The communist system is obviously utopian. It promises *inter alia*, the "withering away of the state," even while it continually strengthens the consistency and breadth of the authority of its despotism. This utopianism is not new in human history. It is the nature of all utopianism—in the words of J. L. Talmon—to postulate "at the same time the free expression of the individual and absolute social cohesion." [1]

The promise of a fulfillment of incompatible goals, such as free-

[1] J. L. Talmon, *Utopianism and Politics*, London, Conservative Political Centre, 1958, p. 13.

dom and absolute social harmony, or of the goals promised in the French Revolution of "liberty, equality, and fraternity," is indeed the final mark of utopianism. For it always reveals blindness to the fact that liberty and harmony (or equality as a principle of ideal harmony) are not absolutely realizable in history. The self-concern of man requires that he be socially restrained; therefore, absolute liberty is not possible. Social co-ordination being dependent upon a social hierarchy, absolute equality is also impossible. In other words, the relationship of perfect liberty and perfect harmony is possible only under the condition of perfect love, and is, therefore, not in the realm of the political order.

Professor Talmon believes that utopianism "assumes the 'perfectibility of man'—a concept which arises only when the religious tradition declines, and particularly the doctrine of 'original sin.'" The Israeli historian of the French Revolution declares: "I am not concerned with the validity of this doctrine theologically, but I think that it contains an extremely important psychological truth. It stands for the terrific mystery contained in the words: '*Video Meliora proboque, deteriora sequor*'—I know and respect what is right but do what is wrong." [2] This Pauline definition of "original sin" does not define all the causes of the perennial rise of evil even in the most ideal social situations. It asserts the contradiction in man between his sense of duty and his inclination; but the tendency of a man to assume that his definition of the right is identical with an ultimate conception of justice is a more potent source of evil. The failure of utopian enthusiasts to recognize the inevitable ideological distortion in their own conceptions of justice creates their fanaticism; and fanaticism in the espousal of contradictory goals engenders chaos in the revolutionary ranks, which chaos is usually suppressed by dictatorship.

Fanaticism is, of course, not purely a revolutionary phenomenon, neither is it merely the fruit of either religion or irreligion per se. The similarity between fanaticism of the sects of the Cromwellian revolution and the fanaticism of the various rationalist sectaries

---

[2] *Ibid.*, p. 10.

of the French revolution refutes the theories both of traditional religion and of secularism, that utopianism is the result either of faith or want of faith. Religious faith or any system of philosophy may create a universe of meaning which transcends, or seems to transcend, all particular historic norms and concepts. Wherever this transcendent meaning is taken seriously a tolerant attitude is developed toward means, ends, and purposes other than our own. But all systems of meaning, whether founded in religion, philosophy, or science, more frequently tempt men to identify their norms and ends with the final meaning, thus generating fanaticism. Oliver Cromwell was quite certain that his victories represented divine validation of his cause, while the various sectaries of his armies looked for signs and portents to justify either the Presbyterian or the Leveller conception of the cause. In the French revolution a similar fanaticism was displayed through the identification of a particular political program with "Reason" or "Justice" or the "Sovereign People." The difference between Girondist and Jacobin, or the radical Paris commune and the divided convention, was similar to the difference between Parliament and Cromwell's army, and the army command of Cromwell and Ireton, on the one hand, and the radical leaders, Lilburne, Walwyn, Wildman, and Rainborough, on the other hand.[3]

The Puritan revolutionaries were all inclined to utopianism. In the words of Haller, "All still shared the sanguine expectation that if they kept straight on in their spiritual striving they could not fail to arrive at the new heaven and new earth." [4] "They were all at pains at every stage of their movement to call upon scripture, history and conscience and reason to justify everything they undertook." [5] The religious dimension of the fanaticism was particularly apparent in the appeal to "scripture." In other respects it was identical to the appeals to "reason" and to "justice" of the French revolutionaries. These similarities in the fanaticism of both the pious and the unbelievers show that fanaticism is not solely the

---

[3] See William Haller, *Liberty and Reformation in the Puritan Revolution*, New York, Columbia University Press, 1955.
[4] *Op. cit.*, p. 299.   [5] Haller, *ibid.*, p. 327.

fruit either of religious belief or of scepticism. It is the consequence of man's incapacity to know or to acknowledge the limited and interested character of his conception of the right.

Both fanaticism and utopianism increase in revolutionary situations particularly for two reasons: first, traditional cultures moderate the demands which men make upon life by custom and habit of the ages. No situation in history represents a perfectly just solution of the claims and counter claims of men in a community. Men do not usually challenge the solution, either because they do not realize the depth of the injustice or because they are hopeless about the possibility of altering the social situation. But in a revolutionary era, as in England in the seventeenth century, in France in the eighteenth century, and Russia in the twentieth century, customary solutions and adjustments are destroyed and every traditional answer is challenged. In consequence contradictory utopian solutions arise which are not modified by experience, and produce the confusion of aims and of parties as shown in the Cromwellian army and in the French revolution. Secondly, gradations of authority by which every community is organized politically or socially, and which are justified by their function of co-ordination, are always involved in unjustified privileges and excesses of power. In a revolutionary era these excesses are resented, or rather, the resentments piled up in traditional ages, erupt violently. Therefore, the function of communal integration of these hierarchies is obscured. Liberty and equality are regarded as simple possibilities and the contradiction between them is obscured. In the case of communist theory a most implausible utopia is constructed which promises liberty as a final fruit of equality through collectivism. The Soviet state organizes itself, as all states must, through a hierarchy of authority, but these hierarchies are the more extravagant because "the dictatorship of the proletariat" (that is, of the party) creates a monopoly of power.

In the Cromwellian revolution the army commanders, Cromwell, Ireton, and Fairfax, were naturally aware of the necessity of political and military co-ordination through a hierarchy of authority; and they also believed that property was an instrument of social peace. But the sectaries in the army had various utopian ideas, sometimes contradictory to each other. The Levellers and Lilburne wanted liberty, while the "Diggers," under the leadership of Gerrard Winstanley, were pre-communist equalitarians who believed that "once the earth was again made a common treasury" all social and political discord would be eliminated.

In the French revolution the competition is between the moderate Girondists and the Jacobins, between the convention and the Paris commune. Babeuf, the radical egalitarian, draws the ultimate conclusions from Rousseau's doctrine, as mediated by the "incorruptible Robespierre." The instrument of equality for him was, of course, Communism. The fact was that the social situation was too confused and there were too many in the revolutionary classes who had some stake in inequality—including the inequality created by property—to make the prospects of success for consistent Communism at all hopeful. The French revolution was, after all, bourgeois. The communist utopianism of Babeuf was destroyed despite, or because of, its intimate logical connection with the thought of Rousseau. One of his disciples, Buonarotti, stated the utopian dream in its most consistent form: "The peoples are advancing toward that goal—equality—the sole institution able to satisfy all our needs, direct our useful passions, to chain the dangerous ones and give society a regime, free, happy, useful and stable. I shall not see it for sure. Let it suffice that I have kept my faith alive and unaltered and that no one can accuse me of inconsistency." [6]

Consistency is of course the primary character of the utopian conviction. Unconscious of the necessity of the morally ambiguous instruments of social integration the utopian consistently projects either the one or the other moral ideals of pure justice, either liberty or equality, each of which, if consistently followed, would destroy the order of society. In a revolutionary era the conflict between the consistent and contradictory ideas destroy the revolu-

---

[6] Quoted from: J. L. Talmon, *The Rise of Totalitarian Democracy*, New York, Beacon Press, 1952, p. 178. (Talmon's volume is one of the most perceptive analyses of relationship of utopianism and totalitarianism.)

tion instead of guaranteeing, "a free, happy and stable society" of Babeuf's vision, the commune sought to enforce equality by terror and the experiment ended in failure to the tremendous relief of the nation.

Talmon's excellent survey of the French revolutionary messianism perhaps may be responsible for his conviction, previously quoted, that utopianism is the fruit of the secularization of culture; for the French revolutionaries were undoubtedly secularized idealists, as are also the communists. Nevertheless, it is not persuasive to derive utopianism merely from the secularized idea of the "perfectibility of man." A comparison between the Cromwellian and the French revolutions prompts this scepticism. The Cromwellian revolution was utopian in religious terms. It transmuted Christian eschatology into utopian visions. Cromwell could mix the "grace" which he experienced as an individual in the most baffling manner with the "grace" that God had vouchsafed in his military victories and which he regarded as proof of divine favor. He was so impressed with this favor that he could compare this "grace" triumphantly with the traditional "grace" which the king had as legitimate ruler.

The Cromwellian appeals to divine "grace," to providence, and to Scripture for authority did not differ markedly from the French appeals to "reason," to "justice," and to the idea of progress, the latter being a secularized version of the idea of providence. In both cases historical destiny and success were used to validate the ideal of the revolutionary utopia.

There was not even too much difference between the secular belief in "man's perfectibility" and the Puritan idea of sin or of "original sin." For the Puritan sectaries conveniently subordinated the idea of the "fall of Adam" which implies universal corruption, to the Biblical story of Cain and Abel. This gave them the chance to make a rigorous distinction between the righteous poor and the unrighteous rich. The distinction was as absolute as the later Marxist distinction between the bourgeoisie and the proletariat. It was, of course, to the poor that the "promise of Christ" was made, according to the "Fifth Monarchy men," who were the explicit apocalypticists of the Cromwellian army. It is Christ's pleasure to "give His Kingdom to the poor," declared a Puritan tract.[7]

If there was a difference between religious and secularized utopianism it consisted in the fact that the religiously inspired utopianism was always a little unclear whether the destiny of the poor was to build a more perfect church or a more perfect commonwealth, and whether the virtue of the poor was merely "existential," that is, guaranteed by their poverty, or whether poverty was one of the conditions under which the righteousness of Christ would develop. The secular position from the French Communists to the Russian revolution was to declare unambiguously the poor "existentially" righteous. As Lenin would have it, the proletariat is the only class endowed with courage and integrity. The righteous class in communist mythology of course is limited to the industrial poor. The poor peasants are not in it because, in Trotsky's phrase, they are "Janus-faced" because their love for their own soil prompts them to be less than consistent advocates of collectivism.

Utopianism, whether of the secular or religious variety, misinterprets one and obscures the other of the two dimensions of human existence. The first dimension, which it misinterprets, arises from the vision of a perfect individual or collective virtue. Men always transcend any given social situation enough to imagine a more perfect one, even to a degree which exceeds the possibilities of history. Utopianism misinterprets this transcendent vision as a simple historical possibility.

The other dimension is created by the persistence and power of man's self-regard. Significantly the instruments of social justice intended to establish a tolerable harmony within the conditions set by the expansive desires of men, accentuate, as well as mitigate, injustice; for both property and government easily may become instruments of injustice. We have sought in a previous chapter (Chapter VI) to show that ideally the Christian faith does justice

<hr>

[7] "Glimpse of Zion's Glory," quoted in Haller *The Rise of Puritanism*, New York, Columbia University Press, 1938, p. 271.

to both of the two dimensions. The figure of Christ is an expression of the validity of the first dimension. Christ is also the expression of the final answer of divine mercy for the perplexities and frustrations in the second dimension. But the truth expressed in these religious symbols is created not by a particular faith but by the human situation. It is validated therefore not by a dogma but by historical experience.

Utopian misconceptions of this situation lead to some very ironic consequences. The pretension of having achieved a more ideal virtue or social harmony than is possible for self-seeking men can be as productive of the abuses of an irresponsible power, as the very evils against which the utopians are in revolt. Thus the utopian pretension of disinterested virtue is merely another form of the human corruption of an ultimate vision. The pretensions of monarchs are the more traditional form of this same corruption.

Marxist utopianism is obviously related historically to the Jacobin utopianism of the French revolution. It also has affinities with the Utopianism of Cromwellian England. The later Marxist became belatedly aware of this affinity.[8] The religious, or partly religious and partly secular, forerunners of Marxism in Russia in the Russian populist movement of the late nineteenth century, which was characterized by a sentimental appreciation of the poor and therefore innocent peasants, were a bridge from the sectarian radicalism of the religious sect, "the old believers," to Plekhanov, the colleague and early collaborator of Lenin.[9]

Revolutionary utopianism thus may be regarded as an eruption of the idealism and the resentments of the poor or of the victims of injustice in a decaying society. These resentments against traditional injustice inevitably obscure the necessity of the restraints and balances which justify the traditional means of social peace, in spite of their corruptions.

The corruptions, therefore, reappear in the heaven on earth of

---

[8] See Eduard Bernstein, *Cromwell and Communism*. London, Allen and Unwin Ltd., 1930.

[9] See James H. Billington, *Mikhailovsky and Russian Populism*, particularly the chapter on "Vision of True Christianity." Oxford, Clarendon Press, 1958.

the utopians, frequently in aggravated form, because the perennial root of injustice is not understood by the utopians.

THE RELATIONSHIP BETWEEN UTOPIANISM AND DICTATORSHIP

As we have noted, the three revolutions in England, France, and Russia which were all accompanied by utopian illusion also all ended in dictatorships. They also gave rise to expansive imperial ventures, though in the case of Cromwell the expansive venture was limited to Ireland.

We must postpone for a moment an inquiry into the relation of utopianism to imperialism in order to study the relation of utopia to dictatorship more carefully. A simple correlation between utopia and despotism is ruled out by the fact that of the three revolutions touched by utopianism only the communist dictatorship was designed. And it alone was not a military dictatorship.

The Cromwellian and French revolutions ended in the dictatorship of Cromwell and Napoleon because there was literally no other way of bringing order in the state. The tensions between various parties, fanatically dedicated to contrasting utopian schemes—which may or may not have embodied parts of the many-sided truth about the relation of equality to justice, and of dominion to community—brought the threat of anarchy. In the case of England the army was originally recruited to fight for parliament against the king. But there was not only tension between the bourgeois parliament and the more radical army, but there was tension within the army itself. The Putney debates, designed as a kind of constitutional convention for the new England, did not resolve the army difference, and Cromwell found it convenient to order the debaters to return to their regiments. Military discipline thus snuffed out democracy in the army, even as the army power had annulled the freedom of parliament. In short, the absence of either a traditional or democratic accommodation of conflicting viewpoints made the military dictatorship necessary, though nothing in the utopian creeds of the contending parties anticipated such a development.

The story of Jacobin fanaticism, and of democratic confusion, leading to Napoleon's coup d'état is well known. France, weary of chaos and intrigued by the ambitious army commander with several victories to his credit, submitted to the government in which Napoleon was the "First Consul." He ultimately proclaimed himself "Emperor." Again dictatorship was not the consequence of utopianism but the fruit of the discord between competitive utopian schemes.

Obviously the communist case is in a different category for its dictatorship was anticipated in the utopian dogma. But the dogma alone would not have guaranteed the dictatorship if the communist fanaticism had not been triumphant in Russia against other utopian fanaticisms, because the social forces supporting them were too weak to challenge the communist power.

The success of the communist dictatorship rests upon many contingent factors which make nonsense of the Hegelian-Marxist conceptions of a "logic of history." Perhaps the most interesting of these contingencies is the character of Lenin himself. Marx was, of course, a utopian revolutionist, but his vague ideas of a "dictatorship of the proletariat" in opposition to what he conceived to be the "dictatorship of the bourgeoisie"—notions drawn from experiences of the commune in the French revolution— would have been politically irrelevant but for Lenin's adaptations and amendments. It was Lenin's genius to combine naïve utopianism with a shrewd and cynical concern for power and to compound absolute fanaticism with tactical flexibility.

Lenin was as utopian as Marx; his vision of the process of the "withering away of the state" was a naïve projection of the eighteenth century utopianism. In his *State and Revolution*, he presents the vision in these terms:

> Only in Communist society, when the resistance of the capitalists have disappeared, when there are no classes (i.e. there is no difference between the members of society in their relation to the social means of production) *only then* 'the State ceases to exist,' and 'it becomes possible to speak of freedom.' Only then will democracy itself begin to wither away due to the simple fact

that, freed from capitalist slavery, from the untold horrors, sav-
agery, absurdities and infamies of capitalist exploitation, people
will gradually become accustomed to the observation of the ele-
mentary rules of social life that have been known for centuries
and repeated for thousands of years in all school books; they will
become accustomed to observing them without force, without
compulsion, without subordination, without the special apparatus
for compulsion which is called the State.

The expression, 'the State withers away,' is very well chosen,
for it indicates both the gradual and the elemental nature of the
process. Only habit can, and undoubtedly will, have such an
effect; for we see around us millions of times how readily people
get accustomed to observe the necessary rules of life in common,
if there is no exploitation, if there is nothing that causes indigna-
tion, that calls forth protest and revolt and has to be suppressed.[10]

It is this anarchistic pinnacle on top of the collectivist structure
of utopia which makes the Leninist dream at once so implausible
and so attractive to the victims of injustice. It provides the ideological basis for the power system which has developed in the
communist world. If we remember that power is never merely
force but always a combination of force and prestige it must become apparent that the ideological framework for the communist power structure has some striking similarities with—as well
as differences from—the traditional power structures which are
maintained through the millennia of human history. In these the
gradations of authority and the centralization of power in government were presented as consonant with the cosmic order as
enjoined by the divine will.

The traditional ideological framework was relatively effective
until social discontents and resentments piled up in periods of
great social change. In these periods of change any identification
of the social order with the unchanging cosmic order became very
implausible; and the moral and religious justification for the
necessary, but morally ambiguous, social gradations and restraints
became odious. What could be more plausible than a revolution-

[10] N. Lenin, *The State and Revolution*. Ch. V. First published early 1918.
English edition, Martin Lawrence Ltd., 1934.

ary creed in which the social order is declared to be in direct contradiction to the essential nature of man and in which the vision
of a radical overturn is held out?

The basis for this ideological system was laid by Marx's utopianism, and, for that matter, by all the utopians of the seventeenth
and eighteenth centuries who preceded him. But it was Lenin's
achievement to transmute this utopian scheme into a structure of
power in which utopia furnished the prestige which force cannot
furnish. Lenin did this very simply by translating the "dictatorship of the proletariat" into the dictatorship of the party and making the party, the "vanguard" of the proletarian class, into a tight-
knit group of dedicated revolutionists. The worker would, if un-
aided, be incapable of rising above a "trade union psychology" in
Lenin's opinion. He would be content, in other words, with
proximate goals, and would not be privy to the "logic of history"
which, if nudged at the proper points, would give him and all
men redemption not only from all injustice but from the "realm
of necessity to the realm of freedom." The phrase is Engels', and
it proves that he mistook the freedom of the self-appointed masters of historical destiny for the freedom of man.

Thus Lenin took the fateful, and politically necessary but
morally catastrophic, step of changing the dictatorship of a class
to the dictatorship of the party. The party was the "New Class,"
which in theory had a monopoly of power, since all remnants of
the community which opposed it were but remnants of the capitalistic class and had to be liquidated. The absolute fanaticism,
joined with the absolute utopianism, eliminated all grades and
shades of interest and opinion, so that those who opposed Stalin's
enforced collectivization program were merely defined as "Kulaks,"
that is, rich peasants, and were marked for "liquidation."

The theory of Communism allowed for one more step in the
hierarchy of authority, historically so inevitable and yet so contradictory to any utopian scheme. The party was governed by a
"central committee" and it must be conceded that the authority
of this central committee, the organ of "democratic centralism,"
which was only acknowledged in theory in Stalin's despotism,
nevertheless established a tradition which has been successfully

revived in the post-Stalin era and offers some hope for the decentralization of authority in the communist power system.

But naturally the central committee was too large to act as an organ of government once the revolution was successful. The next step in building the inevitable hierarchy was not consciously contrived but took place under the pressure of events. Barrington Moore describes these pressures as follows:

> Because of this, just before the November Revolution on October 23, 1917, a small nucleus was created with the Party Central Committee at the suggestion of Dzerzhinsky, later chief of the secret police. The original members were Lenin, Zinoviev, Kamenev, Trotsky, Stalin, Sokol'nikov and Bubnov. The main task envisaged at this time appears to have been little more than the management of the details of the November uprising. Nevertheless, the idea of concentrating decision-making powers in the hands of a very few leaders persisted, owing to the continuing need for immediate and far-reaching decisions in the crises directly following the Revolution. By March 1919 the Eighth Party Congress set up, as a permanently acting body, a Political Bureau consisting of five members, who were "to decide on questions which do not permit delay" and to report bimonthly on all its work to a regular plenary session of the Central Committee. At that time the Politburo consisted of Lenin, Trotsky, Stalin, Kamenev and Bukharin. At no time during the period from 1919 to 1946 did the membership of the Politburo, including candidates, exceed seventeen individuals.
>
> Although originally this elite within an elite was theoretically established to decide upon political questions of an urgent nature, after its first year of existence its range of authority had increased enormously. Lenin, in a report of the Central Committee to the Ninth Party Congress in 1920, stated that not only had the Politburo "decided all questions on international and domestic politics" but that "any question at all could be considered a political question, upon the request of a single member of the Central Committee" to the Politburo, its functions (together with those allocated to the Plenum of the Central Committee, a larger body to which the Politburo was theoretically responsible) covered almost the entire scope of political, economic, social and cultural problems in Soviet life.[11]

[11] Barrington Moore, Jr., *Soviet Politics—The Dilemma of Power*, Cambridge, Harvard University Press, 1950, p. 141.

The contradiction between the original equalitarianism and the gradations of power in such a system—naturally more severe than in any traditional system, either capitalistic or feudal—has been a source of embarrassment to Communism. It could only be justified by constant references to the original dogma, which attributed inequality to property and postponed the "withering away of the State" to the day when all the enemies of the new order would be eliminated. Stalin, in his report to the Seventeenth Party Congress in 1934, presents the rationalization in this way:

> The Party is the highest form of organization of the proletariat. The Party is the fundamental leading element within the class of the proletariat and within the organization of that class. But it does not follow by any means that the Party can be regarded as an end in itself, as a self-sufficing force. The Party is not only the highest form of class association of the proletarians; it is at the same time a weapon in the hands of the proletariat for the achievement of the dictatorship where that has not been achieved; for the consolidation and extension of the dictatorship where it has already been achieved. The Party would not rank so high in importance and it could not overshadow all other forms of organization of the proletariat if the latter were not face to face with the question of power, if the conditions of imperialism, the inevitability of wars and the presence of crisis did not demand the concentration of all the forces of the proletariat on one point and the gathering together of all the threads of the revolutionary movement in one spot, to overthrow the bourgeoisie and to establish the dictatorship of the proletariat. The proletariat needs the Party first of all as its General Staff, which it must have for the successful seizure of power. Needless to say, the Russian proletariat could never have established its revolutionary dictatorship without a Party capable of rallying around itself the mass organizations of the proletariat and of centralizing the leadership of the entire movement during the progress of the struggle.
>
> But the proletariat needs the Party not only to achieve the dictatorship, it needs it still more to maintain, consolidate and extend its dictatorship in order to attain complete victory for socialism.[12]

[12] Stalin's Report to Seventeenth Party Congress in 1934.

Five years later, at the Eighteenth Party Congress in 1939, he placed the emphasis upon "capitalistic encirclement" in international terms. The rationalization was obviously prompted by the experience of the war but the explanation hardly justifies the excessive internal monopoly of power which the organs of the party had achieved. Stalin offered this justification for the suppression of both liberty and equality:

Since the October Revolution, our socialist state has passed through two main phases in its development.

The first phase was the period from the October Revolution to the elimination of the exploiting classes. The principal task in that period was to suppress the resistance of the overthrown classes, to organize the defense of the country against the attack of the interventionists, to restore industry and agriculture, and to prepare the conditions for the elimination of the capitalist elements. Accordingly, in this period our state performed two main functions. The first function was to suppress the overthrown classes inside the country...The second function was the work of economic organization and cultural education performed by our state bodies with the purpose of developing the infant shoots of the new, socialist economic system and re-educating the people in the spirit of socialism. But this new function did not attain to any considerable development in that period.

The second phase was the period from the elimination of the capitalist elements in town and country to the complete victory of the socialist economic system and the adoption of the new Constitution. The principal task in this period was to establish the socialist economic system all over the country and to eliminate the last remnants of the capitalist elements, to bring about a cultural revolution, and to form a thoroughly modern army for the defense of the country. And the functions of our socialist state changed accordingly. The function of military suppression inside the country ceased, died away; for exploitation had been abolished, there were no more exploiters left, and so there was no one to suppress. In place of this function of suppression, the state acquired the function of protecting socialist property from thieves and pilferers of the people's property. The function of defending the country from foreign attack fully remained; consequently, the Red Army and the Navy also fully remained, as did the punitive organs and the intelligence service, which are indispensable for the detection and punishment of the spies, assassins and wreckers sent into our country by foreign espionage services. The function of economic organization and cultural education by the state organs also remained, and was developed to the full . . .

As you see, we now have an entirely new, socialist state, without precedent in history and differing considerably in form and functions from the socialist state of the first phase.

But development cannot stop there. We are going ahead, towards communism. Will our state remain in the period of communism also?

Yes, *it will*, unless the capitalist encirclement is liquidated, and unless the danger of foreign military attack has disappeared. Naturally, of course, the forms of our state will again change in conformity with the change in the situation at home and abroad.

No, it will not remain and will atrophy if the capitalist encirclement is liquidated and a socialist encirclement takes its place.

That is how the question stands with regard to the socialist state.[13]

Meanwhile, Soviet despotism developed in breadth and consistency from year to year, and what Djilas defines as the "New Class" developed. It had the power to manage "collective property" and its power was more unchallenged than that of any previous dominant class. Djilas describes the logic of Communist totalitarianism as follows:

The Communist theory of the state, a theory worked out in detail by Lenin and supplemented by Stalin and others, favors the totalitarian dictatorship of the party bureaucracy. Two elements are fundamental in the theory: The theory of the state alone and the theory of the withering away of the state. Both of these elements are mutually related and together represent the entire theory. Lenin's theory of the state is most completely presented in his document *The State and Revolution*, which was written while he was hiding from the Provisional Government on the eve of the October Revolution. Like everything else of Lenin's the theory leans toward the revolutionary aspects of

---

[13] From his report to the Eighteenth Congress of the Communist Party of the Soviet Union—Stalin, in 1939.

Marxist teaching. In his discussion of the state Lenin developed this aspect further and carried it to extremes, utilizing particularly the experience of the Russian Revolution of 1905. Considered historically, Lenin's document was of much greater significance as an ideological weapon of the revolution than it was as a base for development of a new authority built according to its ideas.

Lenin reduced the state to force, or more precisely, to the organ of tyranny which one class employs for the sake of oppressing the other classes. Trying to formulate the nature of the State in the most forceful way, Lenin noted, "The State is a club."

Lenin perceived other functions of the State too. But in these functions he also uncovered what was for him the most indispensable role of the State—the use of brute force by one class against the others.[14]

These developments must prompt the student of the political order to question Ferrero's definition of legitimate and illegitimate government, which placed the traditional governments in the category of legitimate government because they governed by implicit consent rather than by force and fraud.[15] The question is whether there is not a subjective element in the concept of "fraud" both in traditional and in revolutionary governments. And force must be used to prevent the inspection and the discovery of the fraud. Thus communist tyranny, even more than traditional governments, must use force to cover up the defects of its ideology. The years and experience prove the incompatibility between the utopian vision and the necessities of a community even under a revolutionary government.

It is surely significant that of all the revolutionary governments from the Cromwellian revolution to the communist one, only the communist dictatorship did not result in a military dictatorship, which we have previously attributed to the necessity of maintaining order in the ideological and political confusion of the revolution. Only in Communism has a political party been able to sub-

[14] Djilas, The New Class, New York, Frederick A. Praeger, 1957, pp. 83–84.
[15] See Guglielmo Ferrero, Principles of Power, New York, G. P. Putnam's Sons, 1942.

ordinate the army to the party (and has proved its continued dominance over the military as late as the demotion of Zhukov by Khrushchev). It has been able to do this not because its ideological system was so impressive but because it had been able to establish a monopoly for the system from the beginning through the rigor of its fanaticism and the weakness of any social forces which might have challenged it. But the subordination of the military did not obviate the necessity of force. The more that experience proved the ideological foundations of the system to be fraudulent the more force had to be used to proscribe inspection of the pretensions of the oligarchy. This force used in Stalin's day was not provided by the military but by the police. But the post-Stalin "Thaw" permitted so many people to raise questions which could not be answered satisfactorily that the post-Stalin oligarchy has significantly returned to some, though not all, features of Stalinist repression, even though this return embarrassed all its claims of moral legitimacy. Obviously there is a more intricate relation between force and fraud than Ferrero assumed. It is also obvious that "Fraud" may begin as an honest utopian dream, as in Marx, then become a political tool, as in Lenin, and end in pure fraud, as in Stalin. As this fraud is discovered, or as history transmutes the dream into a nightmare, more force is necessary to protect the ideological basis of the system.

One of the elements of real promise in the present situation is that a power system based upon utopian illusions is discovered more and more to be fraudulent, the further the revolution recedes into the past, and as greater force is needed to prevent the inspection of the fraud.

Bourgeois democracy is rightly regarded in the West as the best form of government because it checks every center of power, and grants no immunity to any form of prestige. The early democratic idealists had utopian illusions similar to those of the Marxists. They thought, for instance, that "reason" would eliminate fraud and therefore the need of force in government. Reason did not eliminate fraud as simply as they anticipated; and force remained a necessary instrument of government. Yet their theories were validated ultimately because force remained a minimal instrument of government, for the pretensions of any particular government could be challenged in the open society which they created, so that confidence that the government would establish justice was not destroyed.

Bourgeois democracy is, therefore, in a more impregnable position, not only in the West but in the world, than are the bourgeois interests which first gave birth to it. But for the time being, the western type of democracy must expect to lose many encounters in the dark continents because its fluid equilibria require a technical civilization, which is beyond the present competence of nations recently introduced to an industrial civilization; and because its high and sometimes extravagant living standards (those of our own nation particularly) will seem vulgar to nations who are anxious to escape the most abject forms of poverty and of injustice prevalent in pre-industrial societies. We must not expect a rapid triumph over these moral and political hazards of democracy.

But in the long run, the form of government which had its inception in the revolt of western middle classes against the aristocratic and feudal forms of agrarian civilizations can achieve a moral validity beyond the peculiar conditions which gave it birth. It can do this for many reasons but chiefly because it is not under the necessity of proving that the morally ambiguous instruments of social cohesion and social co-ordination: government, property, and social hierarchy are either in accordance with a cosmic or divine order, as the traditional ideology of government asserted, or are in the process of disappearing on the other side of a revolution, as the revolutionary ideology asserts. Every year on the other side of the revolution adds to the refutation of the revolutionary ideology, as is apparent in the embarrassments of communist ideology as it faces either the advanced technical civilizations of the West or the growing technical civilizations of the East.

The embarrassment is mitigated to some extent by the fact that there is a measure of democracy in the Soviet oligarchic system through the power of the central committee as the final court of

appeals. It is significant that Khrushchev, who for the moment
seems to have the undisputed dominance in the Soviet hierarchy
of power, found it necessary and possible to appeal from the apex
of the pyramid of power, the "presidium," to the central committee, which supported him against the adverse majority in the
presidium. He has since been able to pack the presidium with his
cohorts, thus proving the limits of the democratic principle in the
Soviet system. But the fact of his appeal to the central committee
and the fact that the Polish leader, Gomulka, came to power in
Poland against Russian pressure because the Polish central committee gave him the victory over the Stalinists, proves that the
central committees of communist parties may be in a category
analogous to the Whig aristocracy in the House of Commons
and Lords in the eighteenth century. There is a bare possibility of
the extension of freedom through rivalry between the various oligarchies in the Soviet system and through their theoretic subordination to the "plenum" of the central committee.

The Soviet oligarchic tyranny contains one other aspect of an
"open society" which, in the polemical tension of the present, we
may have not appreciated properly and thus we may have obscured one of the possible avenues of escape from the rigor of the
dogmatism and absolutism which we have been fated to encounter.
First, the system allows a certain opportunity in education, giving bright children the possibility of education through scholar-
ships. We have suddenly discovered their system of education to
be in some respects superior to our own. This is an aspect of Russian Communism which differs radically from traditional des-
potisms and which cannot be annulled because the system requires technical competence for pursuing its goal of increased
industrialization, thus realizing Lenin's definition of the promise
of Communism: "The Soviets plus electricity."

The other aspect which holds promise of a more open society,
is closely related to the democratic features of the educational
process. It is the reliance of the regime upon the expert in general
and upon the physical scientist in particular. The recent achievements of the Soviets in the field of guided missiles and earth

satellites have suddenly disclosed to the complacent western world the fact that tyranny is not incompatible with the creation of a technically competent class, and that this revolutionary tyranny has the ambition and will to acquire the competence to transmute an agrarian order into an industrial one.

The hopes that this technical competence implies a rational achievement which is finally subversive in a despotic regime are probably too sanguine, for it is possible to harness non-political skills to political ends; but the "New Class," which is not exactly identical with the political oligarchies but which has achieved a significant position in the communist hierarchy, may ultimately provide the leaven for the lump of despotism. Leopold Labedz in an excellent survey of Soviet science in an article, "How Free is Soviet Science" comes to this circumspect conclusion:

> As a rule, the closer the subject is to sensitive ideological points, the smaller its chance of unfettered development. In this respect physics appears to be situated fairly far from the magnetic pole, while genetics and psychology are much closer, and sociology is almost on top of it. The hard core of the dogma is sensitive to independent research in these latter fields. While in medieval times Catholic theology was especially touchy about the finding of natural science which seemed to contradict its view of the universe, Communist ideology is particularly vulnerable to critical findings about social structure and development. Since it pretends to be *the* science of society, Soviet Marxism cannot be basically modified without undermining the position of its guardians.[16]

One may not expect natural scientists and engineers to risk their privileged position for the sake of challenging the ideological foundations of the communist system. Intelligence per se is not as politically subversive as the past centuries believed. It is, nevertheless, apparent that there are dynamic factors in the Soviet system of power and culture which may lead to the same consequences as the dynamic factors in the culture of the West in the seventeenth to the nineteenth century.

[16] Leopold Labedz, "How Free is Soviet Science?" *Commentary*, Vol. XXV, No. 6, June 1958, published by the American Jewish Committee, New York, N. Y.

In short, after four decades of communist success in obscuring the hiatus between utopia and reality, we are still uncertain whether those aspects of the system which do not correspond to the traditional pattern of despotism may gradually change the system, or whether the "New Class" will in desperation use more force to obscure the realities of history which stand in contradiction to the utopian illusions upon which the system is founded. Every turn of the screw of force will, of course, accentuate the contradiction.

The future of mankind may depend upon which tendency will ultimately prevail. Since the tendency to obscure the realities obviously prevails at the moment, and the more obviously since the post-Stalin leadership has been forced to re-institute a policy which it had ostensibly abandoned, we can only hope that the present dominant policy will not create havoc in the whole world before time has a chance to leaven the lump of despotism by giving internal forces of the leavening process the chance to do what was accomplished in the West from the sixteenth to the nineteenth century.

CHAPTER XIV

Communist Universalism and Imperialism

Our consideration of the relation of revolution to utopia and of utopia to despotism, particularly in the communist dogma and history, has not included, for reasons which will become apparent, the universalist elements in the utopian scheme and the relation of this universalism to modern communist imperialism. The communist system denies the necessities of inequality and produces a despotism which annuls both liberty and equality in its search for equality. But inevitably utopia also denies or obscures the perennial character of particular communities and promises instead a universal community which would include all mankind. Inevitably, too, this universalism becomes the instrument of an imperialism in which a particular power in history seeks to dominate all communities in the name of its pseudo-universal community. We have had previous opportunity to note the relation of universalism to imperialism in traditional societies, beginning with Rome and ending in the three medieval empires. In these traditional communities the claim of universality was drawn from a religious faith which was thought to reveal the very nature of the universe or its divine governance. But always there was a particular agent of this universally valid principle of community, whether it be the classical Rome of Cicero's imagination or the Byzantine sacerdotal state or the western Papacy or the western empire, founded by the Frankish kings, or the Arab and Turkish nations who provided the core of power for the Islamic Empire, with its universal pretensions.

Marxist universalism is distinguished from this type of traditional universalism as its utopianism is distinguished from traditional ideology. It does not deny the fact of particular communities. It is conscious of the realities of nationhood. But it projects an ideal international community in which the rivalry between nations will be abolished because that rivalry is ascribed purely to economic causes. Both internal and international friction are ascribed to greed and greed is attributed purely to property ownership. By this double error all power impulses in individuals and groups are attributed to one source. Therefore, the socialization of property is expected to guarantee not only a classless national community but also a harmonious international community.

In one strand of the Marxist theory capitalism is regarded as the very climax of imperialism, making the middle classes—the "bourgeoisie"—the devils in the class struggle. There was another strand of Marxist theory, according to which the capitalistic revolution was not the climax of nationalistic imperialism but the beginning of internationalism. Thus Marx and Engels wrote:

> National differences and antagonisms between peoples are already tending to disappear more and more, owing to the development of the bourgeoisie, the growth of free trade and a world market, and in the increasing uniformity of the industrial processes and of the corresponding conditions of life. The rule of the proletariat will efface these differences and antagonisms even more.[1]

While Marx, and after him all the Marxists, underestimated the power of national loyalties and assumed that the class loyalty of the industrial workers would transcend all other loyalties, he was by no means blind to the persistence of national sentiments in life. At a communist meeting Marx poked fun at a French speaker who assumed that nations would be dissolved into little communes. He reports the encounter as follows:

> The English laughed very much when I began my speech by saying that our friend LaFargue, who had done away with nationalities, had spoken French, a language which nine-tenths of his audience did not understand. I also said that by the negation of nationali-

---

[1] Karl Marx and F. Engels, *Communist Manifesto*.

ties, he appeared, quite unconsciously to understand their absorption into the French nation.[2]

Marx's preoccupation with the economic factor prevented him from being a proponent of the "self-determination of nations." For whether nations were capable of independence depended in his mind on the advancement and cohesion of their industrial process. This reservation was not heeded by either later Marxists or liberals who have made national independence into an absolute value. His preoccupation with industrial and economic factors also made him more complacent toward imperialism than the Leninists. "What we call history," he wrote, "is but the history of successive intruders who founded empires on the passive basis of unresisting and unchanging societies." "Weakness and backwardness" predestined India to conquest and the "question was not whether the English had a right to conquer her," but "whether we are to prefer India conquered by the Turk, the Persian or by the Russian, to India conquered by the British." [3] This note of realism is lost in later Marxist polemics.

It is clear that Marx, who contributed to Soviet despotism only the vague idea of a "dictatorship of the proletariat," which Lenin transformed into the dictatorship of a party of trained revolutionists, contributed even less specific ideas to the development of Soviet imperialism. His contribution was the even more vague utopian idea of an ideal international order in which nations would live in peace with one another, because the "exploitation of man by man" being abolished within the nations, the exploitation of nation by nation would also disappear. Marx, who held Russia in contempt as a backward nation, would have been surprised at the use to which his ideas were put in establishing the Russian hegemony over the "socialist" nations. His contribution was the new form of utopian universalism which was important in a day when the universalisms which had existed in traditional cultures

[2] Quoted from Soloman F. Bloom, *The World of Nations*—A Study of the National Implications in the Work of Karl Marx, p. 29. New York, Columbia University Press, 1940.
[3] Bloom, *ibid.*, p. 51.

had no appeal. Confidence in an "essential" structure of the community had disappeared and so had the religious eschatology, which assumed the completion of the meaning of human existence and the correction of injustice in an ideal community transcending all the possibilities of history.

The loom of history chooses the most disparate and seemingly incompatible ideas and events to weave its pattern of destiny. There is some "logic" in this choice, but not the neat logic which Hegel assumed when he asserted that the "cunning of reason" brought interest and passion under control. The logic of history is steeped in irony. It was "logical" that modern culture would respond only to a this-worldly, and not other-worldly, projection of a communal idea. Modern culture rightly did not believe that "essences" were waiting to be realized in history. It believed that the ideal community would be established when the primary causes of evil were removed. For liberalism that cause was monarchical absolutism. For Marx it was the institution of property. Thus, he merely contributed to the structure of communist imperialism the vision of an ideal universal community from which the only cause of disharmony had been removed. He certainly would have been as surprised by the use which Russian power made of this universalism as Augustine would have been surprised by the use which was made of his conception of the "City of God" by the Cluniac monk, Hildebrand, who ruled as Pope Gregory VII and quoted Augustine to justify the power and prestige of the medieval Papacy. Since authority in nation and empire is always compounded of prestige and force, and since prestige always depends upon an ideological framework, it is inevitable that a dominant community should acquire for its prestige whatever ideological framework is most serviceable for its pretensions.

Even Lenin, who had transmuted the Marxist vision of dictatorship to make it politically relevant and dangerous, could not be accused of being the conscious agent of relating Marxist universalism to communist Russian imperialism. Lenin signed the draconic treaty of Brest-Litovsk because he had the illusion that a revolution would break out in Germany which would correct it. Nor was there much evidence of the ambitions of Russian imperialism when the treaty of Rapallo was signed. The first evidence of the dominance of Russian power in this ideal universal community developed in the relation of the Russian party to the other communist parties of the world through the "Comintern." This development does not yet indicate the flowering of Soviet imperialism for most of these parties had no power in their respective nations. The capstone was placed upon the imperial structure when the Russians, after the Second World War, could use their captive parties as instruments of government in the nations of Eastern Europe which the war had brought under their control; the Red army was, of course, an added and necessary instrument of force.

If there was a conscious agent of the transformation of Marxist universalism into communist Russian imperialism it was not Lenin, but Stalin who was prompted by the growth of Russian power and the ideological prestige of the Communist Party in Russia to give this curious but plausible account of the way in which Russian power supports, and is in turn supported by, the "working classes" of the world. This interpretation was given before the Second World War, that is, to the Seventeenth Party Congress in 1934:

> The working class of the U.S.S.R. is strong, not only because it has a Leninist Party that has been tried in battle; it is strong not only because it enjoys the support of millions of toiling peasants; it is strong also because it is supported and assisted by the world proletariat. The working class of the U.S.S.R. is part of the world proletariat, its vanguard; and our republic is the offspring of the world proletariat. There can be no doubt that if it had not been supported by the working class in the capitalist countries it would not have been able to retain power, it would not have secured for itself the conditions for socialist construction, and hence it would not have achieved the successes that it did achieve. International ties between the working class of the U.S.S.R. and the workers of the capitalist countries, the fraternal alliance between the workers of the U.S.S.R. and the workers of all countries—this is one of the cornerstones of the strength and might

of the Republic of Soviets. The workers in the West say that the working class of the U.S.S.R. is the shock brigade of the world proletariat. That is very good. It shows that the world proletariat is prepared to continue to render all the support it can to the working class of the U.S.S.R. But this imposes a very serious duty upon us. It means that we must prove worthy of the honourable title of the shock brigade of the proletarians of all countries. It imposes upon us the duty to work better, and to fight better, for the final victory of socialism in our country, for the victory of socialism in all countries.

Hence the third conclusion: to remain loyal to the end to the cause of proletarian internationalism, to the cause of the fraternal alliance of the proletarians of all countries.

Such are the conclusions.

Long live the great and invincible banner of Marx, Engels and Lenin.[4]

It is evident that Stalin's interpretation of world events seeks to justify (and from his standpoint plausibly) his policy of "socialism in one country," his ruthless suppression of the Trotskyite opposition, and his policy of industrialization, which proved in the end to contribute more to the Russian hegemony than the Red Army.

Our abhorrence of the chicane of Russian revolutionary politics and the brutality of military intervention in the affairs of nations, whenever Russian interests are involved, must not obscure the obvious fact that the primary instrument of Russian imperialism in the period after the Second World War has become Russian technical and industrial power, which has been used both to bind the satellite nations to the Russian economy, to woo the uncommitted nations in Asia by grants and loans, frequently more generous than our own, and by the supply of military weapons (as in the case of Egypt). The latter extension of power merely proves that in an industrial age not only a democratic nation but a communist one can transmute technical power into military power and can use the possibility of this transmutation as a source of

[4] Stalin, Report of the 1934 Congress, C.P.S.U.

prestige. Economic and industrial potential is in fact a source of both force and prestige for it can be converted into military might and can also hold the promise to nontechnical cultures for the abolition of their poverty through industrialization.

In consequence the brutally enforced industrialization of an agrarian Russian culture in Stalin's era gave Communism the chance to export its creed, not in Trotsky's terms but in Stalin's terms, both by the prestige of its new industrial power and by the actual exportation of capital and technical skill to the undeveloped nations. It could do this the more easily because the living standards of Russia, starting from a very low base, could be improved even slightly and yet offer the oligarchy the chance to export capital to other nations with greater freedom than the other hegemonous nation, the United States. Reliable estimates disclose that the Soviet economy, beginning at a much lower level, is growing at twice the rate of the American economy. Roughly one-half of her gross product is used to satisfy consumer demands in Russia while we give two-thirds. Naturally, the Russian economy is able to produce more for military expenses, capital investments, and foreign aid. The amount expended for foreign aid is, of course, a tremendous source of prestige for the Russian system.

According to the report of the Rockefeller Brothers Fund Panel on Foreign Economic Policy, the industrial nations of the free world spent 72 per cent of their gross product on consumer needs, 20 per cent on investments, and 8 per cent on military expenditures. Russia, on the other hand, devotes 47 per cent to consumers, 27 per cent for investments, and 26 per cent for military expenditures.[5]

Thus a revolutionary creed of yesterday has been transmuted into a competitive alternative for the quick industrialization of backward cultures. The ability to defy the consumer pressure both in Russia and in the new industrialized nations hastens the tempo of industrialization.

---

[5] The *New York Times*, June 16, 1958.

Professor Harvey Wheeler has suggestively and plausibly compared Stalinist industrialization both at home and abroad to the policy of pre-capitalist mercantilism in the period of imperialism of Britain immediately before the American Revolution.[6] Stalinism was probably more brutal in its methods than mercantilism was, but it was effective in developing industrial power and in drawing strength from its dependencies.

Its despotic organization could not prevent consumer revolts after Stalin's death, and Wheeler interprets the problems of the post-Stalin oligarchy chiefly in terms of meeting the revolts both of the consumer and the satellites. Malenkov fell because he yielded too much to consumer pressure and aroused the fears of the military oligarchy. Khrushchev's triumph was possible through an alliance of the military and the heavy industry oligarchy and through his artful acceptance of part of the Malenkov program of promising more consumer goods. This development proves that even under despotism some consideration must be given to the people's needs. If no other problem confronted the post-Stalin oligarchy its triumph in competition with the "free world" might be possible particularly since the launching of the earth satellites has given her the prestige of superior achievements in advanced technology. But the great problem of the post-Stalin era, which was assumed to be solved by Khrushchev's reconciliation with Tito, remains. The fact that it remains is attested by the subsequent hardening of the Russian line of authority over the satellites and the exclusion of Tito. Why was not the original revision of the dogma that "there are many roads to socialism" maintained? Why was it revised into a new Stalinism after Stalin had been discredited? Why was Hungary suppressed so brutally and Nagy murdered a year after the Hungarian revolt? Why was Poland's semi-autonomous status called in question? What prevented the devolution of the monolithic structure of the empire of Russia, particularly after the first steps to that end were taken after Stalin's death?

[6] See his article, "Problems of Stalinism" in *Western Political Science Quarterly*, Vol. X, No. 3, September 1957.

The answers to these questions are not simple because no question of dogma is involved. The idea of the dictatorship of the party was derived from the original dogma of the dictatorship of the class. But the dictatorship of Russia itself is not based on any dogma. It has simply been added by the contingencies of history which have made the first nation to have a revolution also the most powerful nation, and by the added fact that Stalin's enforced industrialization and the subsequent technical successes of a once backward nation have added to the Russian prestige in her empire. But the original necessity of exploiting her "colonies" has disappeared. Russia is exporting both capital and techniques to help the satellite nations to a rapid industrialization at a tempo which the creed demands but which is probably too rapid for the good of the satellites. There is no pressing economic reason for the tightened control. There is, of course, a strategic reason, for Tito has proved no longer a safe ally and if Titoism were to spread the strategic hazards would be multiplied.

But we must find the real reason for the return to Stalinist control of the empire by Russia in the realm of the ideological system from which the prestige of Russia as a ruling nation was drawn. That ideological system was based on utopianism and fanaticism. Russia was not designed to rule the Kingdom of God on Earth according to the Marxist creed. But it was forced to undertake the hegemony of the cohorts of socialism in achieving the victory of the righteous over the unrighteous imperialists. This fanatic and absolute distinction between the righteous and the unrighteous, between the "imperialist" nations and those who were "anti-imperialists by definition," was in conflict with the empirical facts, which anyone could see who was not bound by the dogma. The necessity of a tighter control arose from the dogmatic presuppositions of the communist system. If Russia was not to have this control what was to prevent Tito's policy from proving that the imperialists would not exploit Yugoslavia as the creed asserted? And what was to prevent both Tito and Gomulka from adopting a more melioristic policy toward the peasants than the dogma permitted? It is, of course, still difficult to see why this empirical policy was not permitted, particularly since the Russian oligarchy after Stalin made all kinds of empirical adjustments to the realities, including, for instance, the abolition of the "tractor stations" as a source of power over the collective farms.

But in an empire based upon a creed it is one thing to make slight adjustments to reality at the source of authority, and another to allow "different roads" to develop to such a degree that the original distinction between the socialists and the capitalist world disappears.

It will be remembered that Mao, almost a co-ruler in the communist empire, had committed heresy in 1957 and had spoken of the tension between the people and the bureaucracy, a tension which was not acknowledged in the dogma. He had also made his famous "Let every flower bloom, let every school of thought contend" assertion.[7] But the liberal attitude had caused too many flowers and weeds of criticism to bloom and the Chinese Communists were forced to lay heavy hands upon the critics in their "rectification" program.[8] Perhaps it was this experience which persuaded the Chinese, since that time, to be supporters of Russia as the final seat of authority and power. The Chinese dependence upon Russian heavy industry may have also prompted this passion for Russian orthodoxy. In any event the re-Stalinization of the Russian empire proves that an ideological system so glaringly at variance with the historic realities must not only have a fixed dogma, but also only one source of interpretation of the dogma. The dogma did not provide for Russia to be the authoritative source of interpretation any more than early Christian dogma made Rome the source of authority. In each case history supplied the seat of authority but the dogma supplied the necessity for a single authority.[9]

[7] Mao Tse-Tung, "Correct Handling of Contradictions Among the People," reprinted in the New York Times, June 19, 1957.
[8] Yugoslav observers insist that Mao's "flower" speech was deliberately designed to tempt critics to reveal themselves.
[9] The rather explicit Chinese acceptance of Russia's supremacy as the seat of dogmatic authority is in obvious contrast to China's imperial ambitions in Asia, which developed without explicit Russian consent and to the increasing anxiety of Russia.

No other analogy between the Christian and the communist dogmas is intended, but it is significant that the single source of authority of the Roman Church has given it the advantage of unity which both the Eastern church and Protestantism lack. Such unity may have its disadvantages but the advantages are obvious.

These recent developments are not pleasant to contemplate, for the future of mankind would be more promising if the leavening influences which the world detected in the post-Stalin era had been allowed to take their course, if utopia had been refuted and fanaticism had been allowed to be dissolved for the complex realities of history do not conform to any dogma, even the democratic one. But the fact that the post-Stalin oligarchy, having embarked upon this liberalization, turned back to the original fanaticism suggests that its ideology made this step necessary. There is, in short, no way of allowing freedom to creep into a system which denies the necessity and possibility of freedom. It is always right to hope that somehow freedom will creep in or erupt in a despotic system.

One of the most pressing problems facing the democratic nations is the formulation of policies which are favorable to the gradual disintegration of the Soviet Empire. The most promising policy would seem to be one designed to loosen the ties of the satellite nations with Russia by strengthening their economic means of independence. In this, as in other instances, a policy prompted by a moral abhorrence of despotism does not permit sufficient flexibility for this task; for it is always in danger of making the same absolute distinctions as does communist fanaticism between good and evil, thus obscuring all shades of political and strategic realities.

The hope for the disintegration of the international despotism of Communism must, however, not rely too simply on confidence in the power of national sentiment to challenge the pseudo-universalism of the imperialism. For the bureaucracy which has established itself in the various nations may be, as Milovan Djilas asserts, "an international class bureaucracy," whose loyalty to Russia is prompted by class interests; for it sees in this unity the only possibility of preserving its ascendancy over the masses. Djilas' pessimism about national Communism, coming from the former Vice President of the Yugoslav Party, and expressed before the hardening of the Soviet line toward Tito, is impressive.

Djilas declares:

> The world center of Communist ideology no longer exists; it is in the process of complete disintegration. The unity of the world Communist movement is incurably injured. There are no visible possibilities whatsoever that it can be restored. However, just as the shift from Stalin to "collective leadership" did not alter the nature of the system itself in the U.S.S.R., so too national Communism has been unable, despite ever increasing possibilities for liberation from Moscow, to alter its internal nature, which consists of total control and monopoly of ideas, and ownership by the party bureaucracy. Indeed, it significantly alleviated the pressure and slowed down the rate of establishment of its monopoly over property, particularly in the rural areas. But national Communism neither desires nor is able to transform itself into something other than Communism, and something always spontaneously draws it toward its source—toward the Soviet Union. It will be unable to separate its fate from that which links it with the remaining Communist countries and movements.
>
> National modifications in Communism jeopardize Soviet imperialism, particularly the imperialism of the Stalin epoch, but not Communism either as a whole or in essence. On the contrary, where Communism is in control these changes are able to influence its direction and even to strengthen it and make it acceptable externally. National Communism is in harmony with non-dogmaticism, that is, with the anti-Stalinist phase in the development of Communism. In fact, it is a basic form of this phase.[10]

This testimony from an experienced former communist raises uncertainties about the motives of the recent about-face of Gomulka and the Polish Communist Party when, under pressure, they condemned Tito's policy, which undoubtedly originally in-

---

[10] Milovan Djilas, *The New Class*, New York, Frederick A. Praeger, 1957, pp. 183–84.

spired Gomulka and gave him the prestige to defy the Russians and set up a moderately independent course deviating from orthodoxy on both church and agricultural policy. Yet when Soviet authority tightened, and the reconciled Tito was again thrust into outer darkness, Gomulka was forced to disassociate himself from Tito in the following words: "Yugoslavia can exist as a socialist state only because there is a commonwealth of socialist countries. This is certainly understood by every Communist and every citizen of Yugoslavia. The League of Yugoslav Communists, because of its mistaken revisionist theories, separates and divides Yugoslavia from the whole international workers' movement. International reaction is on the side of Yugoslavia." [11]

The emphasis lies upon orthodoxy for the sake of unity. The absolute division between socialism and reaction, which is the hallmark of communist fanaticism, is made despite the precious freedom which Poland gained through its moderate heterodoxy. The question is whether Gomulka yielded to pressure for the sake of saving some remnant of Polish freedom, or whether Djilas is right and the Polish Communists yielded because they are part of an international class which is doomed unless it preserves unity under Russian power. There is a slightly analogous uncertainty about the motives of the Russian oligarchs. Are they adopting the only policy which would preserve the unity of their empire or are they the victims of their own despotic creed? Knowing no other way to co-ordinate but by rigorous subordination of all forces under a dominant force have they, after adjusting themselves to many new situations, become the victims of their creed and found themselves unable to adjust themselves to the rule of an empire which requires flexibility, rather than inflexibility, because the different parts of the empire face such varying social and economic conditions? If the latter explanation be correct, then communist imperialism would prove itself inferior to the Islamic imperialism with which we have so frequently compared it, because Islamic

[11] Wladyslaw Gomulka, quoted from The New York Times, Dispatch, June 29, 1958.

imperialism fell into this rigidity only in the final period of the decay of the Ottoman Empire.

If this current imperialism, based upon a utopian creed, should continue in this inflexibility it might hasten the disintegration of the system; but it might also threaten the peace of the world by the renewed fanaticism and dogmatism. A survey of the strange history of communist absolutism reveals how many adjustments to new situations it made before it failed to make the final adjustment. Such a survey leaves moral considerations out of account and assumes that communist despotism and imperialism has always outraged the moral sense of mankind by the brutality of its methods in the name of an utopian ideal.

It is possible to summarize briefly the history of this strange imperialism, different from—yet revealing similarities with—the traditional combinations of power and prestige previously studied, as follows: first, there is the original utopian dream of Marx, designed for the alleged climax of injustice in technical civilization but with universalistic overtones. It was a scheme of social redemption for the whole of mankind, involving not only redemption from social injustice but redemption from the ambiguous human situation, namely of man being both creature and creator in history. From this ambiguous situation it promises to help man take the final leap "from the realm of necessity to the realm of freedom." The conditions of early industrialism in the West gave an immediate plausibility to the vision, which the fluid social and political equilibria of a growing democratic society corrected. The vision would have become irrelevant but for the fact that a non-technical society in Russia collapsed under the exertions of the First World War.

Next follows the adaptation of the utopia by Lenin to the new historic situation. This adaptation involved (a) substituting the dictatorial party for the class and thus changing an irrelevant concept into a politically relevant and dangerous instrument, (b) the projection of the goal of industrialization for a non-industrial nation according to Lenin's concept of the "Soviets plus electricity."

Thus Communism embarked upon the same path which had made capitalism so successful in the West. Instead of allowing the capitalists to amass capital investments out of their profits, the all-powerful state postponed the satisfaction of consumer needs until it could create the capital for heavy industry. Stalin embarked upon the industrialization program in the most ruthless and brutal manner. The policy involved the industrialization and collectivization of the peasant, a step necessary both politically and economically: politically because a dictatorship cannot afford to let the peasant or any class possess independent sources of power. The communist dictatorship has from first to last been remarkably successful in bringing both economic and military power under the dominance of political power. It has created a monopoly of power for the party of prophets turned priest-kings; but it has also created an omnicompetent state similar to the bureaucratic absolute states of ancient societies. Economically the collectivization of the peasant, if not necessary, was at least advisable because it introduced techniques into agriculture which would not have been possible with small scale holdings. The deterioration of animal husbandry under conditions too consistently drawn from the industrial civilization in which the communist utopia was born, was, of course, as obvious as the success in cereal agriculture. This industrial program was not only successful in Russia but tremendously attractive for the pre-industrial cultures of Asia and Africa. They could use the same brutal methods as the Russian Communists in pressing capital wealth out of the labors of poor and powerless peasants. They could also draw upon Russia for both capital and skill, thus increasing the prestige of the imperial power. This prestige increased enormously in recent years with the Russian achievements in nuclear technology. Thus Russia has gained the same prestige in the non-technical cultures which western nations once gained when western culture was both capitalist and technically proficient.

Then, finally, the Russian empire could exploit the resentments of the colonial peoples who are or who were under the domination of the western nations. Thus the "anti-imperialistic" part of the communist creed to which we have referred previously became a tremendous source of prestige for the Russian empire. For according to the creed it was not Russia, a particular nation, which exerted the power over the empire but rather Russia the nation who happened to be the "vanguard of the revolution."

It is the latter aspect of communist imperialism which we in the West find so galling, partly because of the fraud involved in this prestige and partly because of its obvious success. The success is so great that the prestige of the empire extends even to those parts of the world, particularly in the Middle East where the original Marxist dogma found no lodging place. Here its pretensions of anti-imperialism were attractive to nations which had originally extricated themselves from the toils of the Islamic Empire only to fall under the dominance of one or another of the western empires.

The communist success in imperial power and prestige is, in short, greater than our own. It lacks only one element for complete success and that is the flexibility which it seemed for a moment to have acquired after the death of Stalin and which then disappeared for reasons which we have sought to analyze.

It is obviously more important for us to compete more successfully with communist economic and technical prestige and power than to speculate on the possible causes of its hoped-for decline. Students of the international situation have become increasingly aware, for instance, of the necessity of a much more generous aid to India than we have been inclined to give. India is the chief symbol of democracy among the large nations of Asia, and the competition between India and China can have fateful consequences. The immediate disadvantages of a democracy like India in this competition is due to the fact that even an imperfect democracy is hampered in such a struggle, not by its weaknesses but by its virtues, for it cannot demand the staggering sacrifices from the consumers for the sake of industrialization such as despotism can exact.

An understanding of the hazards and the fateful consequences of the competition between India and China belongs to our imperial role in world affairs. This competition between the two Asian nations is one of the many examples of the contest between the two ideological systems on many levels, of which the U.S.A. must be cognizant in its role as an imperial power.

CHAPTER XV

Empires, Nations
and Collective Security
in a Global Situation

THROUGHOUT the millennia of civilization, until the dawn of the modern era, two rather constant structures of community were known: the one the integral community, whether city-state or nation; and the other the larger structure of community and dominion, the empire.

Modern civilization, with its rapidly advancing techniques, particularly in the nineteenth and twentieth centuries, has given the nation a new status as the integral community; and has usually encouraged the development of autonomous nations. On the other hand the same technical developments have made for the disintegration of the imperial structures. Technical advances, particularly printing and the invention of gunpowder, seem to have given the nation an advantage over the imperial structure. The art of communications solidified the integral community rather than the imperial one. And gunpowder hastened the end of the feudal structure of society, which was the political cloth out of which the empires were fashioned. Furthermore, the global dimension of the problem of community robbed the imperial community of the pretension that it was, in fact, universal. We have noted in previous chapters how important this claim was for the prestige of the imperial communities in traditional ages.

These rapid developments have persuaded liberal democrats of the West to regard the autonomous nation as an ultimate norm of community, and then to provide for the integration of the nascent global community through the principle of "collective security." The communists, on the other hand, have regarded both nations and empires as outmoded structures, but, using their utopian ideology, have presented a new version of the old claim of universality for what was in fact an imperial dominion. Both the democratic and the communist creeds have, therefore, given an erroneous account of historical developments in the structures of community. Their contrasting errors invite a fresh examination of the impact of technical developments upon forms of dominion. Such an examination must raise the question whether the politically autonomous nation is really an absolute norm of community; and whether all integral or parochial communities are capable of sustaining the burdens of full autonomy. The examination must further inquire whether the empires may not have been prematurely consigned to the limbo of history. The imperial structure of dominion, as it was known in the traditional ages or even in the nineteenth century, is obviously outmoded. But this fact cannot obscure the necessity and inevitability of various forms of supranational community. These modern forms are much more varied than those in former ages; but the variety of forms corresponds to those necessities of history which modern creeds too easily obscure. They include such remnants of the old European empires which may still be viable as, for instance, the French community in black Africa, and the British Commonwealth of Nations, and also the new Russian empire which claims not to be one. They also include all the regional alliances such as NATO as well as the more amorphous global anti-communist entente with its Anglo-Saxon hegemony and its secondary hegemony of the western, chiefly European, nations. Finally, technical developments and the need for economic co operation have created such new forms of economic supranational sovereignty as the European Coal and Steel community, and may yet create the European Common Market.

Both Marxist and liberal democratic theories are, for contrasting reasons, unable to bring their creeds into harmony with these varied and complex historical realities. The discrepancies between theories and realities may be conveniently measured by considering the contrasting policies in the Middle East. In that critical area, the Egyptian nation bids fair to develop an empire, or at least power of imperial proportions, because it exploits supra-national rather than purely national forces of cohesion. It does this while it constantly inveighs against the "imperialism" of the western nations, having vivid memories of its long subjection to foreign rule, most recently to British dominion.

The West has sought to frustrate Nasser's increasing successes in unifying the region. His success depends upon geographic factors, the common economic interests of oil-producing and oil-transporting states, upon whom the economy of Europe depends for oil consumption, and by the common religio-cultural force of the Islamic faith and the common ethnic factor of Arab nationality. The forces of unity for the region far outweigh the forces of integral and autonomous nationhood.

Britain and America (the latter probably because of its uneasy conscience in having frustrated Britain in the Suez crisis) have sought to prevent the expansion of the new imperialism by appealing to the old democratic principle of "the self-determination of nations," i.e., autonomous nationality. The United States landed troops in Lebanon ostensibly to prevent rebellion through infiltration. But Lebanon is a nation in which a precarious balance is maintained between the Christian majority and the Moslem minority. The balance does not permit Lebanon to admit any of the Palestinian refugees to acquire citizenship. This makes for Arab discontent, which Nasser did not create but from which he can profit. Britain landed troops ostensibly to guarantee the independence of Jordan, a nation consisting geographically of desert wastes without oil, and peopled by loyal Bedouins and disgruntled Palestinian Arab refugees. It is the least viable of nations. Actually the British venture was intended to preserve her foothold in the Middle East; primarily to guard her oil supplies from the oil rich sheikdom of Kuwait. The economic motives did not square with the ideological pretensions.

Russia naturally had her own reasons for supporting the Arab dynamism under Nasser. For public consumption she came to the support of the nations suffering from "imperialism." For communist consumption she had a dogma which fitted the case better than the western ideology. The communist dogma allowed, and even enjoined, the provisional support of "bourgeois nationalism." The Middle Eastern dynamism was hardly "bourgeois" and it was certainly supra-national rather than national, as is all so-called "Arab Nationalism"; for the supra-national forces of cohesion are more dominant than the forces which make up integral nationality. We are at such a disadvantage in the political struggle of the Middle East that it is a mystery why the communists have not sooner established their ascendancy.[1]

It would be, of course, unwise and probably impossible for the western nations simply to bow to Nasser's imperial ambitions as the new Saladin. But if his policies are to be frustrated western strategy must recognize the cultural and economic unity of the Middle Eastern region, and refrain from being guided solely by the outmoded principle of the "self-determination of nations," in a region in which only a few nations possess the resources of integral nationhood.

It is even more important that the United States, as the strongest of the democratic nations, acknowledge the imperial dimensions of its power and accept the responsibilities which are the concomitants of power. Disparities of power in the United Nations, particularly the disparity created by our own power, make a policy which relies on the United Nations as the initiator of strategy futile and even dangerous. Strong nations, and all nations for that matter, must have their own policies within the framework of the United Nations Charter. This problem must be considered more fully in the second part of this chapter which analyzes the devotion of the democratic world to the principle of "collective security."

---

[1] For a comprehensive survey of the Middle East see *Communism and Nationalism in the Middle East* by W. Z. Laquer, New York, Frederick A. Praeger, 1958; also article by Hans J. Morgenthau "The Lebanese Crisis" in *New Republic*, Vol. 139, pp. 14–17, August 4, 1958.

OUR RELIANCE ON "COLLECTIVE SECURITY"

If both Communism and liberal democracy are mistaken in estimating the constant and the variable factors in the structure of empires and nations, liberal democracy is particularly mistaken in assuming that it can easily come to terms with the global dimension of the problem of community by appeal to the principle of "collective security." Reliance on this principle is the consistent climax of the voluntarism which has informed so much of modern political thought. In a technical civilization community can rely more and more on the "artifacts" of legal and constitutional arrangements so that it was tempting to forget that communities are composed both of organic and of contrived forms of cohesion. In civilized societies both are necessary. The necessity for both forms is constant, but the proportion between them is variable according to the culture, the degree of education in a nation, and the intensity of the means of communication.

The organic forces may be defined briefly as those which are least subject to conscious political manipulation or control. They are the "given" forces in a political situation. They relate historical communities to the organisms of nature, and, indeed, constitute the historic community as an "organism." Naturally, the forces of cohesion dependent on natural necessity are most clearly organic. Among such the sense of ethnic kinship—derived as it is from the most primeval of all social cohesions, the sense of family kinship —is closest to nature. Men belong to various ethnic groups by nature; and the sense of ethnic kinship is both a binding force in communities and a dividing force between communities. If ethnic types are too variant, as is the case with the Negro in America, great difficulty is encountered in relating the race to the national community. One must hasten to add that even this given factor of race is not absolutely immutable. America prides itself on being a "melting pot" of European races which have not melted in Europe. Nor would they melt under political compulsion. But if "nature," that is, the possibility of intermarriage without compulsion, is allowed to take its course, an ethnic amalgam develops, though the earlier American immigration laws reveal the inclination of the north European original settlers to set a limit to the amalgam, excluding the Asians and placing limits upon the peoples of Latin and Slav origin.

The "given" factors of race are therefore not absolutely immutable but they are least subject to conscious contrivance or control. They do not finally determine the limits of community as is proved by the insistence of the national community in America that the Negro should have equal rights, though local custom resists this constitutional standard, significantly because of the fear of intermarriage and a consequent racial amalgam between very divergent racial types.

Next in the scale of ascent from organism to artifact are the given factors of culture for which language is a convenient symbol. Languages grow and change, and so do the spirits of culture which they express. But the forcible imposition of the language of a given political community, for the sake of the integration of the community, have proved almost universally futile in such border states as Alsace-Lorraine, for instance. Common cultures are binding forces in communities and differences in culture are dividing factors between communities. No conscious political contrivance can wholly alter even this "organic" factor as a constant force in the community.

Next in the scale of ascent from organism to artifact in community is custom which is partially malleable under the pressure of new social conditions, as for instance in the change from an agrarian to an industrial society. But the changes cannot be too rapid because custom represents the unconscious accumulation of habits and responses to the social situation. Custom may be malleable through education, and indeed it must partly be controlled under the rapidly shifting conditions of technical societies, but our difficulties with the problem of racial integration prove that there are limits in the tempo of change in custom. Custom reaches up to the very limits of artifact in community. It would surprise many social voluntarists that the habit of obedience to constitutional authority in advanced democracies, as distinguished from communities in which military power can usurp authority, is guaranteed not so much by the constitution itself as by the long-established habit of obedience to civil authority.

This combination of constitutional and customary sources of authority bring us finally to those dimensions of community which are most clearly contrived, rather than organic. All conscious political adjustments and accommodations, as embodied in laws within a community and treaties between communities, belong in this category. The final pinnacle of artifact is a written constitution, as we have it in this nation, in which a specific covenant is made the basis of the communal unity and integrity.

All shades and degrees of organic and contrived elements are present in all civilized communities but vary between them. Parochial communities with rapidly shifting social conditions will contain more artifact than traditional agrarian communities; and modern civilization contrives consciously more successfully than the cultures of the ancient or medieval world. But no amount of conscious contrivance can eliminate completely the organic element. The organic element must be recognized as necessary in all communities. Efforts to create world community through world government by constitutional enactment are the consequences of convictions, in a highly mobile and fluid modern culture, that laws and constitutions create communities when it is obvious that they can only strengthen and slightly modify what more unconscious factors have created. These illusions are particularly powerful in America for our peculiar history encourages the idea that we constituted ourself as a nation through the covenant of the constitution. Yet this covenant was merely the final contrivance which perfected the union established by the struggle against the common foe as well as by the organic factors of community, including common language, ethnic kinship, and geographic contiguity and integrity.

The idea of unifying the world community through world law is so illusory that it has intrigued only the most abstract idealists and a discussion of such proposals would be irrelevant. But the idea of establishing peace through "collective security" has had a strong appeal, particularly in the two Anglo-Saxon nations. It expressed itself in and after the First World War in the project of the "League of Nations," which Woodrow Wilson passionately espoused but for which he failed to win the adhesion of his own nation for reasons previously discussed. After the Second World War the same project was elaborated in the "United Nations" in which America has played a leading role from the beginning. Despite the superior realism which informs the constitution of the United Nations its policy of collective security has proved almost as ephemeral as that of the League of Nations. Its basic assumption was the hazardous one that the great powers united in the war against Germany would preserve their common purposes in peacetime. It was the more hazardous because wartime alliances frequently disintegrate with the defeat of the common foe; and in this particular instance one of the allies, communist Russia, was informed by a fanatic creed, which made the alliance hazardous.

The League of Nations was a pseudo-constitutional system because it did not endow any organ with the authority to—or enjoin upon it the responsibility of—enforcing its decisions. It was thus a perfect illustration of the ineffectiveness of the vague universalism of liberal democracy in coming to terms with the power realities and the organic and given facts of the world situation. The question is whether the United Nations has advanced as much beyond the League's inadequacy as most men assumed. It called upon the Security Council to dispose of (and upon the member nations to make available to the Council) armed forces and facilities for enforcing its decisions,[2] but this provision remained a dead letter because the Soviet Union refused to make proportionate contributions to a joint force. There remained therefore only the frail reed of the assumption of the essential harmony of the great powers. In the light of subsequent events it is something of a mystery how almost universal was the hope, if not the belief, that this harmony would be

[2] Article 43, par. 1.

preserved. Kenneth Thompson, in analyzing these problems, reports the statement of Stalin, written in October 1944. He asked the question in an article in the "Soviet Information Bulletin" whether the world organization would be effective and answers his own question, probably with his tongue in his cheek, that it would "be effective if the Great Powers, which have borne the brunt of the war against Hitler-Germany, continue to act in the spirit of unanimity and accord." [3]

If Stalin made this answer with tongue in cheek the Western leaders were painfully conscious of the frailty of the reed upon which the enforcement machinery rested. Thus Secretary Stimson in a memorandum to President Truman on September 11, 1945, frankly implied the necessity of mutual trust between the great powers as the basis for the enforcement machinery. He wrote:

> The chief lesson I have learned in a long life is that the only way to make a man trustworthy is to trust him; and the surest way to make him untrustworthy is to distrust him and show your distrust.[4]

Even as wise a statesman as Stimson thus was forced to turn to the personal ethics of trust and mistrust to assure himself about the adequacy of a foundation for the peace of the world which he knew to be dubious. That foundation consisted of the hoped-for accord of the great powers. Russia had already proved, and was about to prove more unmistakably, that it was informed by a fanatic creed, which made mutual trust between capitalist and communist nations impossible, however much we might nerve ourselves to trust them. Even Senator Vandenberg, a convert from isolationism to the idea of collective security, failed to realize the danger inherent in the quasi-constitutionalism of the United Nations machinery of enforcement, or perhaps he realized the danger but in the mood of the time tried to obscure his fears with the observation:

---

[3] Quoted from Kenneth Thompson's chapter "Uses and Limits of Reason" in the Symposium *Isolation and Security*, Alexander Deconde, Durham, Duke University Press, 1957, p. 177.
[4] Quoted from Thompson, *op. cit.*, p. 177.

The alternative is collective security. ... Which is better in the long view from a purely selfish Russian standpoint: to forcefully surround herself with a cordon of unwillingly controlled or partitioned states, thus affronting the opinion of mankind—or to win the priceless asset of world confidence in her by embracing the alternative, namely full and wholehearted cooperation with and reliance upon a vital international organization.[5]

Russia did not follow Vandenberg's advice nor justify his hopes and the result is now a matter of history. In order to circumvent the Russian veto in the Security Council, we emphasized the General Assembly rather than the Security Council as the chief organ of the United Nations, though the Assembly has no authority by the charter to take any definitive action.

Meanwhile Russia's success and our failure in the Middle East has given her the sympathy of the Asian-African-Arab bloc in the General Assembly. The idea of harmony among the big powers as the basis for peace has long since receded. The United Nations is still a valuable forum, chiefly for the debate between the two great power blocs. But these developments suggest that the quasi-constitutionalism of the United Nations, which ostensibly takes account of the power realities may prove as ineffective as the League which took little account of them. For the organic and given facts of the international situation are more powerful than a quasi-constitutional system. In a tragic age we have come upon one of the constant factors in the international situation which men have tried desperately to obscure in their desire for peace. Constitutional authority alone cannot create community, either on the national or international level. Therefore, it can not of itself create authority which is always compounded of the prestige to speak for the community and the right to use force in its behalf. Mr. Thompson sums up his analysis of the inadequacies of the principle of collective security as envisaged in our generation in the words

Collective security has failed us, and has left us with problems it could never solve, and has preserved and increased the gap already existing between theory and practice. ... While isolation

[5] Quoted from Thompson, *op. cit.*, p. 179.

has no theory, collective security gives us a philosophy so abstract and idealized as to provide little guidance in practice.[6]

The obvious lesson about the constant and variable factors in the communities of history is that although the larger community, including the world community, creates the necessity for more artifacts and human contrivances must always make use of, and not be blind to, the organic factors of community. We neglect them to our peril.

Meanwhile the United Nations is a necessary and useful instrument of foreign diplomacy in a global situation. It is a forum in which the policies of nations can contend with each other and gain the respect and adhesion of various nations according to the merit of these policies. It may in time create centers of real authority within itself which would be able to modify the self-will of nations and mitigate the rivalries of power between the nations. But it is idle to expect it to evolve into a world government merely by changing some constitutional device such as the abolition of the veto. For the veto is not the product of the caprice or pride of the great nations but merely the expression of the fact that the United Nations is not a full constitutional system which would have both the authority and the force to coerce recalcitrant nations. It cannot of itself create world community. Perhaps no constitutional contrivance is or will be capable of this task. Perhaps we are fated, for some centuries at least, to live in a situation in which the global community appears to be a necessity because of the interdependence of nations, but an impossibility because there are not enough organic forces of cohesion in the global community. Perhaps there will never be enough of these factors. Certainly the fear of nuclear annihilation, while universal, is not such a factor; for the fear which communities have of each other cannot be a force of cohesion and unity between them. The one remaining hope is that the recognition by both sides of being involved in the common fate of the nuclear dilemma may create the first strands of community which could be enlarged by various forms of mutuality.

[6] Thompson, *op. cit.*, p. 181.

CHAPTER XVI

The Cold War
and the Nuclear Dilemma

THE long history of conflict between communities, whether national or imperial, has reached a climax in the cold war and the nuclear dilemma of the present day. It is a climax which certainly contradicts and refutes most of the philosophies of history in which the wise men of two previous centuries attempted to chart the course of history and to predict its future. The "cold war" means a perpetual tension between the two blocs of nations, communist and anti-communist, of such unique intensity that one may question the adjective used to describe it. Yet it is regarded as "cold" rather than "hot" because there are no overt hostilities on a large scale. These hostilities are prevented by an historical phenomenon as unique as the cold war itself. Both sides have nuclear weapons which have raised military destructiveness to such a degree of suicidal and lethal efficacy that neither side is tempted to initiate the conflict. This is the proportion of the "nuclear dilemma." Both sides have the weapons in fairly equal proportions, so that even a surprise attack would not be certain to grant immunity to the attacker from retaliatory measures of such destructiveness that the conflict might well make any distinction between victor and vanquished irrelevant.

In the arsenals of both sides, bombs are piled on bombs and guided missiles will be piled on guided missiles in an armory of such frightfulness that man's technical progress throughout the ages has taken on a new dimension. The dimension is novel because, for the first time, the balance between the creative and destructive possibilities of the mastery over natural forces would

267

seem to have been destroyed. The destructive possibilities are certainly more apparent and more imminent.

Furthermore, modern technical advances have set man's progress in techniques in a new light. Progress in this field is accomplished, as previously, through human agency, but it outruns human desires so that historical developments become more and more analogous to natural forces "which go on their fateful way unswerved, unswerving and know not what they are."

At the beginning of the atomic age Pope Pius XII hesitantly suggested a moratorium on scientific advances, of the type engaged by Leonardo da Vinci when he refused to continue scientific experiments (submarines?), which might prove to be detrimental to mankind. But the Pope did not enlarge upon his original suggestions, nor has anyone else. For such a moratorium is obviously beyond the competence of any agency.

In this situation of the cold war and the nuclear stalemate two questions inevitably loom large in scanning the dark future. The most immediate question is whether there is any way of abolishing the dread weapons; and the second is whether there is any way of mitigating the animosities of the conflict. The first question, which is the more unanswerable, looms largest; but the second question is of equal importance. Can any light be thrown on these questions by studying the history of the behavior of communities throughout the ages?

If we seek to draw lessons from history to instruct us in our present perplexities it is important to note the radical difference between two problems which communities in past history have faced. In the first case, communities were confronted with a crisis in which they were forced to make a choice between their survival or liberty—and some larger good, or the good of a larger community. In this situation nations chose their own existence, security, or interest rather than the more universal value, such as the peace of Europe or any other region. In such situations of crisis nations and other communities always have responded by protecting their lives and liberties without regard to the more universal value, particularly as the latter was usually too remote or abstract.

The second situation is radically different. It is when communities were pressed by historical circumstances to adjust their interests, usually by gradual and even by unconscious steps to new conditions. In the past, communities have successfully negotiated these adjustments, even when the new conditions presented some radical novelties. The great difference between the two situations is due to the necessity of either a risk or sacrifice of vital interests in the first case, while only an adjustment of interests and a re-interpretation of the peril and promise, given by the new situation, is necessary in the second case.

Thus in the Wars of Religion which followed the Reformation, neither Catholic nor Protestant nations thought of sacrificing their securities for the sake of the peace of Europe. But when it became apparent that neither side could eliminate the power of the other side Catholics and Protestants began those adjustments of a competitive co-existence which gradually transformed the culture of Europe into a religiously pluralistic one.

If the radical distinction between the two situations be validated by this example, and also by many other similar historical instances, it might follow that it is easier to cool off the animosities of the cold war than to agree on nuclear disarmament or the total abolition of nuclear weapons. For nuclear disarmament, even if undertaken mutually, involves some risk to the securities of both sides. There is small prospect that either side would be willing to take the risks. This remains true even if their failure to do so would involve the world in the continued peril of nuclear warfare. One may take for granted that neither side actually intends to begin the dread conflict. But it may come upon them nevertheless by miscalculation or misadventure.

DISARMAMENT AND ABOLITION
OF NUCLEAR WEAPONS

In approaching the first issue it is necessary to recall that, after long negotiations, the two sides have reached some tentative agreement in regard to the abolition of nuclear tests which had seemed unlikely only a year ago. We would not abolish tests without an inspection system and the Russians professed to favor the abolition of both tests and weapons without an inspection system, thus impressing the world with the alleged American preoccupation with nuclear weapons and with their moral superiority in favoring the abolition of all nuclear weapons. Meanwhile, the Russians hesitantly entered scientific conferences for the examination of the feasibility of inspection systems which resulted in a considerable degree of unanimity in regard to their feasibility. Thereupon we proposed to conduct further negotiations on a trial abolition of tests with inspection for one year. Subsequent negotiations did not fulfill the early faint promise. Their failure was due to many reasons, but it is significant that the Russians insisted on a review of our whole strategic position as a basis for further negotiations.

Disarmament negotiations cannot in fact proceed without reviewing the whole power position of the contestants in the negotiations. In such negotiations with the Russians one of the hazards will be that, while there is sufficient parity between us to prevent the ultimate conflict, the Russians have considerable political advantage over us in the Middle East and Asia and strategic advantage in their reputed superiority in intercontinental missiles; that they will not be inclined to any agreement which will not guard these advantages, while we will not be disposed to any agreement which will disturb or imperial our basic security, already somewhat threatened by the Russian advantages.

In order to illustrate the difficulties in coming to an agreement on disarmament Hans Morgenthau has recalled the difficulties of the disarmament conference, called in 1932, in order to implement the promise of the Treaty of Versailles that the forcible disarmament of Germany would finally lead to a general disarmament in Europe. More than a decade was required to produce even the gesture of a conference. The real difficulty according to Morgenthau [1] was that Germany knew herself to be potentially the strongest power on the continent while France tried to preserve, though a weaker power, the advantages she had gained in the

[1] Cf. Hans Joachim Morgenthau *Politics Among Nations*, second edition, New York, Knopf, 1954.

victory of the First World War. "Hence the conflict between Germany and France," declares Morgenthau, "was in essence a conflict about the distribution of their power. Behind what the delegates expressed in ideological terms of security versus equality, retrospective analysis discovers the moving force of international politics: the desire to maintain an existing distribution of power, manifesting itself in the policy of the status quo on the one hand, and the desire to overthrow the existing distribution of power... on the other hand." [2] Armaments are, in short, the fists and arms of the nations; and they cannot be discussed, or their limitation contemplated, without surveying the whole body of the contending nations.

The relations between Russia and America are not exactly analogous to those of Germany and France in 1932. No historical analogies are ever exact. But what is analogous is that both nations are bound to view the disarmament problem in terms of their total power relations, which includes both military capacity and the political prestige of each in and across the continents of the world. It would be difficult to determine which of the two nations has the greatest potential or present power. We have felt secure both in our power of industrial production and in our nuclear armaments. While the Soviets are presently inferior to us in industrial power their power is growing at a faster rate than ours. Moreover they have the capacity to divert more of it for war production than we have because of their lower living standards.

The Soviets have, in addition, a political advantage over us which is potentially very great. They exploit the issue of colonialism to our disadvantage; and their advantage will continue until their imperialism will create the same resentments in Asia which western imperialism once generated. They will export the same technical advantages which we exported; and these advantages will have the same effect in creating integral nations through the higher arts of communication. Their disadvantages in exercising

[2] *Ibid.*, p. 376.

their rule over the integral nations of Eastern Europe is already great and are bound to grow. But they have the further political advantage over us which is that both our system of democracy and our high standard of living seem irrelevant in Asia and Africa. The first, representing achievements which took the technical civilization of the West centuries to accomplish, seems unattainable to nations emerging from either a pastoral or agrarian economy; and the second, our standard of living, seems irrelevant because it is beyond the dreams of avarice of the poor nations. These living standards are, moreover, less attractive than the achievements of a nation which, while living in poverty not dissimilar to that of Asia, has managed to negotiate the path to a technical civilization with sufficient speed to outstrip us in the conquest of outer space. The Russian prestige was tremendously enhanced through the successful launching of the earth satellites because they were the symbols of a technical triumph that seemed to make the cherished freedoms of the West unnecessary.

Both strategic and political advantages seem to rest ultimately with the Communists, though they are immediately with us. If it should be true that armaments are one of the indices of the power of nations it is not likely that a nation which seems to be potentially the stronger will yield anything at the bargaining table. We, on the other hand, cannot yield because the price of an accord seems to endanger our basic securities. There is thus a very rough analogy between France and us and Russia and Germany in the situations of 1932 and 1958. The prospects for an accord on nuclear weapons are, therefore, if historical analogies are indicative, not too bright.

There are men who have the rather desperate hope that the degree of mutual danger will overcome the constant inclination of nations to fear each other more than they fear the danger which their enmity has caused for each and both. Were this to happen a really novel factor would have emerged in history. We cannot rule out the possibility that it will emerge, but we cannot have any confidence in its emergence.

The prospects of an agreement would be tremendously enhanced if both sides were not only more conscious of the common danger which transcends their enmities, but also if they refrained from attributing to the other side the intention of beginning an atomic conflict, which neither side really believes of the other. Since the Geneva conference the Russians seem to have been convinced that it is not the purpose of America to start an atomic conflict; but this has not changed the propaganda of the Soviets against the alleged warlike designs of the "imperialists." As late as the NATO Conference in 1958 the West, on the other hand, has attributed the ambition of world domination by any means, including war, to the communists. The only justification for this charge is that they continue to believe in their dogma of the ultimate triumph of Communism over Capitalism, whatever may be the vicissitudes of history.

During Malenkov's brief period as prime minister he asserted that an atomic war would mean the end of civilization, and made no distinction between Capitalism and Communism. This was a little too heretical and was amended by Khrushchev who, while changing the Leninist prediction of an inevitable war between the Communist and Capitalist civilizations in favor of a plea for "peaceful co-existence," declared that in the event of such a war, Communism would triumph in the end. "The war is not fatalistically inevitable," declared Khrushchev, despite the fact that "millions of people might be plunged into war for the sake of the selfish interests of a handful of millionaires." But their designs will be prevented by the growing strength of the communist nations, who do not want war because they see victory by the inevitable superiority of the socialist system over the capitalist system. The victory is within the frame of "peaceful co-existence," or perhaps more correctly, competitive co-existence; for "the socialist mode of production possesses decisive advantages over the capitalist mode of production. Precisely because of this the ideas of Marxism-Leninism are capturing the minds of the broad masses of the people in the capitalist countries." [3]

[3] From Khrushchev's report to the Twentieth Party Congress of the Soviet Union, February 1956.

The affirmations are within the limits of the Marxist apocalyptic vision. One could have more confidence that Khrushchev believed what he said if he had not spoken of the "broad masses of the capitalists nations," and had confined himself to the historic truth about the triumphs of Communism in Asia and Africa. These are certainly sufficient to make the communist oligarchy hesitant to sacrifice known political advantages to the hazards of an atomic conflict. The communist leadership does not want a war any more than we do. The communist advantage over us on the dark continents has prompted Khrushchev in the memorable interview with Walter Lippmann (New York *Herald Tribune*, November 10 to 13, 1958) not only to assert the undoubted fact that the Russians do not want a war but also to repeat the charge that we do, making it immediately relevant with the explicit prediction that our prospective political and economic defeats, would persuade us to begin the ultimate conflict.

The Russian leader has at least brought his charges up to date while we were inclined to restate the original fear of Communism, as if it were analogous to Hitlerism. But in any case neither side fully realizes the fact that we not only face a common predicament, but that both sides have an identical inclination to attribute the predicament to the foe.

NON-POLITICAL PROPOSALS FOR DISARMAMENT

Since the dawn of the modern era in the seventeenth century it has been one of the fondest dreams of modern culture that the same scientific procedures which were so efficacious in mastering natural forces would be equally effective in mastering the problems and perplexities of human history. This faith, so eloquently expressed by Auguste Comte in the past century, seemed to have a particular relevance in a nuclear age. Scientific advances were undoubtedly responsible for the nuclear dilemma. What could be more logical than to resort to the same "methods of science" to solve the problems created by these methods in the realm of the natural sciences?

Such a point of view is given in Linus Pauling's book *No*

More War.[4] The greater part of the book is devoted to a very interesting and terrifying account of the horrible destructive powers of the nuclear weapons of all types but particularly of the "super-bombs," bigger even than the hydrogen bombs. This description leaves one with the uneasy feeling that we are all, as laymen, not as hysterical as we well might be about the insecurity of the nuclear stalemate because of sheer ignorance.

The description leads Pauling to the conclusion that the nature of the new weapons makes wars simply impossible. The result of this conviction of the impossibility of war in a nuclear age is a proposal for a "World Peace Research Organization" which would carry out "research for preserving the peace of the world. ... This would mean of course carrying out research on how to solve the great world problems of the kind which have in the past led to war." [5] It would "make a thorough analysis of the problems involved in reaching agreements to stop the testing of nuclear weapons." This world peace research organization is conceived in non-political terms. Pauling declares "We cannot expect that the problems of the world can be solved by government officials, who have many duties and who cannot be expected to devote to these problems the long and careful thought that they require for their solution. These problems need to be attacked in the way that other problems are attacked in the modern world—by research, carried out by people who think about the problems year after year. ... If thousands of able investigators are attacking world problems by imaginative and original methods, working on these problems year after year, many of the problems should be solved." [6]

It is clear what form of non-political rationalism lies at the foundation of this proposal for world disarmament. The contest between nations, in which their pride and security is at stake, is reduced to the dimension of a problem of natural science, which can be solved if disinterested specialists devote themselves to it. Statesmen are dismissed from the solution because they are too busy; but it does not seem to occur to Pauling that statesmen,

[4] Linus Pauling, *No More War*, New York, Dodd, Mead & Co., 1958.
[5] *Ibid.*, p. 211.   [6] *Ibid.*, p. 203.

however wise or stupid, have a responsible relation to their communities which no pure specialist can have. He does not consider this facet of the problem of disarmament because it is a scientific rather than a political problem in his mind.

For this reason Pauling's proposals have not been taken seriously by either the statesmen or the political scientists, though everyone recognizes the legitimacy of the moral anguish which prompted them. Significantly many of the scientists who supported Pauling were geneticists who were most aware of the awful peril to which radiation exposed not only this but succeeding generations.[7]

CAPITULATION

The very considerable strategic and political advantages the Russians have over us make disarmament negotiations more difficult, for they are best conducted under conditions of practical parity. Even under such conditions, there would be the rivalries, as previously referred to, for specific strategic advantages in the disarmament treaty. Our handicaps may not be as serious as some now believe, even as our advantages were hitherto not as great as our optimists assumed. But the advantages of the Russians are real. This has prompted a mood of defeatism in some European circles which regards nothing less than capitulation to the Russians as a way out of the nuclear terror.

A recent booklet by the English writer Philip Toynbee expresses the hopelessness of those who think that the Russian ad-

---

[7] Since these lines were written Lord Bertrand Russell's plea for disarmament has been published: "Common Sense and Nuclear Warfare" (Simon Schuster, 1959). While on a higher level of political sophistication than Pauling's book, Russell approaches the nuclear dilemma with that combination of common sense tinged with irony, and naivete, which characterize all the approaches of the eminent philosopher to political issues. He admonishes both sides, perhaps needlessly, not to believe that the other side desires to begin the nuclear conflict. He sees the differences between the two sides as "ideological" which hardly does justice to the dynamics of two contrasting civilizations. He is realistic enough to assert that "The removal of American troops from western Europe cannot become practical politics except as a sequel of an agreement for the abolition of nuclear weapons" (p. 61). In analyzing the prospects for such an agreement he consistently assumes that the rather desperate need for the abolition of nuclear weapons will overcome hazards which we have previously analyzed.

vantage over us has become so impressive that "There is only one step, which is to negotiate with the Russians and get the best terms available to us. There is little reason to think that they would be crushing." [8] Toynbee's proposals are clearly proposals for capitulation. He assumes that the negotiations would proceed in a defeatist mood on the part of the democratic nations. This mood presumably would be engendered both by the acknowledgement of Russian superiority, strategically and politically, and by the conviction that nothing but capitulation would prevent a nuclear holocaust. His proposals also assume that the novelty of the nuclear danger would efface many of the characteristics of national behavior which any careful study of history must reveal as constant characteristics. These perennial characteristics may be defined briefly as consisting of three inclinations of national communities which are generally interwoven. The first is a stubborn will to live and to preserve the liberty and identity of the nation. This will to live may be transmuted into the will to power, but the basis of the will to power is the will to live. The second drive or inclination is a sense of loyalty to an alliance of nations of which the nation is a member; and the third source of action is the sense of devotion to the culture and civilization which may overarch or may be embodied in the alliance.

This complex of interests and loyalties raises questions about identifying the "national interest" with the moral norm of states. The "national interest" accurately describes the dominant motive of autonomous nation-states. But all nations are involved in a web of interests and loyalties. Their problem, therefore, is to choose between their own immediate, perhaps too narrowly conceived, interests and the common interests of their alliance, or more ultimately of their civilization, in which, of course, their "national interest" is also involved.

Toynbee's proposals assume that both vanquished and victors—who would, incidentally, acknowledge their respective status before a real trial of strength has taken place—would not behave according to these interests and loyalties which seem to be the

[8] Philip Toynbee, *The Fearful Choice*, London, Victor Gollancz, 1958, p. 15.

constant characteristics of national behavior. He expects the
vanquished to suppress both their desire for life and freedom, and
their loyalty to their alliance and to their civilization or culture,
for the sake of avoiding an ultimate conflict. He expects his own
nation, Great Britain, to be disloyal to its alliance, though it is
Great Britain which rightly prides itself on its record of loyalty to
the ideals of western civilization and to the European community when this loyalty meant bearing the brunt of the conflict
with Nazism almost alone. If the "Americans" persist in their
nuclear struggle, declares Toynbee, "We must employ the sanction
of unilateral withdrawal." [9] He thinks these novel forms of behavior are possible for nations because of the uniqueness of the
nuclear dilemma. He recognizes that the action proposed has
similarities with the policy of appeasement for which "Munich"
has become a symbol, but claims that "... the situation [of the
nuclear dilemma] is unique in history, and nothing in the past can
instruct us how to conduct ourselves." [10]

The nation which is to gain a victory without a struggle is
expected to behave as uniquely as the nations which have
capitulated without a struggle. He expects a nation which has
no compunction about a monopoly of power, nevertheless, to refrain from grasping the final monopoly of power, namely the
monopoly of nuclear weapons. He thinks that we might press for
the best terms possible "for there is little reason to think that they
will be crushing." [11] He is so confident about Russian moderation
because he thinks of power realities very simply in terms of
"military occupation" and "military conquest" [12] for he, rightly
no doubt, thinks it unlikely that the Russians would occupy the
nations which had thrown themselves upon her mercy. But he
does not realize that such obvious and crude methods would be
unnecessary once all the eminences of power were in Russian
hands. Toynbee does not measure all the cultural and political
consequences which might flow from such a capitulation. Our
predicament is assumed to be so unique that it is expected to
prompt nations to behave quite differently from the way they have

[9] *Ibid.*, p. 20.   [10] *Ibid.*, p. 20.   [11] *Ibid.*, p. 15.   [12] *Ibid.*, pp. 17, 19.

behaved in past history. Nations are expected to sacrifice both their freedom and their dearest possessions for the sake of escaping nuclear terror. If this were mankind's only hope then, indeed, we would be in a desperate situation.

While Philip Toynbee's escape from the modern nuclear dilemma may be naïve, it is no more naïve than the various proposals for disarmament which rightly regard agreements without a complete reign of world law as hazardous, but wrongly assume that the depth of the dilemma may scare the nations into vaulting over all the possibilities of creating world community by the slow processes of history by which communities can be created; and presume to create it instead by endowing an international authority with a monopoly of power.[13]

PROPOSAL FOR "LIMITED WARS"
IN A NUCLEAR AGE

It would not seem fair to include Henry Kissinger's proposals for limited wars in the same category as the unpolitical and implausible proposals for the abolition of nuclear weapons. But it is necessary to include his significant proposal in a total consideration of the nuclear dilemma. Kissinger [14] rightly excoriates a policy which has not learned any of the lessons of the past decade, and which, therefore, still assumes that the only danger is a surprise attack from the Russians. According to this policy the only safeguard against this danger is the mounting of a tremendous nuclear power to act as a deterrent against the surprise attack, accompanied by the promise, on the one hand, that we will never start a war and, on the other, the threat that we will use "massive retaliation" against the surprise attack.

Kissinger points out that this policy has put an undue emphasis on the hydrogen bomb and robbed us of the weapons by which we might successfully fight limited wars. Kissinger defines these wars

---

[13] See, for instance, Granville Clarke and Louis Bruno Sohn, *World Peace Through World Law*, Cambridge, Harvard University Press, 1958.
[14] Henry Kissinger, *Nuclear Weapons and Foreign Policy*, Council of Foreign Relations, New York, Harper Brothers, 1957.

as those which do not involve the survival of either side and are fought with weapons of limited destructive power. He thinks we were probably too hesitant about the possibilities of starting an ultimate conflict in the Korean war; and he envisages Europe as the probable locale of such a limited war in the future. His polemics against preoccupation with the weapons, which are needed only to preserve the balance in the armament race but can never be used, has been widely praised here and in Europe. The dubious part of his plea for limited wars is his assumption that tactical atomic weapons can be useful instruments in such wars. The original arming of NATO troops with tactical weapons for the sake of overcoming Russian superiority in manpower has been overtaken by history as surely as the idea of a surprise attack by the Russians has been refuted by the realization that the Russians have no incentive for such an attack as long as they win victory after victory over the West in the "uncommitted" world.

The idea of limited wars with limited objectives which do not involve the survival of the contestants is always valid. But two emphases in Kissinger's thesis seem dubious. The one is that Europe is a possible battleground for such a war. It has become apparent that no power realities in Europe can be changed without culminating in the ultimate war; for strategic points in Europe are too precious in the policies of each side, even though they do not involve the "survival" of the contestants. The other emphasis is the idea that limited wars can safely be fought with "tactical" atomic weapons. Some of these tactical weapons are as destructive today as the bombs which fell on Hiroshima and Nagasaki were in their day. The general use of tactical weapons obscures the necessary absolute dividing line between the limited war and the ultimate war. This is too dangerous even though that dividing line is symbolic and psychological rather than actual in terms of comparative destructive power. There is no chance of avoiding the ultimate conflict if this line is obscured.

The prospects either of abolishing the nuclear terror altogether or of limiting nuclear weapons to tactical dimensions are not too bright. The possibility that the uniqueness of the danger may negate some of the factors in the behavior of communities which our study has defined as "constant" forces, cannot be excluded. But the presumption must remain strong that the collective impulse for survival and loyalty to a civilization which an alliance embodies are certainly more powerful than the proposals for either disarmament or the limitation of weapons assume.

RELAXING THE "COLD WAR"

While the prospect of abolishing the nuclear threat completely is slight, we are also confronted with the less difficult task of sharing the world with a despotic system which we abhor and which decades of polemics have made the more abhorrent. Yet unless we annihilate each other in a nuclear war we must come to terms with the possibilities of co-existence with this regime. This task is easier than the abolition of nuclear weapons but it is not as interesting and does not excite the same devotion among the idealists. It is easier because it does not demand that the impulse for survival of each collective system be challenged directly. It is only required that each side allow historical developments to modify the animosities and to change the power realities within each system.

The first precondition of survival in such competitive co-existence is that both sides come to a full recognition of their involvement in a common fate. Included in this common fate are fear of mutual annihilation and also the common inclination to attribute malice to the other side, particularly the evil design of initiating the ultimate conflict. It would be sobering to the West to make an honest analysis of the situation of a common fate. Such an analysis might well prompt the conclusion that the temptation to begin the ultimate conflict probably is greater on the western side than on the Russian, because the Russians have all the immediate political advantages in the Middle East and in Asia and Africa; and their prospective victories there are much more likely to lead to desperation in the democratic alliance. We have the absurd situation that a system which some of our leaders regard as ephemeral because of its inflexible dogmas and fanaticism seems much more plausible and available to the nascent nations of the new continents. It will, of course, suffer some defeats in Europe where the communist system is an economic blight even to the less advanced nations of eastern Europe, and where its imperialism is an affront to historically established nations. At the same time, it offers emancipation, economically and politically, to the nations of the Orient.

The task of managing to share the world without bringing disaster on a common civilization must include, on our part, a less rigid and self-righteous attitude toward the power realities of the world and a more hopeful attitude toward the possibilities of internal developments in the Russian despotism. Our rigid and self-righteous attitude is manifest particularly in our insistence that Chinese Communism is "ephemeral" and will disappear if we oppose it rigorously enough. Communist despotism in China is undoubtedly more absolute than in Russia. But the system which, according to our official dogma, is fated to extinction has meanwhile gained enough power to influence the Russian strategy, chiefly by exchanging loyalty to Russian hegemony for the tangible benefits of technical equipment and guidance. Our China policy appears to the uncommitted world as dogmatic as anything in the rigid dogmatism of the communist world.

We have considered in another chapter the irrelevant dogmatism of our policy in the Middle East, where the more flexible policy of the Russians has outflanked us and breached our military alliances and made profitless our defense of certain unviable nations.

The other side of the problem of co-existence is to hope for, and abet, those aspects of the communist system which offer some promise of gradual change in the despotic rigidity of the communist totalitarianism. It would be foolish to expect an inflexible system either quickly or even gradually to develop into an open society. But it is not wrong to reflect on historical analogies between the monarchical absolutism which gripped Europe only a few centuries ago and the present Russian system. Monarchical absolutism succumbed in France to the Revolution, but in Britain

it evolved into an open society because a group of Whig aristo-
crats, who controlled Parliament, disputed the authority of the
monarch; and the tension between King and Parliament gradually
benefited the common people of Britain. It may not be too sanguine to draw the analogy and to point to the fact that the remnant and the beginning of democracy in the communist system
may be the Central Committee of the party. Its power seemed
to be qualified by the more closely knit oligarchy, originally de-
vised in purely *ad hoc* terms, of the "Politbureau" and now the
"Presidium" of the party. Stalin managed to dominate both this
little oligarchy and the party through terror. Much has been said
about the ease with which this despotism established itself in the
name of "democratic centralism"; but with the death of Stalin
new forces expressed themselves in Soviet society, and the execu-
tion of Beria and the abolition of the police terror showed that
the surviving oligarchs could express a will to resist absolute
tyranny. The system still allows shrewd and ruthless leaders to
emerge with almost absolute power; but it is wise to remember
that Khrushchev has achieved his present eminence partly by appealing to the central committee against the Presidium where he
was outvoted. Evidently there is something like a Whig aristocracy
in the Russian system of the Central Committee. One remembers
too that Gomulka, who almost lost his life in one of Stalin's
purges, came to power through the vote of the Central Committee
of the Polish Communist Party and tries to preserve the quasi-
independence of the Polish nation in the communist imperialistic
system, sustained by the partially communist and partially nationalist convictions of the Polish people. Clearly there is a possibility of
historical development within this system, though one must not
paint the prospects in too bright colors.

The second aspect of the communist system in Russia which
offers the prospect for dynamic internal developments, which we
must not discount, is the educational system. In Russia children
of peasants can receive a university education if their intelligence
merits it. The political system may be despotic but the rudiments
of democracy are in the educational system. Only a short time ago

we regarded Russia condescendingly as a backward community; but now we wonder whether we can match the Russians in training technicians for a technical society. This despotism differs from the traditional despotic communities because it is a dynamic society which requires a great deal of competence for its health on all levels of the community. Technical competence is not synonymous with a humanistic training, aware of all the nuances of culture. Russia probably will be "vulgar" for decades to come; and we might reflect that the vulgarity of our own mass culture may be destroying the humanities as rapidly as the Russians may be becoming conscious of the limits of their technical achievements.

There is, of course, no immediate prospect of achieving political emancipation by raising the level of intellectual competence. Dictatorships have co-opted a technical oligarchy for their purposes; and have kept them quiet and docile by finding the point of concurrence between the prestige and security of the technicians and the ambitions of the oligarchy. We cannot think in short-term goals when we think of leavening the lump of despotism by intellect alone. But the long-term result must be that a technically competent culture cannot avoid a rational ferment which yet may prove politically subversive. We cannot build any immediate hopes on these probabilities. But we must realize that we are not fated to share the world with the present despotism forever. It is under the ferment of a culture which is bound to produce political effects in the long run.

Two characteristics of the communist system discourage even those rather desperate hopes which we have enumerated. One is that it is the first system of government which identifies without reservation the ideal and the real, claiming for its system of power if not the immediate then the ultimate realization of an ideal justice. The only despotic system which made an analogous identification was the Islamic one. Both Stoic Rome and Western and Eastern Christian empires had conceptions of an ideal justice which transcended the historic possibilities or at least realities. Perhaps this identification in Russia is related to the consistent subordination of the individual to the social whole, thus giving the individual conscience no leavening influence in the community. The artists and writers have tried in the post-Stalin era to exploit this leavening influence of the individual; but they have not succeeded markedly in defying the canons of "socialist realism," which means the canons of conformity which make the glorification of the given historic reality of the Soviet State into the norm of art and morals.

The other characteristic of the communist system which tempts even the most hopeful to lose their hope is that none of the oligarchies—rivalry between which must be one of the conditions of increasing freedom—have independent sources of power, not related to the state bureaucracy. The managerial oligarchy, for instance, is distinguished from the rising business class of western history in early modernity by the fact that they have no property of their own but are only the managers of state property.

The twin forces of freedom in western history were property and conscience. They are also the sources of freedom in some of the newer countries like Tunisia. There seems no room in the communist system for either of these forces.

The sharp distinction made in this analysis between the perennially manifest behavior of nations and empires with reference to their collective self-regard and the more hopeful attitude toward the possible transformation of the communist system can be justified by observing that political systems and communities are subject to various developments by the shift of historic circumstances; and that systems built on revolutionary ardor are particularly subject to development as the revolutionary enthusiasm abates and the oligarchy acquires a sense of responsibility for the preservation of order and the adjustment of interests within the growing system. It must be understood, of course, that these hoped-for developments do not change the common characteristics of communities. They can only mitigate the uncommon characteristics of Communism, including the fury of its fanaticism and the rigor of its despotism. It would be foolish to expect the development of a democratic system within the foreseeable future, or to hope for any other than a collective self-regard within the communist system, even if a full-blown democracy should develop. All that can be expected is that historical developments finally will reduce the communist system to more or less the same dimensions which are universally manifest in the traditional communities of history. Such a development might make accommodation between the democratic and the communist alliance easier, but it would not eliminate the peril of war. That peril may be avoided in the future, as in the present, by the fear of mutual annihilation and the processes of diplomacy. The peril will be lessened, also, by mutualities of trade and culture which will increase as the revolutionary animus abates in Russia in the second and third generations of post-revolutionary leaders.

CHAPTER XVII

The Creative
and Destructive Possibilities
of Human Freedom

IT IS fitting to close our study of dominion and community in nations and empires by tracing, as summary and conclusion, the sources of those constant and variable factors, to which we have often referred, as they are revealed in the communities of history. We must also try to discover the sources of the creative and destructive tendencies displayed in the life and rivalries of the nations and empires.

The behavior of collective man naturally has its source in the anatomy of human nature. The most apparent constant factors are obviously derived from those aspects of human nature which constitute man a creature of nature, namely his natural hungers and needs, and the natural forces of cohesion in his communities, such as the sense of kinship. But natural necessity is not the only source of the constant factors. Some are derived from the unvarying way in which man's unique freedom manifests itself, though that freedom is also the source of the unique and variable factors in history.

Man is that curious creature who, though partly determined and limited by the necessities of nature, also possesses a rational freedom which enables him to harness the forces of nature in the world and to transmute the natural appetites and drives in his own nature so that he can conceive ends and entertain ambitions which exceed the limits which pure nature sets for all her creatures except man. Man's freedom consists not only of the rational capacity

287

for analysis and conceptual understanding which enables human beings to transcend the flux of temporal events by conceiving the patterns which give meaning to the flux. It consists, in addition, of the unique capacity to transcend himself and the flux of finite causes in which he, himself, is involved. Therefore he is able to choose between various alternative ends which present themselves to him and also to choose between the various forces which presumably determine his actions. This freedom prevents any one of the causal sequences in which man is involved from finally determining his actions.

This unique freedom is certainly the obvious source of the unpredictable character of historical events and of the variable nature of many of those events. Classical philosophies had no place for genuine variables or contingencies in history because they conceived history as being—in common with nature—subject to "essences" as potentialities which were inevitably realized in actual events of history. But there are no "essences" in history because every historical configuration represents an amalgam of natural necessity and human freedom.

Human freedom is undoubtedly capable of historical growth. Civilized man enjoys a degree of freedom which primitive man did not have. In the same way the mature man has greater freedom over nature than does the child. This growth of freedom imparts a forward movement to human history. Developing freedom manifests itself in all the arts of culture; but it is most obvious in man's increasing mastery of nature. This forward movement gave rise to many optimistic interpretations of history, particularly since the eighteenth century. The optimism was derived from the assumption that increasing freedom meant increasing rationality, and therefore the emancipation of the community from those elements which were due to man's relation to nature and to the community's early dependence upon natural forces of cohesion. Thus, historical development would guarantee both justice in the parochial community (in which rationality would generate disinterested, rather than interested, attitudes) and the gradual development of a universal community through man's gradual emancipation from the forces and limits of nature. But, as we have previously noted, the natural forces of cohesion in the community remain operative even in the most civilized communities, though they are variously compounded with historical political contrivances. The rise of the modern nation is a rather ironic refutation of the hope for the establishment of a universal community through pure contrivance because it represents a victory of the more primal forces of community, particularly the force of ethnic kinship, over the artifacts which the ancient and medieval empires introduced into history. The triumph of the parochial community was, of course, not a pure victory of nature over artifact because the victory was made possible by the development of the arts of communication, particularly the invention of printing.

Modern optimistic interpretations of the historical and political problem easily obscured the possibility both of destructiveness and of creativity in the growth of freedom. The historical development of freedom was believed to be purely creative, partly because it was believed that increasing freedom meant increasing rationality; and increasing reason was tantamount to increasing disinterestedness which would overcome both injustice and parochialism in the community, thus establishing by gradual process the ideal community. This was the burden of the "idea of progress." Unfortunately, the growth of freedom had more ambiguous consequences than the optimists assumed. Reason, despite every refinement, could always become the servant of interest and passion, even if the general tendency of rational growth was increasing disinterestedness. Reason also could become the servant of the parochial rather than of the ideal universal community. Thus, historical development did not solve any of the problems of the community. Instead, it constantly enlarged them until our generation faces these problems in a global dimension.

Some modern philosophies of history were encouraged in their optimism by another, rather plausible, error. They assumed that man's mastery of nature automatically would redound to human welfare. Yet it should have been obvious long before the nuclear age that the mastery over natural forces increased man's power;

and that this greater power could be used—and in a sense was bound to be used—destructively as well as creatively. The possibility of destruction was given not only in the fact that it might be used in the service of parochial, rather than universally valid interests, but also because it could be used for the actual destruction of life. A nuclear age, ironically, has refuted the optimism of the previous centuries because nuclear energy has much more imminent destructive possibilities than creative ones, though we talk hopefully about "Atoms for Peace" projects. Plans for the abolition of the nuclear peril which are based on erroneous identification of nature and history trust the "scientific" method to abolish the bombs which science has created. These plans are belated expressions of an approach to historical problems which modern experience has refuted.

The growth of freedom, in short, creates some constant factors in history, but among them is not the hoped-for, constant emancipation of man from nature. Man remains throughout history, partly a creature of nature and partly a creature of the very historical environment which he has helped create.

It is significant that man's desire for a more unambiguous status, expressed in his yearning for an ultimate good, establishes yet another constant tendency in history, just as clearly as his involvement in nature creates the first obvious constant tendencies. Man is a creature who has a strange yearning for the ultimate, transcending all the limitations and conditions of a history which has its basis in nature. Man refuses to set limits, not only to his desires for power and glory but also to his sense of the right and of justice. This sense of the ultimate can be defined as the religious dimension of human existence. But history has proved that it can manifest itself almost as powerfully in a secular as in a religious age. This shows that it is derived from the very structure of human existence, if it is understood that a part of the anatomy of human selfhood is the capacity of man to stand beyond and outside himself and his communities. It was the mistake of the religious ages to regard the religious dimension as good in itself, and an equal mistake of the secular age to regard it as purely the source of evil.

It can be both destructive and creative. It is creative when an ultimate norm or value is set in judgment over the historically relative and ambiguous achievements of man's existence. It is destructive and a source of evil if a simple identification is made between the ultimate norm and the norms and values which we cherish.

The sense of the ultimate may express itself both in individual and in social terms. In individual terms it sets, when creative, standards and frames of meaning which transcend the ambiguities of the political order and make the conscience of the individual the leaven of the community. It can also prompt to escapism when it sets standards which are so pure as to be irrelevant to the life of the community. Such religious escapism is manifest in Catholic asceticism, in liberal perfectionism, and in the Lutheran doctrine of the "two Realms" in which the "Heavenly Realm" consists in a perfect virtue which is politically irresponsible and irrelevant. The individual sense of the ultimate, when creative, proves that the freedom of man, expressed in artistic, religious, and scientific pursuits, is bound to place the community in the category of frustration—as well as fulfillment—of the human spirit. This refutes all collectivist theories which regard the community as man's "concrete universality," in the words of Hegel, making the community purely into the fulfillment of the human spirit. Properly balanced, the individual sense of the ultimate is a leavening influence in the community in which the uneasy conscience of the individual acts as a creative force to raise the norms of the community. Hence, the demand in an "open society," that man have social freedom consonant with the essential structure of his existence, is helpful to the community even when it seems to encourage liberties which are immediately irrelevant or even dangerous to the community.

The sense of the ultimate expresses itself in political terms in both conservative and radical versions. Our encounter with Communism proves that not only the conservative but the radical sense of the ultimate may be dangerous. The conservative sense of the ultimate was manifest in all the classical and medieval millennia of history when a particular and historically contingent form of political order was identified with the cosmic order, and the ruler claimed to be either divine or divinely ordained.

But the radical sense of the ultimate, which places the status quo of any community under the judgment of an ultimate justice, may be as dangerous as it can be creative. It is creative when it challenges any given status quo by comparing it with a more ultimate norm of community and justice. In both Stoicism and Hebraic Prophetism the more ultimate norm is defined in terms of a more equal justice and a more universal community than the particular communities of history. In modern history the conflicting utopian visions of seventeenth century puritanism led, on the one hand, to Cromwell's dictatorship because they were conflicting; but, on the other hand, they spread the seeds of a creative justice in an open society insofar as they expressed visions of a more perfect justice. The very conflict of ideals, libertarian and equalitarian, helped to create a pluralistic society once the Cromwellian dictatorship had been proved to be too vexatious. Thus, utopian visions were partly creative in the formation of an open society in the West. Western democracy was the fruit not only of cultural and religious pluralism but also of the multiplicity of centers of power, economic and political.

The Marxist-Communist utopianism proved dangerous and only incidentally creative, inasmuch as it destroyed the injustices of traditional civilization. It was also creative insofar as it lifted the educational standards of a whole community and created a dynamic, rather than static, society. It was dangerous insofar as it substituted a new and more plausible ultimate norm amid historical contingencies and gave a new oligarchy a religious sanction for its rule. It was the more dangerous because it endowed this oligarchy with a monopoly of power which created (as all such monopolies do) monstrous injustices. These were certainly analogous to the injustices of the traditional societies. Thus, the recurring factor of irresponsible power emerged among the variables of traditional and revolutionary societies.

The utopian basis of a revolutionary despotism clearly creates

as many perils to justice as do the claims of ultimacy of a traditional society. Taken together, these perils prove that men are
dangerous not only because they have unlimited appetites and
unlimited yearning for power, but because they are creatures with
dreams; and their extravagant dreams turn into nightmares if they
seek to realize them in history.

The only safe way of building communities is to assume that the
dominion which the community needs for its cohesion always is
ambiguous morally and that both the traditional and the revolutionary method of obscuring the ambiguity increases it. A purely
naturalistic approach to problems of community, interest, and
power is too one-dimensional to uncover the complex facts of
man's need for, and corruption of, community. The sober facts
about the communities of men and the corresponding necessity
of balancing every power with a countervailing power, and of allowing freedom to place every center of power and of ideology under
review, were not discovered by an objective science. These truths
were discovered by the fortuitous circumstance that the open
societies of the western world had cultural pluralism thrust upon
them by the vicissitudes of history, and that different centers of
economic and political power were developed, not by design, but
by the pressures of history. The rising middle class developed its
own economic power which challenged the economic power of
the soldier, the priest, and the landlord but could not defeat these
authorities without reluctantly granting the industrial worker the
right to use his own organized power. The tortuous processes of
western destiny bequeathed treasures of wisdom upon our culture
which no group was disinterested enough to discover.

To be sure, the unities and cohesive power of western communities were not accomplished merely by the fortuitous introduction of many centers of power and of ideological prestige into
the culture. The stability of these communities would not have
emerged if there had not been educational, moral, and spiritual
resources for the achievement of the tolerance which such a pluralistic community requires. It must be understood, also, that the
unity of a pluralistic culture would not be possible if the divergent

elements of the culture did not possess basic affinities. The civilization of the West possessed these affinities in the two versions of the Christian faith and Judaism; or, in other words, the three forms of Biblical faith. Moreover, secular humanism did not seriously diverge from, and sometimes reinforced, the basic tenets of the common faith. This made for an underlying unity amidst the divergences. Moreover, the culture required a level of economic well-being which would mitigate the social competition between the classes, and an equilibrium of power which was finally achieved by the balance of power between big labor and big business. This contrivance of justice was not planned or anticipated by the classical liberal democracy of the eighteenth century.

The basis for these achievements was laid by historical developments not designed by man or class. The virtues and the stabilities of western pluralistic cultures and communities are thus a bequest of historical "providence" transcending the intentions of any of the agents in history. This "secular" providence was more complex than the "laws of motion" in which the Marxist dogma tried to confine historical fate, and it certainly produced quite different consequences than the Marxist dogma anticipated. The virtues and achievements of the pluralistic communities of the West were, in short, the consequence of an interaction between unintended historical contingencies and human responses to these contingencies.

Before congratulating ourselves too much as members of the "open societies" of the West, which have achieved a tolerable answer to the problems of the community (chiefly the one problem of making freedom compatible with justice and stability), it is necessary to reflect that these virtues are more or less limited to the domestic scene and tend to evaporate in the heat of international competition. The nascent global community is certainly culturally and economically pluralistic. It contains integral communities in every stage of culture and economy and with a wide diversity of political organization. It is torn asunder by the conflict of power between two alliances, one of which is under the domination of Russia, which has negotiated the step from agrarian "backwardness" to the technical competence that was the original monopoly of the western culture. It has done this under the guidance of a creed which is abhorrent to the moral and political sensibilities of the West.

In the other alliance the United States is the most powerful nation. It has accepted the credos of liberal democracy with fewer qualifications than a longer history has introduced into the orientation of the democracies of Europe. With these eighteenth century political dogmas the rather incongruous fruits of a mass culture are combined. We have elaborated both of them with greater consistency than have any of the European nations. Yet we are tempted to the fanatic dogma that our form of community is not only more valid, ultimately, than any other but that is more feasible for all communities on all continents. We have made our position the more unpalatable by overemphasizing our military power. It may seem strange that a nation without a military tradition should suddenly put so much weight on military power; and should persist in the emphasis long after our original nuclear monopoly has been destroyed. The uniqueness of this development probably can only be explained by the fact that economic power is more readily transmuted into military power than into political power. For the latter requires a prestige which cannot be gained easily in a pluralistic world community where our systems of belief do not have the same plausibility as in our own community or in the West.

Thus, we are in the strange predicament that, as the leading exponents of an "open society," we introduce a stubborn insistence on our own kind of openness (including the alleged virtues of the "free enterprise" system) as the only basis for a free society. In consequence of this fanatic protagonism of a non-fanatic culture we are threatened with the alienation of the sympathies of the uncommitted nations, of which Mr. Nehru has made himself the spokesman. He declares that the dogmas of Communism are too inflexible to the changing conditions of the world and that the

"Economics of the West, though helpful, have little bearing on present day problems." [1]

It is difficult to deny the ironic quality in this historic development when the principles of liberal democracy, fashioned in a domestically pluralistic culture, should appear more inflexible, in a pluralistic global community, than the pretensions of a despotic culture which has distilled despotism from utopia but meanwhile found another avenue, than that of the West, to the technical competence which all modern nations seek in their war against poverty and misery.

We may well be baffled by these strange historical developments and ask whether there is any genuinely "ultimate" judgment for historically conditioned man. Perhaps the only ultimate political judgment is the negative one that despotism is always dangerous. Its monopoly of power is dangerous to justice, and its exclusion of the private and peculiar dimension from the realm of meaning, subordinating all human ambitions to collective ends, is always dangerous to the integrity of the human spirit. But we cannot affirm that the emancipation which western society has achieved from the despotic conditions is an ultimate form of emancipation. It also is conditioned by historical contingencies which cannot be reproduced in the unique histories of the Asian and African nations who are trying to develop both autonomous nationhood and technical competence in this century against a background of colonial dependence and agrarian or pastoral economies. Both the cultural and economic conditions of their life are not analogous to those of our western history.

It would be tragic, as well as ironic, if the tolerance and modesty which we learned or had forced upon us in the peculiar conditions of western life should become the basis of fanaticism and immodesty in our international relations. We would be declaring, in effect, that our cultural and economic pluralism, the basis of our domestic health, is the only possible approach to the world's problems. We, thereby, change domestic tolerance into self-

[1] Quoted from an article by Nehru, Jawaharlal, "The Tragic Paradox of our Age," *New York Times* Magazine Section, September 7, 1958, p. 13ff.

righteous attitudes in international affairs. We have forgotten that an open society is, on the one hand, the only condition for justice in society, but that, on the other hand, the peculiar form of the open society which has developed in the West is a luxury which not many nations can afford. To present a value which is both a necessity and a luxury in such a guise that only the aspect of luxury impresses the world is to make the unique forms of relativism in western life the basis of a false ultimate.

Perhaps it is as difficult for western democracy as it is for communist ideology to come to terms with the inconclusive character of human history. The communists believed in bringing the problems of community to an end by the naïve expedient of a revolution which would abolish the institution of property, the alleged source of all evil. They are being disillusioned by the reemergence of all the perennial problems of justice in the community which are bound to manifest themselves in every culture and in any age.

Western democracy, despite its pluralism, on the other hand, really had one regnant faith to which all other schemes of meaning were subordinated. That faith was in the idea of progress, in the notion that historical development would solve all the unsolved problems of the human community. But western civilization is in the throes of the tragic refutation of this faith by the events and predicaments of current history, and more particularly by the dilemma that it cannot guard its treasures, accumulated through the ages, against a new despotism without running the risk of a suicidal war. All the old problems are there, but in larger dimension than in any previous age. The drama of history remains inconclusive to the end of history; and men must be prepared to assume a responsible attitude toward their treasures of culture even though they realize the fragmentary character of their treasures and achievements. The facts of current history refute both the simple secular moralism of our culture and the moralistic versions of the Christian faith which pretend that there is a moral answer to the nuclear dilemma, or a moral way of removing the ambiguity of power and dominion in the community. Modern history has given us a vivid illustration of the fact that the history of communities accentuates, rather than mitigates, the moral ambiguities of our existence, particularly the ambiguities of our common life. Only a religious faith and a humanism more profound than many extant varieties can make sense out of these terrifying facts of modern history, particularly those facts which prove that all historic responsibilities must be borne without the certainty that meeting them will lead to any ultimate solution of the problem, but with only the certainty that there are immediate dangers which may be avoided and immediate injustices which may be eliminated. Thus modern men of whatever persuasion of faith must learn the modesty of acting on the principle, "Sufficient unto the day is the evil thereof."

It is man's ineluctable fate to work on tasks which he cannot complete in his brief span of years, to accept responsibilities the true ends of which he cannot fulfill, and to build communities which cannot realize the perfection of his visions. The heaven of traditional faith is a symbolic expression of the fact that "our reach is beyond our grasp." It is incredible, but the utopias of modern men, these heavens on earth, are as incredible and much more dangerous. The utopias include those which are implicit in many of the "liberal" views of history, as well as those which are explicit in communist theory.

Most traditional forms of faith followed Plato in finding the source of evil in the passions of the body. They were wrong. But the modern views which find the source of evil in the inertia of nature are just as wrong. In the collective life of man, at least, most evil arises because finite men involved in the flux of time pretend that they are not so involved. They make claims of virtue, of wisdom, and of power which are beyond their competence as creatures. These pretensions are the source of evil, whether they are expressed by kings and emperors or by commissars and revolutionary statesmen. But among the lesser culprits of history are the bland fanatics of western civilization who regard the highly contingent achievements of our culture as the final form and norm of human existence. In all these forms of fanaticism and pride, men prove that while men's freedom is the source of creativity, the pretension that they are more free of finite conditions than mortals can be generates destructiveness amidst the creativity of freedom. Our best hope, both of a tolerable political harmony and of an inner peace, rests upon our ability to observe the limits of human freedom even while we responsibly exploit its creative possibilities.

It is particularly difficult for nations to discern the limits of human striving and especially difficult for a nation which is not accustomed to the frustrations of history to achieve this moderation. It is not sloth or the failure to exploit our potentialities but undue self-assurance which tempts the strong, particularly those who are both young and strong.

INDEX

INDEX

303